Carnival Song and Society

EXPLORATIONS IN ANTHROPOLOGY
A University College London Series

Series Editors: Barbara Bender, John Gledhill and Bruce Kapferer

Carnival Song and Society

Gossip, Sexuality, and Creativity in Andalusia

Jerome R. Mintz

BERG

Oxford • New York

First published in 1997 by
Berg
Editorial offices:
150 Cowley Road, Oxford, OX4 1JJ, UK
70 Washington Square South, New York, NY 10012, USA

Berg is an imprint of Oxford International Publishers Ltd.

Library of Congress Cataloging-in-Publication Data

Mintz, Jerome R.
    Carnival song and society : gossip, sexuality, and creativity in
Andalusia / Jerome R. Mintz.
        p. cm. -- (Explorations in Anthropology)
    Includes index.
    ISBN 1-85973-183-X (alk. paper). --ISBN 1-85973-188-0 (pbk. : alk.
paper)
        1. Carnival--Spain--Cádiz (Province).   2. Carnival--Spain--
Cádiz.   3. Cádiz (Spain)--Social life and customs.   I. Title.
    II. Series.
    GR4262.A3C336 1997   96-46239
    394.25´0946´88--dc21   CIP

British Library Cataloguing-in-Publication Data

A catalogue record for this book is available from the British Library.

ISBN 1 85973 183 X (Cloth)
      1 85973 188 0 (Paper)

Typeset by JS Typesetting, Wellingborough, Northants.
Printed in the United Kingdom by WBC Book Manufacturers, Bridgend,
Mid Glamorgan.

to Sigal, the little drummer

Contents

Acknowledgements

Carnival Song and Society has an independent but complimentary relationship with a documentary film, *Carnaval de Pueblo* (Town Carnival), which I photographed in Benalup depicting the carnival of 1982.[1] I believe that the two forms, book and film, prove to be a good match. Film has dramatic and evocative powers; a book allows expanded discussion and detailed descriptive analysis.

This work also has close ties with an earlier publication, *The Anarchists of Casas Viejas*.[2] That book concerned the development of the anarchist movement in the town of Casas Viejas (which later took the name Benalup de Sidonia). An anarchist uprising there in 1933 had far reaching tragic consequences. The earlier work examined social and political affairs from 1914 until the Spanish Civil War. Since the two books and the film share a common research base, it is necessary for me to express once again my appreciation for the support of the foundations and granting agencies already acknowledged in the earlier works. In addition, I thank the Program for Cultural Cooperation between Spain's Ministry of Culture and United States Universities, and Indiana University.

The remarkable range of poetry and song included here is a tribute to the rich Andalusian creativity. I am grateful to the people in the cities and towns of the province of Cádiz, particularly Cádiz the capital, Benalup, Trebujena, Ubrique, and San José de Malcocinado, for their artistic and intellectual contributions. Alberto Ramos Santana, in person and through his works, generously extended help and hospitality. I am grateful to Diego Caro Cancela for his aid. Special thanks are due to Manolo Lago Barberán, Jesús Mañez Moya, and Carmen García García of Benalup; Manuel Moreno Riobo and María López Liboreiro of Cádiz; and Antonio Olivero Gómez and Juan Antonio Cordero Moyano of Trebujena, all of whom generously provided a variety of texts and useful information. Many others who were helpful, poets and participants, are cited in the text. Ann Bristow of the Indiana University Library has my gratitude for her assistance. I thank Michael Herzfeld for his good counsel.

The translations of the carnival songs were completed by Juan A. Suárez, Elena Frabroschi, and Enrique Torner Montoya. The usual difficulties of translation were exacerbated by idiosyncracies of the Andaluz dialect and at times by composers' efforts to maintain the measure of their verses. There are omitted syllables and letters (*pá* is the common abbreviation of para; *contao* = contado; *marío* = marido; *tó* = toda) as well as omitted words. There are also localisms, unusual variations, enigmatic nicknames, double-entendres, and an extraordinary range of sexual euphemisms.

Much of the material concerning women is the product of the interviews and insights of my wife, Betty. We shared in the fieldwork as well as in the realization of this book.

Notes

1. The film (or video) can be rented or purchased from Documentary Educational Resources; 101 Morse Street; Watertown, MA 02172 USA. Telephone: (617) 926-0491. It can also be rented from Instructional Support Services; Indiana University; Bloomington, IN 47405--5901. Telephone 001(800) 552-8620. The other films in the series are cited when they are related to specific circumstances. The other titles are: *Romería, Day of the Virgin; Pepe's Family; The Shoemaker; The Shepherd's Family;* and *Perico the bowlmaker.*
2. Jerome R. Mintz, *The Anarchists of Casas Viejas* (Bloomington, Ind.: Indiana University Press, 1994 [1982]), [Spanish edition: *Los Anarquistas de Casas Viejas* (Cádiz: Diputación de Cádiz, 1994)].

A carnival group sings its repertoire on a Cadiz street.

A carnival composer in Benalup recites a comic love poem.

Prologue

Festivals in Spain

This work is about carnival in Cádiz, a festival that celebrates in song the affairs and sentiments of the Andalusian people.

In the yearly round of feasts, fairs, and holy days in tradition-minded Spain, communities generate their own entertainments. Because of the time and resources that go into such celebrations, the people of each hamlet, town, and city customarily concentrate their creative energies on a single holiday, be it a secular or religious festival. Each celebration calls for specific and often elaborate arrangements, including sewing costumes, building floats, furnishing food and decorations, and preparing songs and dances. As a result of each community's collective efforts, certain locales are identified with particular festivals: the *Fallas* (fire festivals) are tied to Valencia along the eastern coast of Spain, while *Semana Santa* (Holy Week) is associated with the city and province of Seville in southwestern Andalusia. In the province of Cádiz, south of Seville, *Carnaval* is the preeminent festival.[1] As a carnival singing group, "Los Llaveros Solitarios," proclaims:

San Fermines in Pamplona,	San Fermines en Pamplona,
Castellers in Tarragona,	Castellers en Tarragona
and bonfires in Alicante.	y hogueras en Alicante.
Huelva with its pilgrimages in Altamonte,	Huelva con su Romería
What a joy to see pilgrims in their flounced dresses!	en Altamonte que alegría ver romeras con volante.
San José takes to Valencia all the fire – the essence of Mediterranean folklore.	San José lleva a Valencia todo el fuego que es la esencia del folklor mediterráneo.
In April Seville is like an Empress	En abril Sevilla es la emperaora
of the fairs, beautiful singer,	de las ferias cantaora

pride of the Sevillano.	orgullo del sevillano.
In all these provinces,	En todas estas provincias
in all their towns and their surroundings,	todos sus pueblos y alrededores
people support unconditionally these festivities.	apoyan la primacía de estos festejos sin condiciones.
But that doesn't happen among us,	No pasa aquí lo mismo
where some people question our carnival.	y se cuestiona nuestro Carnaval.
Everybody in the province must know	Sepa la provincia
that even in Franco's times,	que aún en los tiempos de dictadura
and in spite of the censorship,	a pesar de la censura
they couldn't silence us.	no nos pudieron callar.
It is easy to jump	Es fácil subirse al carro de La Victoria:
on the wagon of victory.	No admitimos más historias.
Let's not accept more stories.	Recuerden que el Santuario
Remember that the sanctuary of our festivities is the Falla [theater],	de nuestras fiestas se llama Falla
and it is in our capital.	y está en la capital.

(Paco Rosado, Los Llaveros Solitarios, 1984)

Carnival Song and Society examines the Cádiz carnival and the world in which it is celebrated. The period covered in this study is primarily from 1966 to 1990. Following decades of severe repression, Andalusians found their voice, and carnival enjoyed an extraordinary florescence. The songs of carnival are created anew each year by local composers. The songwriters speak in their own voices on subjects they have chosen, utilizing their own forms of speech and imagery. They provide us immediate access to the Andalusian people and their concerns.[2] Although the songs in these pages spring from a specific corner of Andalusia, they provide a broad perspective of traditional life. The songs illuminate the last years of the dictatorship of Francisco Franco (which ended with Franco's death in 1975) and the succeeding period of the new constitutional monarchy.

In order to consider distinctions between rural and urban carnivals, the social dimensions of carnival are studied in town and city in several locales: the towns of Benalup (earlier called Casas Viejas), Trebujena, and Ubrique, the agricultural settlement of San José de Malcocinado, and the city of Cádiz. The rural town of Benalup and San José de Malcocinado are in the grazing and cereal zone of the province; the town of Trebujena lies to the north in the rolling vineyard region; Ubrique is perched in the mountains in the northwest; Cádiz is the capital city of the province, the seat of government, and a principal port and shipbuilding center on the Atlantic. The town carnival is the focus of chapters 1-8 and chapter 12. Carnival in the capital is examined in chapters 9-11.

Almost all of the songs considered in the first six chapters are printed here for the first time. The songs of Los Llorones were scribbled on scraps of paper by the composers. The poems of Esteben Moreno in chapter 5 and Isabel R. in chapter 8 were memorized and never written down until I recorded and transcribed them. Most of the remaining songs appeared in *folletos* (pamphlets) that were sold in the street by the singers during carnival time. Passages in the text marked by quotation marks are from my interviews; passages cited by a footnote (and without quotation marks) refer to a variety of printed sources.

The History of Carnival in Cádiz

The holiday of carnival has perished in much of the Old and New Worlds. Where it survives, it has assumed many different forms, from the elaborate costumes and parties of Venice to the sensual dancing and near nudity of Rio de Janeiro. While the *gaditanos* (citizens of Cádiz) enjoy their share of street revelry, imaginative costumes, sparkling parades, and parties, the Cádiz carnival is a unique celebration of freedom of expression, verbal wit, and acerbic and poetic commentary. Cádiz is the theater of carnival song.

Antecedents of carnival can be found in pagan times, but the festival has more direct and immediate ties to Christianity and the Christian calendar of the late Middle Ages.[3] The profane and prurient carnival revelry was traditionally celebrated in the week before Ash Wednesday, which signals the austere forty-day Lenten period leading to Easter Sunday. Today, however, the carnival celebration extends through the weekend past Ash Wednesday into the Lenten season.[4]

The contemporary Cádiz carnival reflects centuries of historical change. It contains elements from the Old World and the New, with conspicuous contributions from points as distant and diverse as Venice, Nice, and Cuba. By the early eighteenth century, settlers and traders from Genoa, Italy, had placed their mark on the Cádiz carnival. After centuries of a simpler celebration, the patrician practices of Genoese [and ultimately Venetian] origin won the favor of the Cádiz bourgeoisie and aristocracy, and carnival in the capital became distinguished by dances, balls, and operas held at the theater as well as in private homes.[5]

A more raucous public carnival thrived in the streets, as well. In the public walkways and at street corners, there was music and dancing, as well as feasts, games, and contests. Practices described by officials as unlawful help to define the holiday during this period. Sexually provocative displays were repeatedly banned. Particularly cited were obscene dancing (at times by gypsies and others), costumes exaggerating male and female sexuality, and men and women cross-dressing. Satirical discourses with political overtones were frequently prohibited, as well as costumes mimicking members of religious orders, the military, and the government. Offenders were fined and sometimes jailed. Despite complaints by the upper classes and the authorities, passersby continued to be affronted and humiliated by various forms of mischief. These included making lewd comments and gestures, throwing confetti (or candy), spraying water from syringes, setting off rockets and fire crackers, and tossing buckets of water and flour bombs from balconies, as well as swinging sacks of sand to knock off the hats of men strolling below.[6]

In the nineteenth century, singing gradually superseded dancing and the costume ball as the most celebrated activity of the Cádiz carnival. While modest compared with the program of today's carnival, performances were given by *comparsas* and *coros* at private parties and on the streets.[7] They sang a range of patriotic songs as well as *coplas* (popular songs). Local historians recall that during this time bands of singers dressed up in costumes and informally marched through the streets singing and accompanied by drums and cymbals. "*Murgas* (bands of singers) would walk around singing picaresque songs, but it was nothing as regulated as it is now. The *coplas* had no instrumental accompaniment. They were sung to improvised rhythms. Then they started to be sung to the music of guitars and bandores, and these instruments continue to be the main ones in carnival." (Eugenio Mariscal, Secretario de Sociedad de Autores)

In time, the singers became the voices of the working classes. As satirical expressions and criticism increased in the *coplas*, a long-lasting tension began between the singers and the government authorities who sought to retain control over carnival antics and plebeian political criticism.

From the New World

As the carnival *copla* (popular song) was taking shape in the last half of the nineteenth century, the music of the Cadiz carnival showed the influence of exotic rhythms. Throughout the eighteenth century, Cádiz had been the principal port of call for merchants and slavers trading in the New World. During that time, a bounty of song and dance was transported dockside by crews, both slave and free. The citizens of Cádiz admired the rhythm and dance of groups of blacks working the cargo and parading on the streets. Caribbean musical styles were also introduced by well-traveled Spanish crews and *Indianos* (as Spaniards who returned to Spain from the Caribbean were called) and their mulatto servants.[8]

Ramon Solís Llorente charted the diverse forces shaping the Cádiz carnival:

> How did the Cádiz carnival originate? There is no doubt that it is a creation, albeit totally of Cádiz, inspired by rhythms from overseas.
>
> We must remember here the uninterrupted traffic maintained between Cádiz and Havana. The lower classes from Cádiz made up the crews of ships traveling between Cádiz and Havana; aboard these ships, *gaditanos* worked as cooks, waiters, or sailors. These are also the years during which the ships of the Spanish navy – old wooden hulls – guarded over the Antilles and the Philippines, the last portions of a huge crumbling empire. Many *gaditano* crews would learn the sweet and rhythmical music from overseas. The population of Cádiz, coming and going in those ships, renewed itself from year to year. Those returning from abroad brought back with them a longing that tightened their bonds with the ports on the other side of the ocean. In its folklore, of all these ports, Cádiz is most closely linked with Havana. Only a yearning *gaditano* could have sung:

In the morning	Me gusta por la mañana
after drinking coffee	después del café bebío
I enjoy strolling through	pasearme por La Habana
Havana smoking a cigarette.	con mi cigarro encendío.

Many are misled by the fact that carnival was well established in Cádiz since antiquity. They think that Cádiz exported the carnival to America. This is possible, but it was actually America who sent it back to us, centuries afterwards, refined and Americanized.[9]

Musical ties to Cuba continue to resonate in Carnival song:

Who doesn't carry the beat	Quién no lleva los compases
of some habanera in his soul?	de una habanera en el alma.
(Paco Rosado, Los Cubatas, 1987)	

Over the course of time, the music of the Cádiz carnival has continued to be eclectic, borrowing and reshaping contemporary forms:

...the Cádiz carnival has not created a rhythm of its own, although the carnival tango or tanguillo – not to be confused with the gypsy tango – is perhaps close to being so. . . . The *comparsista* makes use of rhythms in fashion at the time. In this way, besides the ever current carnival *tango*, they formerly sang polkas, *cuplés*, *pasodobles*, and flamenco rhythms. Later on came the times of the fox-trot and the Argentinean tango, the *danzón*, and the rumba. There is not a definite musical form. The common factor is the instruments used, the rhythm, and the movements of the singers.[10]

In recent decades music from the United States has profoundly affected carnival musical modes. This influence is most obvious when the groups offer a customary *popurrí* (medley) of short *cuplés* with music taken from popular songs heard on radio, television, or film.

Carnival Song

Carnival *coplas* are sung by bands of street singers and choruses – *murga, chirigota, comparsa, cuarteto, coro,* and *charanga.* These groups share some features in common but also have identifying characteristics of their own (in terms of the number of participants, song genres, use of instruments, harmonies employed, comic or serious intent, urban or rural ties, and periods of popularity and decline).

Most noticeably missing from the Cádiz carnival is the cante flamenco, for some the apex of Andalusian song. With its emphasis on individual performance, Moorish modalities, and vocal pyrotechnics, the flamenco *cante hondo* (deep song) enables the singer to "ventilate turbulent emotions like jealousy, hate, rage, guilt, despair, death wish, grief, or any kind of profound physical or metaphysical ordeal."[11] In style and content the cante flamenco stands in sharp contrast to the carnival *copla*:

> The *copla* is completely different in character from flamenco songs. The first trait of the *copla* is that it is sung in groups with various voices, which contradicts the tradition of individualism in Andalusian folklore. Furthermore, the *copla* is not defined by its music or singing style, but by the intentions underlying the lyrics and its rhythm.[12]

There are no bravura solos in carnival. *Coplas* are the commentary of a chorus. Themes are realistic rather than romantic. Events usually concern familiar figures and circumstances. Passion is expressed through the content rather than evoked by the musical style.

Music and Lyrics

Song composition for carnival begins with the music. Each year local composers initiate a new beat and a fresh melodic line for their bands of singers. Although carnival composers rarely have any formal musical training, a composer, usually playing a guitar, establishes the rhythms and melody for the lyricist (*coplista*) to shape his thoughts. Sometimes the music is lifted from current popular songs. The music sets the number of lines, the entrances, the length of the line, and the repetitions to which the librettist must adhere. When the composer realizes a line, he sings it to the lyricist and, nowadays, additionally records it on tape.

The lyricist starts his work only after he has absorbed the tempo and melody.[13] Music generates the rhythm and style of the songs; however, as Ramón Solís affirms: ". . .the music holds a secondary place. The most important element is the lyrics, charged with critical content, and acute yet benevolent satire."[14]

The lyricist has a great deal of freedom in matching words and rhythm. There are no hard and fast prescriptions, only artistic and practical considerations, in determining the number of lines for each song. Lyricists and singers recognize the flexibility of form available to them: "There are no rules as to the number of lines. Songs have, in general, twenty or twenty-five lines. A tango has five or six *cuartetas* [stanzas of four verses]. *Pasodobles* tend to have *cuartetas*. The *chirigota's pasodoble* may be a little shorter." (Ricardo Villa, Cádiz)

The same liberties are given to rhyme schemes. Rhymes, when needed, can be shaped by the elimination of words, by the creation of new and often meaningless words, or possibly by a double-entendre, frequently with a risqué and comic connotation.[15] Every detail is then mastered in secluded practices held for months before carnival by lyricists and singers. The result is that at times the language may appear to be seamless and at the same time so perplexing that it is difficult or even impossible for outsiders to comprehend every nuance.

Carnival Themes

Carnival songs relate the news of the pueblo (town). Strolling bands of singers serenade in the streets and pack the bars with renditions of the year's events and circumstances. Gossip is celebrated and the secrets of the pueblo are disclosed and criticized, usually from the point of view of the workers.

Carnival songs range from the serious and thoughtful to the suggestive and vulgar. Most carnival lyrics have a sense of immediacy since they report on activities of the previous year. Charted over time, the hard news and local gossip reflect enduring social and economic conditions and provide an index of historical circumstances and social change. Songs of previous decades detail images of life under the Franco dictatorship and, since 1978, the changes taking place under a constitutional monarchy.[16]

The songs span rural and urban environments. In the towns, the creative strength of carnival derives from the rural and working classes who are the composers, players, and audience. In these towns, rich landowners and other well-to-do citizens often stay out of sight during the most raucous times. In the capital city, however, carnival is celebrated across the social spectrum. Composers and players are generally from the working class, but participation is widespread; the affluent and the government officials exert strong influence over the organization and present-ation of the festival. Some see carnival as entertainment, and others consider it as the opportunity for social protest. A few in the city view carnival as a commercial opportunity.

Carnival Banned

The present period of the contemporary carnival in Andalusia is marked, ironically, by General Franco's prohibition of carnival in February 1937 when the nation was in the midst of the Spanish Civil War. Although the majority of the people in Andalusia supported the Republic, and the region was a center of anarcho-syndicalism, the Nationalists' surprise attack in July 1936 enabled them to take over the southwestern provinces of Cádiz and Seville in the first days of the struggle. With much of the south in Franco's hands, the battle to defend the Republic moved to the central and northern regions of the country. When carnival time approached seven months later, the Nationalists were concerned that the festival might unleash protest in the conquered regions. Carnival masks and costumes seemed especially worrisome. They feared that under the cover of carnival revelry, opposition gunmen could make use of disguises to conceal their identities and settle accounts for atrocities that had occurred.[17] On February 3, 1937, a week before Ash Wednesday, General Franco ordered the suspension of carnival.

The Civil War itself ended in the spring of 1939. On March 28, the Nationalists entered Madrid and on April 1 all Republican forces surrendered. A harsh repression followed. Outstanding Republicans and leftist militants who had escaped capture at the outset of the war were either executed or sent to prison. Soldiers in the Republican ranks were imprisoned, interrogated, and investigated. Eventually most were released but returned to their homes under conditions of parole, being denied military pensions and government aid if they were wounded, forbidden to own firearms, and put permanently under the surveillance of the *Guardia Civil*.

Following the Nationalist victory, the right to organize and to hold public meetings required government approval. Of course there were no strikes. Questions of land reform, workers' rights, and unemployment were no longer broached. Expressions of protest and criticism in print or in public were not permitted. Outstanding intellectuals, poets, and writers had been murdered or were in exile, and the creative spirit of the country was stilled. Even the voices of unknown poets, some whose verses had earned only fleeting local fame in the celebration of carnival, could no longer to be heard.

Across Spain the new ruling class and their supporters guarded an oppressive and tense tranquillity. Conformity in conduct and dress characterized all of daily life. In the rural towns, attendance at Mass was considered an appropriate sign of obeisance to the State and Church. Such signs of piety were necessary to gain the favor of local officials as well as employers. Others who could be found hat in hand at Mass Saturday night or Sunday morning included lesser administrators, foremen on the estates, workers intimidated by fear of losing their place, and even members of the bourgeoisie who had previously expressed favorable views on socialism and skeptical thoughts on religion.

On matters political and social, there was silence. Conversations between friends in cafés, bars, and other public places hewed to uncontroversial subjects. Even in working class households, a submissive quiet existed. In Andalusia, parents, no matter how radical they had been in thought and deed in their youth, rarely spoke of their social ideas to their children. Unable to forget the terror and the countless tragedies that had occurred during the war, the women of households usually forbade such talk.

The suspension of carnival had been intended as a wartime precaution; however, the yearly peal of criticism by carnival singers that had rung out in past times remained hushed for decades after the war. Carnival continued to be prohibited throughout Spain during the 1940s, 1950s, and early 1960s. The English anthropologist Julian Pitt-Rivers, who came in the early 1950s to the northern sierra of Cádiz to study the values and social structure of the people of Grazalema, could only guess at the role of the ancient holiday of carnival. He was told of the shamelessness of the Andalusian carnival "where anything goes" in the years before the Civil War.[18]

When Pitt-Rivers published *The People of the Sierra* in 1954, he explained that the holiday was no longer in vogue and he had been forced to work with informants who could only recall its special ambiance. There were scattered *coplas* and few details. Indeed, the collapsed and abandoned houses set in a dreary halo around the heart of the mountain town of Grazalema were testimony that the former inhabitants had disappeared. The workers, who had been the principal carnival singers and players, had fled the town, some during the war and others in the exodus that took place afterward. With their departure went the memory of the old songs and much of the vitality for creating new ones. Voices of protest and criticism were absent or repressed, and the uneasy silence that had settled over the streets of Grazalema was commonplace throughout Spain.

"Carnival is dead"

Inevitably, investigation of the revival of carnival in Cádiz must account for the festival's presumed demise. In 1965, Julio Caro Baroja, one of Spain's best known cultural historians, of Basque descent but with familial and personal ties to Andalusia as well, published a comprehensive historical and cultural study of carnival. Unlike Pitt-Rivers who had worked a decade earlier doing field research, Caro Baroja was an archivist and library scholar. His examination provided the most oft quoted appraisal of the state of carnival in modern times. Caro Baroja pronounced carnival to be dead and beyond resuscitation:

> Carnival is dead. It is dead, and it will not be resuscitated again each year as in past times. Carnival was an old festival. Nowadays we want to be modern above all.[19]

He had given his dire verdict after carefully surveying social change related to carnival from the beginning of the century. From his point of view, secularization rather than the government's ban had brought about the festival's demise.[20]

> Pious people say its death is all to the better, since carnival is a last remnant of paganism. Yet those of rationalist leanings do not have much sympathy for it either. However, neither the vogue of religious spirit nor actions from the "Left," killed the carnival. A whole

conception of life did; however, this conception of life is neither Christian nor pagan, but simply secular. It consists in a bureaucratic laicism, and it has been alive for quite a few decades now. In fact, the notion that carnival was in decline, and even dead, is already present during the first two decades of the century. . . .while man believed that in one way or another his life was controlled by supernatural forces, carnival had been possible. But the moment everything, even festivals, are regulated according to political criteria concerned about social order, good taste, etc., etc., the carnival becomes a pretentious clubhouse amusement. All its charms and turbulences die out.[21]

Carnival Rekindled

Caro Baroja's melancholy pronouncement, however, was premature. While carnival appeared to have been fatally suffocated in most of the country, in southern Spain, and particularly in the province of Cádiz, the old festival had refused to die. The story of its survival and resurrection in the capital has been well told by historian Alberto Ramos Santana in his *Historia del Carnaval de Cádiz*. As early as 1940, the first year after the war, there were signs that the *gaditanos* would not surrender forever to political expedience. As part of a show at the Gran Teatro, aficionados staged a program of memories of carnival featuring choral performances of prewar *tangos* and *pasodobles*.[22]

A similar memorial celebration to carnival was held that same year in the Spanish protectorate in Morocco, but with a perverted and servile intent. As Santana angrily noted:

> The program's hypocritical connotations became especially blatant when the music of old tangos was used as propaganda to support the regime in power. If it was already painful to witness how the powers manipulated a popular celebration to its advantage while forbidding the people's spontaneous celebrations, it must have been even more so hearing [carnival] tango music used to celebrate precisely those who forbade carnival.[23]

Small groups of devotees continued to honor the lost holiday by singing favorite old carnival *coplas*. For the moment, however, there were no new songs. Cádiz's unique tradition of carnival song had nurtured loyal devotees of every class, including the new mayor of the city, José León de Carranza, whose vigorous efforts won over the more cautious governor of the province, Carlos

Rodríguez de Valcárcel. In 1948, *coros* reappeared in a public performance with the governor in the audience.[24] The following year, 1949, the governor permitted a parade of *coros* and *chirigotas*, although the word *Carnaval* dared not be mentioned, and the songs fell under strict rules of censorship. Nonetheless, one introductory tango was, as Santana characterized it, "full of sentiment and contained rage."[25]

In 1950, a committee chosen by the mayor established *Las fiestas típicas gaditanas* (Typical Cádiz Festivals) with the goal of "establishing the new format of the traditional festivals":

> [In the coming seasons] These councilmen brought back the group contests, albeit controlled by censorship. Costumes were gradually allowed once again, although not the masks. Society balls recovered their former vogue, and the contest for the "queen of the festivals" was established. The contest gained political character, since most of the time the winners were daughters, granddaughters, or acquaintances of personalities of the regime. Last names like Varela, Navarro-Rubio, Fraga, Orol, Guillén, or even Franco's own granddaughter, make up the roster of "typical festival" queens – either adult or "child queens." These festivals had to steer between the permitted and the permissible; between tradition and the proscriptions of the period. They wanted to be refined. . . [and] "avoid coarseness, the carnival quality of communal festivals."[26]

The contest to determine the most favored groups became dominant. A well-organized and popular parade now brought the festival to an end. Some folkloric traditions were sloughed off. Burning the witch at the conclusion of the festival became less important, as well as ceremonially signaling a halt in eating meat by burying the *sardina* (actually the *cerdito*, the remains of a pig) at the end of carnival.[27]

Though the word *Carnaval* was still outlawed, the festival had crept back into Cádiz dressed appropriately in disguise. The subterfuge of a new name, *fiestas típicas*, seemed to be in keeping with the spirit of Andalusia, where language is an art form among common people as well as poets, and where matters are never what they appear to be. By avoiding the word *Carnaval*, the *fiestas típicas* appeared to skirt the major restriction of the law banning the holiday. But were the *fiestas típicas* the incarnation of the ancient festival or a new hybrid holiday? After considering the censorship and other imposed constraints, Ramos Santana characterized the new festival in the capital as "a tamed, de-caffeinated carnival, but one that at least allowed carnival traditions to survive among recent generations of *gaditanos*" (citizens of Cádiz).[28]

In the Towns

With the new festival safely moored in the capital, after years of midwinter silence, carnival slipped back into the smaller rural towns such as Benalup de Sidonia. As had occurred in the capital, the festival arrived incognito and under its assumed name, *fiestas típicas*. In Benalup in 1958, José Marín, the owner of a small *huerta* (garden) just below the town, organized a *chirigota* called Para Luchar Luchar, Para Vencer Vencer (In Order to Struggle, Struggle; in Order to Conquer, Conquer.)[29] The following year, Andrés Ordoñez Garcia, known by his nickname *Andrés el Pito* (Andrés the Whistle) led a group called Los Soleros (Aged Wine). In each of the following half-dozen years at carnival time, new *murgas* (strolling bands of singers) appeared on the streets of Benalup.

The scenario was repeated a year later, 1959, in Trebujena, a small town north of Cádiz in the wine growing region of the province. The townspeople were well aware of the tentative renaissance that had taken place in the capital nearby, and it did not take much to revive long suppressed feelings, as Luis de la Rosa records:

> It was impossible. . .for our people to forget by decree the folklore that allowed us to express ourselves as we were. In spite of all pressures to the contrary, masks kept coming out on the streets around Lent, and were often chased by the constabulary. In bars, many sang in a low voice and on the sly those songs that, transmitted from generation to generation, had been preserved in the soul of the people.[30]

The following year, disregarding the governor's opposition, the transformation was complete.

> In spite of everything, the first *murgas* came out again in 1960 under the mayor's own personal responsibility.[31]

Renewal

In the capital during the early 1960s, carnival was still under wraps. Singing in the streets of the city was forbidden.

"People could only sing in the bars. There wasn't anything going on in the street, really. There was a parade and a contest, and so on, but nothing spontaneous from the people. And they used to set up a fair in the *alameda* (public promenade). This was the idea of some fascist city councilmen, who wanted to erase the carnival. The church had always considered carnival something negative and sinful, and so they wanted to get rid of it. They changed the dates, they moved it to after Easter, in May or June; they changed the name – it was called *Fiestas Típicas*. A lot of the carnival folklore was lost. They set it up like the Seville fair. They put up these kiosks where groups used to play; there were costumes, but you could not cover your face. There were parades and costume contests, and so on. Banks and firms set up kiosks, where you had to pay to go in. It was an attempt to diffuse carnival. The Franco regime just wanted to get rid of carnival, because carnival was too critical and said too many things. At that time, *chirigoteros* were sometimes arrested for what they said. Carnival gives people a chance to say what they think. Usually the voice of the people is not heard, but carnival changes that; it gives people the chance to speak up. That's why the dictatorship didn't like it." (Manuel Moreno and Maria López, Cádiz, a shipyard worker and a student)

By the mid-1960s, however, although the word carnival could not be mentioned and masks were banned, the spirit of carnival had shaken itself free of the confines of memory and the crudest official shackles and had moved into the street. In towns and cities throughout the province, a renaissance similar to that occurring in the capital and in Benalup and Trebujena was taking place. With or without the approval of the government of Francisco Franco, carnival was being re-created, and it was not going to be a pleasant interlude to sweeten tourism, but, as it was in the past, a raucous and liberating stimulant in community life.

Everybody in the province must know	Sepa la provincia
that even in Franco's times,	que aún en los tiempos de dictura
and in spite of the censorship,	a pesar de la censura
they couldn't silence us.	no nos pudieron callares

(Paco Rosado, Los Llaveros Solitarios, 1984)

In 1965, the same year that Caro Baroja's funereal dismissal of carnival appeared in print with the publication of *El Carnaval*, I settled in for a yearlong visit to Benalup de Sidonia (also known as Casas Viejas), together with my wife Betty and my two and a half year old daughter, Carla. I had come to collect and study oral accounts of the anarchist uprising of Casas Viejas in 1933. Having read Caro Baroja's book and taken it to heart, I had no thought of ever viewing a reportedly defunct festival. In Benalup, however, carnival singers had been rehearsing their songs in secret for months, as is the common practice. Therefore, the week before Ash Wednesday, in February 1966, carnival time, I was surprised to hear the advancing thunder of a bass drum and the rattle of a snare drum and then see four bands of strolling singers parading in costume through the streets of the town.

Notes

1. For a brief account of the major festivals of Spain, see Salvador Rodríguez Becerra, "Cultura Popular y Fiestas" in *Los Andaluces* (Madrid: Ediciones Istmo, 1980), pp.447–94. For articles covering the culture and folklore of the province of Cádiz, see *Cádiz y su provincia*, 4 vols. (Sevilla: Ediciones Geyer, 1984–85), vol. 4.

2. Carlo Ginzburg pointed out: ". . .the principal failing in Bakhtin's fine book [Mikhail Bakhtin, *Rabelais and His World*, tr. Hélène Iswolsky (Bloomington, Ind.: Indiana University Press, 1984 [1968], (written in Russian in 1940 but denied publication until 1965)] is. . .[that] the protagonists of popular culture whom he has tried to describe, the peasants and the artisans, speak to us almost exclusively through the words of Rabelais. The very wealth of research possibilities indicated by Bakhtin makes us wish for a direct study of lower-class society free of inter-mediaries." Carlo Ginzburg, *The Cheese and the Worms, The Cosmos of a Sixteenth-Century Miller* (New York: Penguin, 1980), p. xvii.

3. "The winter rhythm starts in Advent [four Sundays before Christmas in the Christian calendar], a time of work followed

by Christmas, a period of happiness and celebration. After Christmas comes the carnival season, which starts around January 20, the day of San Sebastian. Carnival is a time of licentiousness, reaching its climax three days before Ash Wednesday. After the season of freedom comes the repressive Lent, and then sad Easter." Alberto Ramos Santana, *Historia del Carnaval de Cádiz (Epoca contemporánea)*, (Cádiz: Caja de Ahorros de Cádiz, 1985), p. 10. The issue of origins is discussed in Julio Caro Baroja, *El Carnaval (Análisis Histórico-Cultural)*, (Madrid: Taurus, 1965), pp. 27–45. The context and the historical details cited here are drawn largely from A. Ramos Santana's account.

4. There are variances in the schedule of events in the capital and in the towns. In the towns the *pregón* (public proclamation) that inaugurates the carnival usually takes place on the Friday (or Saturday) evening preceding Ash Wednesday. This is followed by the presentation of the repertoires of the carnival singers. During this first weekend an exhuberant parade of *murgas*, *chirigotas* and *comparsas* crisscrosses the town performing in the bars and cafés and in the street. The singers usually pass the hat to recoup some of their expenses. The coronation of the carnival queen is celebrated; there are public and private dances, and parties for children and young people. On Sunday the children flock to the *alameda* to capture candies spilling from a *piñata* smashed by a lucky (or skillful) masked player swinging a stick. The carnival ebbs on Monday and Tuesday, falls sharply on Ash Wednesday and, with many of the men away at work, the streets and taverns remain quiescent for the remainder of the week. Carnival roars back to life the following weekend with renewed singing in the bars and cafés. A masked ball is usually held on Saturday night. On this second Sunday in some towns, the Witch Piti (or Dios Momo) is burned. The carnival takes its departure with a final parade through the town led by the singers and other costumed participants and disappears until the following year.

5. ". . .the Cádiz carnival had its own peculiarities. It is, logically, an urban carnival which borrowed traits from the Italian carnivals. Italian influence is easily explained by the important Genoese presence in Cádiz." A. Ramos Santana, *Historia del Carnaval de Cádiz*, pp. 11–12. As the author explains, traders and settlers from Genoa were much in evidence in Cádiz

beginning in the sixteenth and seventeenth centuries when, driven westward by Turkish control over the Mediterranean, they sought new ports from which to trade with north and central Africa.

6. A. Ramos Santana, *Historia del Carnaval de Cádiz*, pp. 14–17. A similar carnival prank is cited in Miguel de Cervantes' *Don Quijote* when tavern merrymakers toss Sancho Panza high in a blanket much as they would a dog at carnival. (Chapter xvii.)

7. See A. Ramos Santana, *Historia del Carnval de Cádiz*, pp. 12–13, concerning the shift from dance to song. A bit later he writes: "*Cuadrillas* (singing groups) came out on foot or on carriages accompanied by bands. . .some Cádiz merchants hired music bands to play in their homes. . .*Cuadrillas* who used to meet to rehearse before going out on the streets were called *comparsas*. . . In 1858 the editor of the newspaper *La Moda* suggested that the origin of the *comparsas* was in the groups of rich *gaditanos*, who, a month or so before the festivals started, gathered to rehearse dances and songs, and to prepare a pantomime. . .Such groups became the main interest at private parties, to the extent that they often spied on each other to find out the themes, clothing, and content of their parodies or pantomimes." pp. 30–1. As the author describes, other evidence from *La Moda,* citing the poor quality of the material used for the disguises, indicates that mostly low-income people participated in the *comparsas*. A. Ramos Santana, *Historia del Carnaval de Cádiz*, p. 34.

8. As Ramon Solís Llorente observed: "The *chirigota* and the *comparsa*, when sung in parades, evidence a marching rhythm clearly influenced by Afro-Cuban music forms, like the samba. These black rhythms are accompanied by the *murgistas* [members of a strolling band of singers, a *murga*] with movements and gestures fashioned after those of the rumba. The instruments used by the *comparsistas* are alien to Andalusian folklore. With the exception of the bass drum and the rattle drum, also called *caja* or *redoblante*, they hardly use any musical instruments, but simple everyday objects able to produce rhythmic sounds, such as graters, etc. The indispensable tool in the *comparsa* is the *guiro* or cane whistle." Ramon Solis Llorente, *Coros y Chirigotas, Carnaval en Cádiz*, (Madrid: Silex, 1988 [1966]), pp. 17–18.

9. As R. Solís Llorente observed: ". . .It was not until well into the second half of the nineteenth century that the carnival *copla*

was defined," and by then an amalgam of Afro-Caribbean rhythms and styles had reshaped musical forms. R. Solís Llorente, *Coros y Chirigotas, Carnaval en Cádiz*, pp. 21–2.

10. R. Solis Llorente, *Coros y Chirigotas, Carnaval en Cádiz*, pp. 20–1.

11. Timothy Mitchell, *Flamenco Deep Song* (New Haven: Yale University Press, 1994), p. 1.

12. R. Solis Llorente, *Coros y Chirigotas, Carnaval en Cádiz*, pp. 17.

13. American songwriters of Tin Pan Alley usually followed the same order of music first and words second. Philip Furia cites "Ira Gershwin's axiom that the art of lyric writing consists of fitting words 'mosaically' to music already composed." For further discussion of variations in the writing of lyrics and music see Philip Furia, *The Poets of Tin Pan Alley* (New York: Oxford University Press, 1990), p. 190.

14. As proof of the music's lesser place than the lyrics, Solís observes: ". . .the Cádiz carnival has not created a ryhthm of its own, although the carnival *tango* or *tanguillo*. . .is perhaps close to being so." R. Solís Llorente, *Coros y Chirigotas, Carnaval en Cádiz*, p. 20.

15. "The rhymes of the carnival lyrics are highly arbitrary, since they are not written to be sung, but are born at the beat of the music and then transcribed. When necessary – for example, when the idea does not fit the length of the verse – the rhythm is tampered with, or the poet leaves some words out. Sometimes he changes the ending of a word to help the rhyme. These freedoms increase the comic overtones of the songs." R. Solis Llorente, *Coros y Chirigotas, Carnaval en Cádiz*, p. 24.

16. A number of studies have been concerned with carnival and society. The French historian LeRoy Ladurie utilized a single carnival in the city of Romans in the year 1580 to chart politics, class, conflict, and insurrection. See *Le Carnaval du Romans* (Paris: Editions Gallimard, 1979) [English edition: *Carnival in Romans* (New York: George Braziller, Inc., 1979)]. A study by Peter Sahlins, *Forest Rites, The War of the Demoiselles in Nineteenth-Century France* (Cambridge: Harvard University Press, 1994), described (p. 82) the War of the Demoiselles as "a concrete historical and interested realization of the structure of Carnival."

David D. Gilmore examined the social and historical scope of carnival in a town in Seville. See *Aggression and Community: Paradoxes of Andalusian Culture* (New Haven: Yale University

Press, 1987) chapter 6, "Carnaval"; "Carnaval in Fuenmayor:
Class Conflict and Social Cohesion in an Andalusian Town,"
in *Journal of Anthropological Research*, vol. 31, pp. 331–49, 1975;
and "Politics and Ritual: Fifty Years of Andalusian Carnival"
in *Iberian Studies*, vol. 17, 1988. With Margaret M. Gilmore, he
considered psychodynamic aspects of carnival songs in the
province of Seville in "Machismo: A Psychodynamic Approach
– Spain" in *Journal of Psychological Anthropology*, vol. 2, pp.
281–99, 1979.

17. There were many precedents for Franco's action. Carnival had
been banned by Spanish authorities from time to time since
the sixteenth century. See S. Rodríguez Becerra, "Cultura
Popular y Fiestas" in *Los Andaluces*, pp. 480–1. Carnival masks
in particular had been outlawed in at least the following years:
1745, 1773, 1797, 1816, and 1857. See A. Ramos Santana,
Historia del Carnaval de Cádiz, pp. 13–33. The reality of the threat
of violence was supported by the assassination of Gustavus
III, the King of Sweden, at a masked ball in 1792. An ever-
lasting reminder of the event could be seen in Giuseppe Verdi's
Un ballo in maschera (A Masked Ball), first performed in 1859.
Gilmore describes the sort of tumultuous scene feared by
authorities during carnival in 1933 in the town of Fuenmayor
(Seville) in *Aggression and Community: Paradoxes of Andalusian
Culture*, p. 98.

18. J.A. Pitt-Rivers, *The People of the Sierra*, 2d ed. (Chicago:
University of Chicago Press), p. 176.

19. "El Carnaval ha muerto; ha muerto, y no para resucitar como
en otro tiempo resucitaba anualmente. Era una fiesta de corte
antiguo. Hoy queremos ser modernos ante todo." J. Caro
Baroja, *El Carnaval*, p. 21.

20. Of course, since he was writing under the eye of the Franco
regime, it is difficult to guess to what extent political concerns
may have skewed his vision or shifted the weight of his words.
During my visit with him at his home in Madrid in 1965–1966,
he commented that he was already in hot water for his research
into the Jewish ancestry of distinguished Spanish families. See
Los Judíos en la España Moderna y Contemporanes, 3 vols.
(Madrid: Arion, 1961). For commentary on J. Caro Baroja's
analysis, see A. Ramos Santana, *Historia del Carnval de Cádiz*,
pp. 5–12; and S. Rodríguez Becerra, "Cultura Popular y
Fiestas" in *Los Andaluces*, pp. 479–82.

21. J. Caro Baroja, *El Carnaval*, p. 21–2.
22. At the first staged reminiscence of the prohibited holiday, the program announced: "To enhance the carnival atmosphere, the audience in the boxes will throw confetti and serpentines as soon as the *coro* enters the stage." A. Ramos Santana, *Historia del Carnaval de Cádiz*, p. 101.
23. A. Ramos Santana, *Historia del Carnaval de Cádiz*, pp. 102.
24. A. Ramos Santana writes: "In Cádiz carnival remained latent – frozen in people's feelings. Hence, in the years after the war, nostalgic groups of people often gathered in wine shops and bars during February to remember the banned carnivals and sing its coplas." (*Historia del Carnaval de Cádiz*, p. 101) A bit further on he adds: "The next step was to bring the celebration of carnival back to the streets, ending the clandestine period." (p. 104)
25. A. Ramos Santana, *Historia del Carnaval de Cádiz*, pp. 104–5. The singers, called *Piñata Gaditana*, and accompanied by *Los Chisperos* (The Sparks), expressed with new lyrics their loyalty to the old forbidden festival and its songs.
26. Ibid., p. 106. The final brief quotation cited is from an article by Curro Plaza in the *Diario de Cádiz* (15 de febrero de 1951).
27. Burying the *sardina* had nothing to do with sardines. The word derives from *cerdo, cerdito* (pig, pig remains) which accounts for the confusion of terms. During the days of Lent, it was forbidden to eat the meat of a pig. The *vientre* (guts) of the pig, called *cerdito*, is the only part remaining after the pig is slaughtered and prepared for eating. These remains are buried. Since the pig is also a symbol of fertility, it was considered an aid to make the land fertile. (Alberto Ramos Santana, personal communication.)
28. A. Ramos Santana, *Historia del Carnaval de Càdiz*, p. 106.
29. In the film *Carnaval de Pueblo* (Town Carnival), which I photographed in Benalup in 1982, José Marín, then an old man, returned to the town from Valencia (where he had retired to live with his daughter) to form a *chirigota* called *Kokorokos* ("Cock-a-doodle-do"). The group is one of the centerpieces of the film.
30. Luis de la Rosa, *¡¡Esto es Carnaval!! Breve Historia del Carnaval de Trebujena* (Cádiz, 1992), p. 27.
31. Ibid., p. 28.

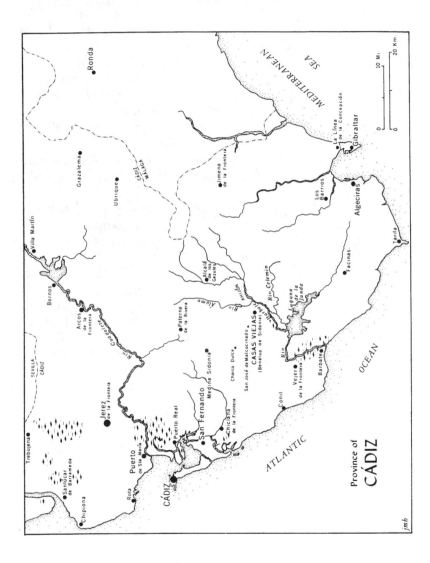

Province of
CÁDIZ

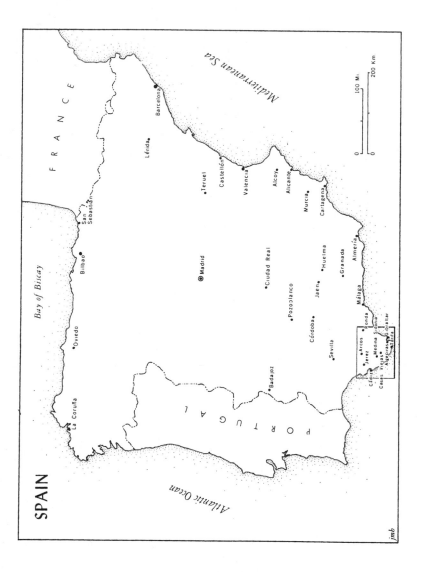

Chapter 1

Carnival in a Rural Town

Benalup (Casas Viejas) 1966

In the town of Benalup, as in the capital, carnival is the major festival in the yearly cycle, involving months of preparation and rehearsal before the holiday. This passion for carnival is not true of every town and city in the province. Alcalá de los Gazules, eighteen kilometers distant from Benalup, celebrates as its primary festival a yearly *romería* (pilgrimage) in September to a countryside shrine dedicated to the Virgin of Alcalá, María de los Santos.[1] Benalup's town carnival, unlike the *romería* that devours the energy of nearby Alcalá, has no higher purpose than its social one. Its focus is not on miracles but on human foibles.

Carnival, carnival, how pretty carnival is,	Carnaval, Carnaval, qué bonito el Carnaval
four months of rehearsals just to come and sing to you about the little events of the year during the days of carnival.	cuatro meses ensayando para venirte a cantar los sucesillos del año en días de Carnaval.
Carnival, carnival, how pretty is	Carnaval, Carnaval, qué bonito
the carnival when I sing for you and criticize the rest.	el Carnaval cuando canto para ti y critico a los demás.
(Los Amarados, 1981, Benalup)	

Town and Countryside

Benalup de Sidonia is a rural town of approximately 5,000 people in the southern part of the province of Cádiz.[2] A relatively new town, Benalup had developed in the previous century from a cluster of *chozas* (thatched huts), a hermitage (dating from the mid-sixteenth century), and an inn located at a crossroads leading south

1

to Algeciras and Gibraltar. It was better known by its earlier folk
designation, *Casas Viejas* (Old Houses).[3] The growth of the town
had been fostered by the sale of nearby common lands in the mid-
nineteenth century. As parcels of the once public lands were resold
and united with other parcels, *hortelanos* (gardeners) and day-
workers were needed to cultivate the gardens and orchards that
were fed by nearby springs and to sow the pasture lands in the
campo (countryside). The location of the growing town at the outer
boundaries of the townships of Medina Sidonia, Alcalá de los
Gazules, and Vejer de la Frontera assured new settlers of seasonal
work on the large estates that were distant from the other
population centers.

In 1933 the town was the site of an anarchist uprising, and the
name *Casas Viejas* became a symbol for rural injustice and mar-
tyrdom.[4] Rural poverty, however, continued unabated. In 1966,
three decades after the start of the civil war, Benalup remained a
poor agricultural town whose lands were concentrated in the
hands of a very few and without industry of any sort.

Benalup lies on a slope below the rim of an uneven plateau
that extends the sixty-eight kilometers from the town to the capital,
Cádiz. The eroded caves on the hillsides neighboring Benalup, a
very few with faded prehistoric line drawings, testify that the area
has been habitable for the last twenty millennia. Southward, below
the town, lies the valley floor and the normally gentle rivers of
Barbate and Celemín. At the far edge of the valley, some seventy
kilometers distant by roadway, a narrow mountain chain shields
Gibraltar from view. A remote corner of the landscape provides a
tantalizing keyhole glimpse of the sea. To the south lies the Strait
of Gibraltar and fourteen kilometers of open sea to the coast of
Africa and the country of Morocco. The Strait is a migratory
avenue for the seasonal passage of birds between the two con-
tinents.[5] In February, when carnival often falls, waves of swallows,
hoopoes and cuckoos pass over the Strait to nesting sites in
Gibraltar and in the swamp land of the Laguna Janda.[6] At month's
end, flights of storks begin, followed by kites soaring over the Strait
with long pointed wings and by goshawks pumping with short
powerful strokes. In March, almost as if to share in the remains of
the prelenten feasting, vultures, snake buzzards and harrier eagles
cross and light in the rocky cliffs of the mountains.

The countryside nearby Benalup is a mix of pasture and hillside,
with scattered fields planted in shimmering green wheat. Cattle

and sometimes brave bulls feed in the pastures, and herds of goats thread their way through narrow paths in the thick brush. Strands of wild cork trees lie scattered on the hillsides, while close to the town and fed by natural springs are gardens and groves. The irrigated gardens had been lined with fig, orange and quince trees until recent times, when it became more profitable to keep cattle and to plant a feed crop. The lands of Benalup, as well as Alcalá de los Gazules and Tarifa, had recently been declared as a cattle zone, which meant that the landowners were not obligated to sow crops (in contrast to Seville, for example, where landowners had to plant at least a percentage of their land). Dry farming was a particular gamble in these areas not because of the soil but rather due to the *levante*, the intermittent hot wind in the spring and summer that razes the wheat, barley, and chickpeas.

In comparison with the rich winter-green countryside, in 1966 the streets of Benalup appeared ragged. The two principal streets were set with cobblestones, but elsewhere the paths were unpaved and showed scant signs of municipal concern. Benalup, legally a hamlet pertaining to the township of Medina Sidonia, was not yet independent and had little power and few funds to act on its own behalf. A deputy mayor for Benalup was chosen by Medina's mayor from among the two local councilmen selected in the municipal elections. For continuity most official matters were handled by a permanent administrative secretary also appointed by Medina.

There were few shops in Benalup and often as not a typical village store was the converted front room of an ordinary streetside house. The larger houses and the old mill in the center of town were made of stone and cement and capped with tile roofs. Many of the homes further up the lane, however, were *chozas*, huts made of thatch and cane and usually set on a low base made of mud, lime, and small stones. Along the short main street, there were a half-dozen bars where men took coffee in the morning and wine in the evening, and whiled away workless days playing cards and dominoes. There were two classes of wine sold: the common wines of the Barberá bodega in Chiclana and the wines of a higher category (usually in bottles) from Jerez.[7] The *campesinos* drank the former from short plain glasses; the gentry drank the bottled wine from Jerez in wineglasses. One or two of the bars could boast of a new novelty – a black-and-white television set which featured a single state-run channel that was operational a few hours a day.

The most popular programs were the bullfights beamed from Algeciras, Seville, or Madrid. There was a rickety movie theater on the main street which opened on the weekends and all too frequently featured Johnny Weissmuller as Tarzan of the Apes.

The church was located at the village center where the two principal streets intersected. It was a physically imposing but architecturally undistinguished structure whose construction had been undertaken in 1915 to replace the earlier community's small and crumbling rural hermitage. In front of the church was the *alameda*, the promenade where townspeople strolled up and back every Friday night. Couples walked locked arm in arm. Young men found occasion to salute attractive girls with *piropos* (compliments) as the strollers measured the chances of finding a *novio* or *novia* (sweetheart). On Sundays and fair days, for recreation and greater intimacy, couples and groups would take longer walks in the countryside.

The Community

Most of the population of Benalup were *campesinos*, landless workers who once hired out for the season or for a particular task during the agricultural cycle. A small number were considered *hortelanos* (gardeners) skilled in the agricultural arts, but many knew little more than gang labor in the fields. The failure of most of the landowners to sow their lands, and increased mechanization by the few who did, promised permanent unemployment for agricultural workers. Since the 1950s, the *campesinos* had been forced to look beyond the pueblo for employment. Many signed contracts to work for a term abroad in the fields and factories of other more industrialized countries. *Campesinos* were increasingly leaving the fields to become itinerant construction workers at the hotels and chalets being built to accommodate tourists along the Mediterranean. Commonly they signed on as peons but many quickly acquired the skill to be masons.

There were other local workers and artisans for whom demand had greatly diminished. The need for men skilled as woodcutters and *corcheros* (cork harvesters) was spinning into oblivion in the countryside, as was the place in town for artisans such as blacksmiths, bakers, and shoemakers. Sewing shoes had once been an important craft in the town, with several scores of men making boots for trade in city shops, but the success of factory-made shoes had reduced the market for handsewn boots, and there were now only a half-dozen shoemakers left in town.

A very few independent-minded men subsisted by dry farming a modest number of *fanegas*[8] and keeping some milk cows. A handful of such *haciendas* lay on the mesa above the town and below on the hillside. Their efforts at surviving and supporting a family were prodigious. Since the land lacked irrigation, a yeoman farmer would dig a deep well on his property in order to plant crops that included tomatoes, potatoes, corn, onions, garlic, and sugarbeets. The sandy soil was hospitable to a variety of trees, including apple, pear, quince, almond and fig, as well as grape-vines and even camomile. The milk from the cows would be carried daily to the stores, and the male yearlings would be sold. A couple of pigs and several laying hens helped their larder and added a few coins to purchase other necessary goods.

A handful of middle-class families owned the principal shops in the town and the *huertas*, the nine irrigated gardens and groves below the hillside. These lands were distinguished from other holdings by their access to the run-off water from the fountains. With irrigation one could produce a rich variety of crops on only a very few *fanegas*.[9]

Two interrelated families, the Velas and the Espinas, were the town's principal landowners and landlords. They were the offspring of a brother and sister, Don Antonio Vela (who was licensed as a medical doctor although he didn't practice) and his sister Nicolasa. They had moved from Medina Sidonia to Benalup in 1882 in order to oversee their estates, which were composed for the most part of parcels of once common land purchased in the preceding twenty years by their father (Francisco Vela).[10] Their wealth had increased still further along with the growth of the two families, and both branches were rich when they divided the holdings in 1908. Eventually many townspeople would be beholden to the two families in one way or another, either through subletting a few hectares of land, working on one of their estates, receiving medical treatment, renting a rundown apartment in town (usually without running water or any facilities), or shopping in one of their stores. They were reputed to be sharp in their business dealings, and penurious with workers and house servants.[11]

Although they were the wealthiest families in the town, only one member, Ana Barca (the wife of Juan Vela, Don Antonio's son), was known for her charity and concern for the poor.

February 1966

The carnival of February 1966 arrived during a trying time. An incessant winter rain had soaked the fields and made them impassable. In the meanwhile, poets and singers prepared and practiced new repertoires. Some townswomen sewed costumes for their husbands and children to strut in the streets. Several couples planned to swap outfits with their spouses or friends and appear as members of the opposite sex. A few of the older men who had participated in carnival before Franco's ban planned skits to be acted out in the *alameda,* such as one man leading another dressed as a bear on a chain, or playing two men quarreling over a debt.

Since carnival in Benalup belonged to those at the lower end of the social scale, it was not surprising that members of the town's upper classes planned to remain under wraps during the holiday. Some were concerned with being the butt of unbridled gossip and criticism; a few were put off by the vulgarity of the occasion; some did not care to be pelted disrespectfully with confetti; and others of the upper classes were frightened by the disavowal of the civil restraints that otherwise helped to maintain social order.[12]

The most devoted aficionados in the lower classes joined one of the four bands of singers who were preparing their repertoire of carnival songs. Two of the singing groups, *Los Llorones* (the Weepers), a *murga,* and *Los Turistas del Figuras* (the Tourists of the Cave Drawings), a *chirigota,* were composed of adult men. The other two were made up of young boys: *Los Maletillas* (the Assistant Bullfighters) and *Los Algodoneros* (the Cotton Pickers), with songs composed for them by men in the other groups. The range of ages of the singers was a sign that carnival enthusiasts had constructed a bridge from the past to the present that enlisted all the generations.

The *Murga* Los Llorones (The Weepers)

Almost all of the eleven men of the *murga* named Los Llorones were *campesinos*. Their costumes revealed their meager means. They had spent a total of 1,500 *pesetas* for drab, long, tan coats made of coarse cotton and simple caps. As props they had pacifiers normally employed to keep infants quiet. The *murga* used a bass drum and a snare drum to set their pace through town. No guitars or other instruments provided accompaniment for the songs, except for the *pitos* (kazoos) that the men sounded to provide the musical key at the start of each verse.

The leader of Los Llorones, Manuel Lagos Barberán, known as Manolo el Zapatero (shoemaker), was then thirty years of age. Manolo had served as an apprentice for several years before earning a full day's wage. He had no shop of his own, and he worked for two older, former shoemakers who farmed out orders from individuals and suppliers in the city. In order to earn even a minimum wage, Manolo had to complete at least one pair of boots (to sew and trim the soles to the upper leather) each day. Most days he sat hunched over a low workbench in a dark, low-ceilinged room in the company of two other journeymen shoemakers. The three men worked without pause and rarely looked up as they sewed and pounded leather. At other times Manolo worked alone. Since his own small house was crowded with his young children, he often returned to a room in his mother's house, sometimes cutting and trimming leather while seated on the doorway step to catch the slanting winter sun.

Despite the long hours and hard work, to some the trade of shoemaking still seemed preferable to laboring on the land of other men or to work as an itinerant construction laborer, the only opportunities available to men without education or a craft. While *campesinos* were locked in a struggle with hardship and the weather, shoemakers were at least able to avoid the heat of the summer sun. During the days of winter rain when the fields were impassable and unemployed *campesinos* slipped deeper into debt, shoemakers could continue to earn a wage and pay their bills to the local shopkeepers. Shoemaking also enabled the men to remain in the town and spend the nights with their families. In contrast, masons and peons had to travel by motorcycle, bus, or in a car pool to sites in the boom towns along the coasts and then stay away for the week, sleeping and eating in makeshift circumstances, often in the basement of the building under construction.

As maestro of the *murga*, Manolo guarded a single rolled-up copy of their songs. He usually kept them in his hand for reference, but often the tattered roll served as a baton to keep time. Manolo not only directed the singing, he had written the words of more than half of the fifty-six songs in their repertoire. Most of the remaining songs were written by Antonio Capitas, a construction worker, who served only as a writer and did not march and sing with the others. A third member of the *murga*, Rafael Cruz, a field laborer known as Raphael Canta[d]or (the Flamenco Singer), created two songs for the group's repertoire. The source of the music for Los Llorones was a simple matter: it came from the radio.

Aside from Manolo and Antonio, all of the other members of Los Llorones were field workers. Several were better known by their nicknames: Luis Orellana, called *Torrijas* (French Toast), and Francisco Sánchez Bancalero, referred to as *Felipe el Mono* (Felipe the Monkey) and his son Manuel Sánchez Bancalero, *Hijo de el Mono* (Son of the Monkey). With their limited education, the men could with some difficulty read a page of script to themselves, but they could not be pressed to sight-read aloud. They committed the songs to memory by reciting them over and over in the months preceding the festival. For the last two or three months, as the holiday drew nearer, the nightly hours of practice had increased. For the most part the singing was fluid, but on occasion the men stumbled over less familiar literary and rhetorical phrases.

On carnival day in February 1966, the *murga* assembled in the street. Most of the men wore the simple tan cotton coats sewn for the occasion. The two Sánchez Bancaleros, *los monos*, father and son, however, were dressed as women, using hand-me-downs from the women in their family. At a signal from Manolo, everyone sounded the lead note through the vibrating paper in their *pitos* (kazoos), paused for breath, and then launched into the verse. As they sang, they set off at a lively pace through town, the beat of their march set by the booming resonance of a bass drum and the sharp rattle of a snare drum.

February is frequently the wettest month of the year. In some years the sun breaks through the heavy, drifting winter clouds with startling clarity to dry the land and warm the people. In February 1966, however, a persistent rain soaked the region, and the men of Los Llorones were a spirited but bedraggled-looking chorus as they piped their way from corner to corner of the town and from bar to bar. Desperately poor men, they had risked a monetary investment in their costumes which they hoped to recoup and perhaps even turn a bit of profit if they were lucky, passing the hat in the street and bars in Benalup, and in visits to other nearby towns.

The Repertoire of Los Llorones: The Vela Family

The subject matter of the songs of Los Llorones drew on the direct observations and experiences of the lyricist or of other members of the group. In the capital a large number of songs were based on general news, on accounts in the press or broadcast on television. In the towns, however, matters of local concern attracted the most attention. The songs provided commentary on the events of the year, some notable and some of little significance except to local citizens. Several accounts of minor pecadillos stirred laughter. Some songs were critical if the matter was more serious or revealed a stingy or hostile character. A few songs lauded individuals well-known and well-liked in the town.

One complimentary *copla* of Los Llorones was dedicated to the memory of Ana Barca (the recently deceased widow of Juan Vela, the past scion of one of the principal landowning families in town). But it was not her place in the social hierarchy of the town that brought her the high tribute of a *piropo* (compliment); it was said that Ana Barca always had a pot of food cooking on the stove for the poor.[13] The fifty-seven laudatory lines were a sincere tribute to one of the few of the local rich regarded with affection.

She was mother and protector	Fue madre y fue protectora
of the whole town in general	de todo el pueblo en general
because all her life consisted	porque toda su vida fue
of sacrifice and charity.	sacrificio y caridad.

Ana Barca was the mother of Nicolás Vela, a councilman, former deputy mayor, and a person of wealth and influence in the town.

We have had for some time	Hace tiempo que tenemos
the market on San Juan Street.	el Mercado en la Calle San Juan
We owe this	eso se lo agradecemos
to former mayor Nicolás.	al ex-alcalde Nicolás.

A fortunate heir of his grandfather and great grandfather who had built up the family's holdings, Nicolás Vela possessed pasture land in the nearby countryside and he owned the town's principal hardware store.[14] Recently he had formed a fledgling construction company, taking advantage of the construction skills newly acquired by displaced *campesinos*. Vela had an imposing chest, a forceful, strutting manner, and a deep voice perfectly placed for shouting commands. Energetic in every way, he had pursued and captured as his wife one of the prettiest girls in the pueblo, and they lived in a well-appointed house next to the *alameda* and the church. To show his appreciation for the homage paid his mother, Vela tipped the *murga* a thousand *pesetas*.

The respect shown Ana Barca was unusual. The remainder of the Vela family, including Nicolás, were looked on warily. Not only did they control considerable wealth and power, but at times they used that power arbitrarily. Some fifteen years earlier (between 1949 and 1952), Nicolás mistakenly suspected one of his mother's workers of being a thief and brought his accusation to the *cuartel*. The *Guardia Civil* then carried out their well-known propensity to force suspects to confess.

> "Paco el Rebuzco [the nickname of Francisco Estudillo], a trusted worker, was responsible for the storehouse of the threshing floor on the property of Ana Barca. The manager of the property was Ana Barca's son, Nicolás Vela. He had taken a certain number of sacks to the threshing floor to be filled with grain. A few of the sacks, however, were stuffed inside of other sacks. When the sacks were filled these few were missing. [It was reported that Paco confessed to filling the missing sacks and stealing them.] The suspicion was that Paco el Rebuzco, an honorable man and a diligent worker, was beaten [by the *Guardia Civil*] until he confessed to the deed to avoid further mistreatment. Later it was verified, after emptying the sacks in the storehouse, that in the bottom of the filled sacks were some additional sacks, the ones that were missing in the *campo*, proving that Paco el Rebuzco had not robbed anything.
>
> The Vela family lost face from this incident when the truth was discovered. A servant in the Vela family, with the nickname la Jurela, related it to various people, demonstrating the honesty of Paco el Rebuzco, although this man never received from the Vela family any excuse or satisfaction." (José R.)

Over the years the townspeople developed a mixed view of Vela. Although he was considered by most to be gruff and crude, he was not generally disliked: "He's not a bad fellow, just *muy bruto*." He lacked the Andalusian grace which ordinarily moderated social conflicts; in his use of language, an ability much admired by Andalusians of every class, he was crude rather than clever.

At weeding and at harvest time, agricultural crews frequently worked *a destajo* (piece work). Rather than be paid a daily wage, a price would be set for an entire field and then the workers would complete the job as soon as possible. The landowners would thus be assured that the work would be completed; fewer workers would be employed, but these would earn a greater profit the faster they worked. Such arrangements often led to disagreements among workers and between landowners and workers. If he was dissatisfied, Nicolás would complain to the crew in his inimitable style:

> "He [Nicolás] had men weeding the cotton paid by *a destajo*. But they were in a rush and did a bad job [chopping out weeds and thinning the plants]. He came down and saw it and said, 'My sister could do better with the tip of her twat.' So the men spent a little more time making another pass chopping out some more weeds and he paid them. He's very *bruto* – a mule without any sense [shrugging his shoulder to indicate one should not speak like that]."

It was inevitable that Nicolás also serve as the subject for songs describing actions taking place in the town. In the *copla* complimenting him for building the market on San Juan Street, a frustrating failure was also cited: as mayor, Nicolás had purchased a field and had the *chozas* (thatch huts) torn down in preparation for rows of duplex apartments to be built of cement blocks. Unfortunately, the endless delay in completing the project also made it a topic for criticism and ridicule:

When he was in power	Estando él en el mando,
he bought the fenced-in field	el cercado se compró
to build some little houses	para hacernos unas casitas
and tear down the shacks.	y quitar las chozas todas.
The houses have not been built,	Las casitas no se han hecho,
I don't know why.	no sé por lo que será
The motives we don't know.	los motivos, no sabemos,
We can't explain it.	no lo podemos explicar.

The song offers a clear explanation. The well-to-do property owners in the town possessed plumbing and running water. Deputy Mayor Nicolás and the contractors, however, had been unable to arrange such amenities for the apartments. It was not for lack of water: the town's fountains flowed endlessly and a reservoir had been built above the town. Fourteen years earlier, in 1952, twenty families had paid 5,000 *pesetas* each for a water line to run to their houses. Since that time an additional five or so families had hooked on. That list of names can be read as a who's who of the town. Lack of plumbing and open sewers were nagging problems for the growing population. A modern solution was available and long overdue.

In the same song as the measured criticism of Nicolás Vela, there were compliments to his successor, the new deputy mayor, Don Salvador, for contracting to put in a water line for the new apartments and for everyone down the main street.

We will soon have the town	Pronto tendremos al pueblo
just like the capital,	al estilo de capital,
with water in every house.	con el agua en todas las casas.
That's some comfort!	¡Vaya una comodidad!
We advise the whole town	Nosotros le aconsejamos
in general not to leave the	a todo el pueblo en general
faucet open because they	que no dejen el grifo abierto,
can wake up flooded.	pueden amanecer agrios.

Don Salvador

Don Salvador had married into the Espina family (the descendants of Nicolasa, the sister of Don Antonio Vela) twenty-five years earlier and by default had come to administer the considerable holdings of that branch of the extended family.[15] He had earned his courtesy title, *Don*, by virtue of his university degree in chemistry. He was a quiet, introverted man who spoke with a slight stammer. Since he was not a native son, after more than two decades of marriage, Don Salvador was still regarded as a newcomer to the town. In truth Don Salvador was unfamiliar with rural ways. Unlike his counterpart Nicolás Vela, who was a native son born to wealth, he could not give orders with the assurance that they would be obeyed. Although he was friendly and cordial, he could not exchange repartee and easy banter. In previous years,

Don Salvador had engaged much of his time on the education of his three sons, but now they were enrolled in school in Cádiz and he was left to his own devices. Much of his time he spent in the house reading and studying. "I have lived as a monk for twenty-five years," he was wont to say.

Although it was located in town, the Espina house was designed as a country estate, with a large interior garden protected from the winds, a second floor to store the yearly harvest of wheat, chickpeas, and rye, and stables along one side of the house for two dozen working oxen and mules. Since the lands were now idle, the storerooms and stables were empty and the tack room containing the halters and tools was dark. On the other side of the house, they had built a garage to park a car, one of less than five motor vehicles then owned and operated in town. With few decisions to make concerning the crops and land, Don Salvador spent much of his time in a cold, damp room on the first floor which he designated as his study. He would wrap himself in a blanket and sit before a heater drawing bottled gas, which he preferred to the less efficient brazier of simmering charcoal. Don Salvador was engrossed in the study of English and he would listen to tapes and drill himself in grammar. At least once a week he would drive to Cádiz where he could obtain copies of the latest English and American magazines and practice speaking with the tourists and visiting American naval personnel stationed in nearby Rota.

Despite his impractical air it was thought that as deputy mayor Don Salvador had the best interests of the town at heart.

We also wish luck	También le deseamos suerte
to Don Salvador	al Señor Don Salvador
so he can build the houses	porque pueda hacer las casas
and tear down all the shacks.	y quite las chozas todas.

Good Fellows All

A few of the songs of Los Llorones were buoyed by waves of good feeling. They offered good wishes, for example, to the carnival queen, "*carita de emperatriz*" (dear face of an empress) and a cordial tribute to Barbate, a busy fishing town on the Atlantic below Vejer de la Frontera that the *murga* planned to visit in hopes of adding extra coin to their kitty. The *piropo* tactfully ignored the flaws of the raw fishing town, with its aging fleet and its workers housed in shacks of flattened tin cans.

We have fallen in love with its beauty, for instead of looking like a village it resembles the capital	Hemos quedado prendados de su belleza juncal, que en vez de parecer un pueblo parece una capital.

Praise was also sung to specific individuals in Benalup, such as Juan Sánchez, one of the three local taxi drivers, who had earned the good will of the townspeople. Juan was a tall stout man, energetic, and with an easy smile. Most *campesinos* scarcely ever had cash to hire his taxi, but on occasion he had made his taxi available without charge. Los Llorones recognized his generosity in a *copla* all his own:

When a trip turns up, he's always ready. With money or without he'll go just the same. He has done favors for nearly all the poor people in town. He once took a sick woman and even donated his blood. We salute him. Without depreciating anyone, Juan Sánchez is the best taxi driver that there is in our town.	Cuando le sale un viaje siempre dispuesto él está, con dinero o sin dinero siempre va igual de normal. El ha hecho grandes favores a los pobres, casi a todos. El ha llevado una enferma y hasta su sangre le dio. Nosotros lo saludamos. Sin a ninguno depreciar, Juan Sánchez es el mejor taxi que hay aquí en nuestra ciudad.

Others in town sung about favorably were Antonio the barkeeper, also new to the town, who had opened a new "first class" bar, "el Resbalón," in the center of town opposite the movie theater. Two brothers, Antonio Rivera and Faselito, ages 18 and 21, were admired as rising *novilleros* (fledgling bullfighters). They had been raised in Barbate, but with their earnings their father had purchased an estate in Benalup. Their father had been a torero himself in his youth but had failed to win fame; their mother was known to go to watch them work the bulls in the arena and was reported to have said that she would rather see them die in the plaza than be told the bad news on the telephone. The two young men had reputations for wild behavior at times, but no one questioned their bravery or skill in the plaza. The song reported that Antonio was:

so phenomenal	cosa tan fenomenal
that in the ring of Tarifa	que en la plaza de Tarifa
they even threw him a pheasant	hasta le echaron un faisán

and Faisito was carried through the main street in Madrid and in Seville on the shoulders of his supporters.

Another newcomer to the town winning plaudits was Don José, the veterinarian. Don José was a tall, handsome man, with dark curly hair and a thin mustache. He and his good-looking and well-dressed wife seemed to be almost too elegant for a simple agricultural town. The veterinarian cut a far more dashing figure than the town doctor, and everyone knew he was also far more important than the doctor to the economy of the pueblo. Don José was paid by the state to supervise the slaughterhouse, as well as the fish and other food products sold in the market. He also certified (along with the *Guardia Civil*) the branding of the *brava* animals. Apart from these responsibilities he had a private practice as a veterinarian from which he earned many times his salary as an official of the state. Don José charged for each visit to care for a sick animal and a second fee for each injection administered, and he was continually hurrying out to the countryside in his Land Rover. It was clear to everyone that Don José would soon be a rich man and that in due time the construction company of Nicolás Vela would move him from his present modest apartment to a fine house.[16] Many already thought of him as a logical successor to be deputy mayor in Benalup, or even mayor of the township of Medina Sidonia.

One *copla* congratulated the veterinarian for vaccinating calves on the nearby estates to prevent an epidemic:

Gentlemen, we are going to tell you	Le vamos a contar señores
what happened in Los Altos.	el caso que sucedió en lo alto.
There were masons,	Había albañiles
water and all the materials.	el agua y los materiales todos,
When the boy saw that,	el muchacho al ver aquello

he came running to give warning.	corriendo vino a avisar,
"I come to tell you gentlemen that a calf has died."	vengo a avisarles señores que un becerro ha muerto ya,
"Go tell the veterinarian for we'll have to vaccinate."	pues avisa al veterinario porque habrá que vacunar;
And when they got there, there was another calf limping.	y cuando llegaron allí, otro cojo había ya.
He didn't have a needle to perform the operation.	Ahora no tenía tarin para hacer la operación,
And he borrowed one from Don Juan Belmonte.	y al Señor Don Juan Belmonte prestado se lo pidió,
And Don José was laughing upon seeing the commotion	y Don José se reía una vez la revolución
because even the masons were all acting as cowhands.	porque hasta los albañiles de vaquero estaban todos
The operation began and there one could hear	empezó la operación y allí se pudo escuchar,
"We will have to finish this up even if it's by gas light."	esto habrá que terminarlo aunque sea con luz de gas.
Gentlemen, it was finished with the good will of all,	Señores se ha terminado con la voluntad de todos,
and thanks to Don José not even one of them died.	y gracias a Don José, ni uno más se le murió.

Of course Don José was not always popular with those of limited means who had only a few cattle:

> "One day I had a sick animal, and I tried to get him to come up. He didn't want to come up because he was going out somewhere to have a good time. Finally I went down and got him to come up and we drove up in his Land Rover. He is a stuck-up guy. He doesn't want to give anyone credit for knowing anything, and he said, 'Why don't you call me before the animal is ready to die?' And I said, 'Because you charge too much.' He didn't say anything." (Enrique)

A Visiting Priest

Plaudits from Los Llorones also went to a stranger to the town, Father Juan Antonio, one of three priests of the Dominican order in Cádiz. Roused by the vigor of Pope Juan XXIII, for ten days they brought their holy mission from the capital to Benalup. One spent his time in the church, another gave talks in the movie theater, and a third went to the Tajo, the heights above the town where the poorest workers had built *chozas* along the public way. These workers had inherited no land from their forebears, and their agricultural skills were often limited to gang labor, poaching, or gathering wild asparagus and chard. Father Juan Antonio began his preaching in the mission building on the Tajo early in the morning before the sun rose; and he lectured again to adults in the afternoons. As in all of Andalusia, church matters were given scant attention by most workingmen; nonetheless, this evangelizing priest won widespread admiration by making good on two promises he had made soon after his arrival: to bring electricity to the Tajo and to form classes for the children in the mission building there.

It was well known that the parish priest, Don Manuel Muriel Guerra, frequently asked the wealthier townspeople for charity which he personally distributed to those he felt were the most needy. He had also undertaken the task of asking for money and for community labor to build a school for the Tajo where many of the town's neediest families lived.[17] To meet Don Manuel's request for a new schoolhouse, those with means gave *pesetas* and the workers contributed their labor. The results, however, brought bitter disappointment and resentment.

"The priest asked for money to build a school in El Tajo. And many people gave him money, including the workers. Once the school was finished, they made it into a church [mission]. The workers were angered by that, but being afraid they did not say a word." (Juan)

Don Manuel was a strict watchdog of town morality, and he especially monitored the appearance of the women. At times on the street he would turn his head to avoid speaking to someone with whose behavior he found fault. He could be critical even in the church, accusing women of wearing their dresses open at the neck.[18] He could say things deeply offensive to the hard-working *campesino* families:

"He would point to people in church: 'Why aren't you wearing stockings?' 'Why are you wearing a low-necked dress?' He wanted women to wear long sleeves and not to wear lipstick. 'Why are you going to the bar and not feeding your children? Why don't you come to church? You run to the circus but not to the church.' He would see women on the street chatting, carrying water or something, and he'd say: 'You have time for that but no time for church. If you don't have stockings you can tie rags around your legs.' The people didn't like it, but they could not protest. In their own house each says, 'In my house I'll do as I like.' He had a raffle to ask money from the poor, and he even had them write to family members working in Germany. He gave each person an envelope with their name on it and, although they didn't want to, they gave out of embarrassment. Those in Germany who went there because they didn't have money to feed their children, had to send money back to him. And one of the things he bought was a crown for the Virgin." (Isabel)

The *campesinos* in their turn were sharply critical of the fact that the priest had used his influence to provide jobs for his brother, nephews and the husband of his niece, jobs that might have gone to local men. One collected fees for the electricity, another was a postman, a third was responsible for the lottery for the blind and in addition was a municipal *guardia*, although he actually put in his time as a clerk in the *ayuntamiento* (town hall). The priest's niece and her husband were given nearby church land to build a house and a garage. As Isabel Vidal put it, "El que anda con la miel se chupa el dedo." (He who handles honey licks his finger.)

Then in 1965 the missionaries arrived for their brief stay to revitalize faith.

"During the year some missionaries came, and one of them went every day to the Tajo where the church was. One day the missionary went into a *choza* where a family with five children lived. He comes and says: 'Good afternoon. May I come in?'

The worker answers: 'Come in.'
. . .He asks the worker: 'You don't go to church?'
The worker answers: 'Of course not.'
The missionary asks: 'Why not?
The worker replies: 'Because of the church that is there. I and my children worked five days for it, since we were told it was for a school, and then they put in a church.'
The missionary takes notes on a piece of paper, and he tells the worker: 'Before I leave this pueblo you will have electricity and the church will be a school.' And he kept his word. There was light and a school."
(Juan Moreno y Vidal)

At night one of the three missionaries spoke in the movie theater.

"The movie theater was full. The *señoritos* were there. He said: 'Speaking of the *señoritos* who say that the workers never go to church, if you don't speak to them in the street, if you don't even look at them, how do you want them to go to church and sit by you? I speak to you who are interested in nothing more than to see the evening come and weigh how much cotton has been picked. But you do not realize that many of the children who pick the cotton do not know how to read or write. If you gave a better wage to the parents then the children would not have to pick cotton.' There was a great deal of applause."

Everyone was amazed that after the talk the missionary danced and sang *coplas*, especially since Don Manuel had banned dancing.[19]

Happiness and joy reigned in us all when he came to bid farewell; "The mission is over. I hope that this work will remain engraved in our souls." We felt such affection for him and there had been such good will that some could not contain themselves and even started to cry. He made us several promises which have all been fulfilled: to bring light to the Tajo, and to form a school group. For this reason a cheer goes up from all our dilapidated huts. Long live Father Juan Antonio, Long live the holy mission.	Y ha reinado la alegría y la felicidad de todos cuando vino a despedirse la mision termina ya; espero que esta labor quede en nuestras almas grabada. Le teníamos tanto afecto y con tanta voluntad que hubo quien no pudo aguantarse, y hasta se echará a llorar; el nos hizo varias promesas que todas están cumplidas ya, de traer la luz al tajo, y hacernos un grupo escolar, por eso le damos un visia ven todo nuestro casarones, viva el Padre Juan Antonio, viva la Santa Misión.

With the missionaries gone, a sense of reality returned to the workers. The need for education would fall before the cynicism of the landowners. In another *copla*, Antonio wrote:

Apparently here in town	Por lo visto aquí en el pueblo
there is no longer any talk	ya no se escucha de hablar
of the literacy project.	del plan de los analfabetos;
Everyone already knows	es porque todos saben ya
how important it is	como se puso tan serio
to end illiteracy, but	de quitar el analfabetismo,
whether we know much or little,	sepa mucho o sepa poco
things will always be the same.	siempre tendremos lo mismo.
The other day one boss	El otro día un patrón
was talking to another,	con otro estaba charlando:
"We can't have any of those	no se puede tener obreros
workers who know too much	de esos que ya saben tanto
thanks to their friends.	por mediación de amistades.
You give them work	Te los llevas a trabajar
and after some time	y cuando pasa algún tiempo
they begin to claim	te empiezan a reclamar
worker's rights and	los derechos del trabajo
tie your shoes together.	y amárrate los zapatos,
And if you don't pay them,	que si tú no se los pagas
they'll bring it to the syndicate."	te pone en el sindicato;
And the other one answered him:	y el otro le contestó:
"I won't pay for bad workers	a unas malas yo no pago
because I've won over the ones	porque los que tengo yo
I have now." [they don't belong to the syndicate]	de momento me los gano.

Notes

1. While other towns in the region, such as Medina Sidonia, Conil, and Vejer de la Frontera, also have ancient shrines to the Virgin, the brotherhood at Alcalá is the most vital in the region, and its *romería* attracts the most attention. A documentary film, *Romeria: Day of the Virgin*, which I shot in 1982–83, depicts the day of the pilgrimage, the ambiguities of the religious beliefs of the participants, and other related circumstances. (For viewing information, see footnote 1 in "Acknowledgments.")

For a comparison of worship of the Virgin at Alcalá and a new shrine (since 1968) at Palmar de Troyas in the province of Seville, see Jerome R. Mintz, "Comfortable Old Shrines; Divisive New Visions," *Natural History*, April 1974. To consider the scope of such shrines in other areas, see William A. Christian Jr., *Person and God in a Spanish Valley*, New rev. ed. (Princeton: Princeton University Press, 1989 [1972]) and other works by the same author.

2. For discussion of population growth, see Antonio L. Rodríguez Cabanas, *Benalup (Casas Viejas)*, Los Pueblos de la Provincia de Cádiz, no. 43 (Diputación de Cádiz, 1985), pp. 23–8.

3. As a sign of its improved cachet, in 1926 the local bourgeoisie and clergy successfully petitioned the township authorities in Medina Sidonia to change the name of the town from Casas Viejas to Benalup de Sidonia, hoping thereby to identify the town's image with the nearby ancient Moorish tower of Benalup rather than with the thatch huts that served as the homes of the *campesinos*. In both local currency and in the historical record, however, the name Casas Viejas lived on. Only in recent years, with the struggle for independence from Medina Sidonia, has the name Benalup come to be completely accepted by the townspeople.

4. The events are described in Jerome R. Mintz, *The Anarchists of Casas Viejas*.

5. The other major migratory path is the Strait of Bosporus between the Sea of Marmara and the Black Sea.

6. The Laguna Janda is a marsh that lies in the neighboring township of Vejer de la Frontera. In the year 711 it was the site of a crucial battle between the invading Berbers and the Visigoths. The defeat of the Visigoths signaled the beginning of the Moorish occupation of the country.

7. The vine growing lands around Chiclana were classified as second class until the 1970s and 1980s when they were purchased by the bodegas of Jerez and reclassified as first class.

8. A *fanega* is 5,480 meters, a little more than half a hectare, or 1.6 acres.

9. For a description of the social classes of Casas Viejas before the Civil War see Mintz, *The Anarchists of Casas Viejas*, chapters 2 and 3, pp. 33–46, 47–61.

10. They had increased their holdings by joining various parcels into estates, buying houses in town, and snaring other

properties from members of the nobility who needed cash. Before the Spanish Civil War, the two families had rented estates from absentee landlords which they then utilized to feed cattle or subdivided to lease at a higher price to small renters.

11. See for example Mintz, *The Anarchists of Casas Viejas*, pp. 37–40, 49–53.

12. In the 1970s, when the festival had become more commonplace, a few landowners and the town doctor would hold a private party and dance which would allow them to invite a select few and discretely enjoy the pleasures of the festival.

13. Los Turistas del Figuras, the other group of singers, also sang the praises of Ana Barca:

> In her house there never lacked   En su casa no faltaba
> a pot of stew for the poor,   el puchero para el pobre,
> counsel for everyone,   un consejo para todos
> and charity envelopes for the   y de la Iglesia los sobres.
> church.

14. In a half dozen years, he would also operate the government gasoline station at the crossroads above the town.

15. Don Salvador's own family circumstances were more modest. His father opened a little shop fixing watches and making cases for watches. His craftsmanship caught the eye of Don Juan Pedro Domecq y Núñez de Villavicencio who had him come to the family home to make repairs. Eventually Don Juan Pedro loaned him money to go to England to study chronometry (the measurement of time used to determine longitude). In the navy he was responsible for the chronometer aboard ship.

16. In 1966 Don José and his wife were living in modest quarters provided by the state, but in five years he would purchase the smaller Espina residence adjacent to the *alameda* and the church, and have it completely refurbished. It stood next door to the home of Nicolás Vela. The house was part of the history of the town. In 1933, during the uprising, the anarchists took cover behind its half-built walls and fired on the *Guardia Civiles*, fatally wounding two of them.

17. There were only nine teachers in Benalup, four men and five women, all of whom taught in the main primary school below

in the town. There were so many children in Benalup that the children could attend classes only half-time. Class time was divided between day and night, since many of the children of school age did seasonal work in the fields during the day. In 1965–66 there were no teachers in the Tajo and no schoolroom, and few of the children living there could read and write. Since teaching positions were based on seniority on a national list, teachers from outside the town frequently moved on to better assignments after earning a year or two of experience.

18. In the years before tourism revolutionized fashion, clothing was modest and generally uniform. Older women, so frequently in mourning, almost always wore black or at best dark brown. Men wore suits and caps. Even *campesinos*, who might not have a complete change of clothing, wore jackets (albeit made of thin cotton) to work in the fields. In one town the pants might be black, in another striped black, and in a third gray, but in each town one style dominated. Similarly, in some towns men wore caps and in another berets. All this changed in the 1960s once the younger workers viewed the attire of tourists to the Mediterranean.

19. Before the war, carnival had not been perceived of as a potential threat, and a former priest, Don Manuel Barberá Zaborido, who had been priest of the town from 1918 to 1925, had on occasion even participated in carnival: "The second day of carnival he would say: 'Let's make a chorus.'. . .The priest was not in the chorus but he followed behind. He would write the verses but the others did not have enough time to learn the words so they always sang the same verse. The music they played was 'La Cucaracha.' They sang and the priest followed. When they would reach a bar, they would close the door and he would take off his cassock and dance. He would say, 'Very well done. We've been practicing for a whole year.' Actually they practiced one day." (Isabel Vidal)

Chapter 2

A Round of Criticism

Public Censure

It is clear that *piropos* offering good will and congratulations were not extended to everyone. On occasion the songs of Los Llorones were critical and biting, and some drew clearly identifiable and unflattering portraits. The criticisms primarily concerned behavior that in one way or another violated the pueblo's sense of courtesy and fairness. Carnival time might find the world topsy-turvy, but the judgment and censure offered by the singers were based on viewing the year's activities from the perspective of commonly accepted principles of conduct. In most instances, if the offense given was slight (and some matters discussed were trivial), the criticism was limited to a mild rebuke:

In Medina street,	En la calle Medina,
gentlemen pay attention,	señores, poner atención,
there are two neighbors	se encuentran dos vecinitos
who are both very fat.	que muy gordos son los dos;
As soon as summer arrives	en cuanto llega el verano
they can't stand it any longer,	ya no se pueden aguantar
and at four in the morning	y a las cuatro de la mañana
they usually wake up.	se suelen de levantar
They begin to call each other,	se empieza a llamar uno al otro,
"Hey, get up already,	"Oye levántate ya
there's a sea breeze	que ha saltado una mareíta
and we're going to take	y lo vamos a aprovechar."
advantage of it."	
Their voices are very loud,	Tienen un torrente muy alto
but even if they speak lower,	pero que hablan más bajito
none of the neighbors	y a ninguno los vecinos
can get any rest.	me los dejan descansar.
When noon comes	Cuando llega el mediodía
they've had it.	ya no se pueden aguantar

One has bought a refrigerator	y uno ha comprado una nevera
and they are always hovering	y sobre ella siempre están.
over it.	
We, the neighbors, tell them	Los vecinos, les decimos
that they can get up	que se pueden levantar
and begin to chat,	y empiezan los dos a charlar,
but let us have our rest.	y nos dejan descansar.

Another song censured a family who continually complained about the neighbors, although they themselves kept everyone up late at night:

It was one a.m.	Era la una de la noche,
and I was sick of waiting	ya jartito d'esperar
for the party to be over	que se acabara la fiesta
so I could get some rest.	para poder descansar.
Gentlemen, it seems	Señores, parece que este
that this is not a normal	caso no es normal.
occurrence.	
When there's a party at the bar	Cuando hay fiesta en la venta
she is the first	ella es la primera que
who begins to criticize.	empieza a criticar.

Praise and blame concerning neighborliness are equally distributed in another song. One townsman, Perico Taparollo, is thanked as a man of good will for loaning his kazoos to the *murga*; another townsman, unnamed, is criticized for refusing to help fix one that was broken:

"I'll tell you how it can be fixed	"Te digo como se arregla
in case you can do it.	por si tú lo puedes arreglá,
But I won't fix it.	pero yo no te lo arreglo
Don't bother to ask."	no me lo vaya a mandar."

Manolo reported the matter to the other singers. It was a blow to men without ready cash, and the uncooperative neighbor was repaid in song with public scorn:

"Gentlemen, I tell you,	" Señores, les digo a ustedes
that I'll go and buy a new one."	que nuevo lo voy a comprar."
I didn't believe such things	Me parecía que estas cosas
happened in carnival.	no existían en Carnaval.

The singers expressed indignation toward a couple who wrote a letter to El Cordobés, the popular bullfighter, asking for money. They actually needed a mule, but in their letter they took a tack designed to elicit pity from the great matador:

"We are telling you the truth,	"Le decimos de verdad,
we have a son who has been sick	que tenemos un hijo enfermo
for quite some time.	hace ya un temporal;
You who are a famous man,	usted que es hombre de fama,
if you would be kind enough	si tuviera la bondad
to help us out with something	de socorrernos con algo
to cure him."	para poderlo curar."

The owners of the local movie theater, who for decades had presented little more than early Tarzan movies, were criticized for their unbridled envy when a visiting traveling circus temporarily cut into movie attendance. The theater owners operated the adjacent candy store, as well; to attract the audience back, they gave away a free movie ticket with every popsicle sold. When that failed to overcome the novelty of the circus, they gave it up and charged for tickets as usual.

When something new comes	Cuando viene algo nuevo
some people even get sick	hay quien se pone hasta malo,
and sometimes they even spend	y a veces que hasta se llena
four and five days in bed.	cuatro y cinco días en la cama,
Since they are so envious	como son tan envidiosos
all they want is money;	no quieren más que dinero
if someone sets up a business,	cuando uno monta un negocio
right away they do the same;	de seguida lo montan ellos;
the way they do things	el prose[?] de que ello
should not be,	eso no debe ser así,
nice words for everyone	con palabritas de bueno
but they won't let anyone live.	y a nadie dejan vivir.

Other songs were an index of community values and concerns. The account of the aftermath of a practical joke dealt harshly with the self-serving and false friendship displayed by the director of the local branch of a provincial bank. It was reported that a young man from the nearby estate of Las Lomas had won the lottery. As the news spread, many came to offer congratulations to the young man and his parents. The director of the bank (one of the bank's two employees) was in the countryside nearby in his car and, eager to seek out new accounts, picked up the happy family and drove them into town to collect the winnings. When the joke was revealed, however, the bank director left them beached in town without a ride home.[1]

They came together	Ellos venían todos juntos,
happy and full of joy,	contentos y con alegría,
but they didn't realize	pero no se daban cuenta
that everything was	que toíto era
hypocritical,	una falsería,
because he thought of them	porque los consideraba
as great millionaires	como grandes millonarios
and he believed that the money	y creía aquel dinero
would be put here in the bank.	lo ingresara aquí en el Banco.
When they arrived	Cuando llegaron aquí
they realized it was a	y vieron que era un
practical joke.	engaño a ellos,
They were brought in by car	lo trajeron en coche
and they had to go back	y tuvieron que
on foot.	irse andando.
Here we have an example	Allí tenemos un ejemplo
of the nature of self-interest	de lo que es el interés,
for if it had been true,	que si hubiera sido verdad
he would have driven them back.	los vuelven a llevar otra vez;
This truly showed the town	bien lo demostró al pueblo
that proverb we all know	ese refrán que se sabe,
which is often said,	que se suele de decir,
"One is worth as much as one	"tanto tienes, tanto vales."
has."	

Lyrics Censored

In Franco's Spain someone had to approve the songs before they were sung in the street. In previous years, the parish priest, Don Manuel Muriel Guerra, had served as the town's censor for the carnival songs; but in February 1966, Don Manuel was not in good health.[2] The matter now rested with Antonio Fernández Pérez-Blanco, the executive secretary of the *ayuntamiento* (the town hall). In point of fact, Antonio Fernández could recognize the individuals and circumstances referred to in the songs far better than the priest.

Antonio Fernández, a protégé of Don Manuel, the priest, was a pillar of the government as well as the church. As executive secretary he was the town's indispensible bureaucrat (more permanent than the deputy mayor selected by Medina Sidonia after every election), and he was a fixed presence at the Mass. Given his aloof personality and his clear loyalty to established authority, if he had been posted as an official to Benalup, his circle would have been very narrow. His social contacts with other townsmen, however, were enlarged by virtue of his being a native son with ties to the large extended family of two brothers, Antonio and Juan Perez-Blanco.[3] They were among the few prosperous middle-class families, with farm lands and gardens, as well as property in the town. Antonio concentrated on his holdings in the *campo*, while Juan had developed enterprises in the town. They were conservative in politics and supporters of the Church. Antonio Fernández's mother was the daughter of Juan Pérez-Blanco. The family had a large stone house facing the *alameda* and the church, with a general merchandise store on the first floor and a residence above for the family.

Though he was tall, somber, and a man of few words, Antonio Fernández was nonetheless known by a nickname he had held since he had been his family's much admired and pampered infant: "Nono" (or more properly: no! no!). His social circle was also increased by his love of hunting. February, carnival time, was in fact the height of the hunting season, and on occasion Antonio spent a morning in the fields with other hunters. Each year he also participated in the marksmanship contest which cut across all social classes. Despite this familiarity, Antonio's presence in a café augured careful, controlled conversation by the working class patrons. Sense of his arrival could in a flash turn a bitter jibe about the church and the priest's relatives into harmless chatter about bullfighting.

Manolo brought the sheaf of songs to Antonio Fernández for review. It was Antonio's task to censor any songs that were objectionable to individuals or were threats to social order. To avoid any possible error, Antonio also carried the songs to Don Salvador for his consideration.

It was not that any political problems were expected. The war and its aftermath had settled any possibility of overt protest. Of course Casas Viejas had already been traumatized by the uprising in January 1933 and the massacre and imprisonments that followed. Three and a-half years later, in July 1936, at the outset of the war, the towns of Andalusia were scarred when Falangist forces arrested and murdered outstanding socialists and anarchists. To avoid the possibility of future retribution, purges were usually carried out by strangers to the town. Late one night, ten people, all said to be socialists, were brought from Alcalá de los Gazules to Casas Viejas and murdered at the crossroads above the town. In Medina Sidonia they shot the socialist mayor of the town, who was also the schoolteacher, and the lieutenant mayor. They tied the mayor's body to a car and dragged it through the streets.[4] A few days later, a Falangist force raided Casas Viejas searching for anarchists and socialists. The men who had been active in the town government or in the *sindicato* fled the town to hide in the countryside or to pass over to the other side and join up with Republican troops.

Since no views opposing the regime were permitted, the only discord possible in the carnival of 1966 would come from insults and affronts in the songs that could generate arguments between individuals.[5] After reading the lyrics of Los Llorones, Antonio cited just one song that should be omitted outright. It told of a secret tryst and Antonio marked it with a "no – prohibida." Since common gossip, right or wrong, had already identified the culprits as being married to other people, he was fearful it could be inflamatory to broadcast the song.

Things have always happened and they never stop happening.	Pues siempre han pasado cosas, y no paran de pasar,
Since now the village is bigger each day more things happen.	como ya el pueblo es mayor, cada día pasan más.
Some time ago I found out, and according to what they told me,	Hace tiempo me enteré y según a mí me dijeron
that there was a house under construction	que era una casa en obra
where a secret was discovered.	y un secreto descubrieron,
A boy hung around for a few moments	un muchacho que de entrar
at the entrance.	tardaron pocos momentos
A man also arrived	y un hombre tambien llegó
and, so that he would know it,	y para que él lo supiera
a woman whispered to him.	ella también siseó,
They began their task	emprendieron su tarea
and the boy heard her say	y a ella le escuchó decir
"If this is discovered	como esto sea descubierto

I don't know what will become of me."	no sé que será de mí,
And the man answered her reassuringly,	y el hombre le contestó con mucha tranquilidad,
"This is the opportune place. Here no one will see anything."	esto es un sitio oportuno, aquí nadie verá nada,
And a short while after that everyone found out,	y a la temporal de aquello ya todo el mundo entero,
and everyone agrees,	y se está conforme con todo,
but since then nothing has happened.	y por aquí nada ha pasado.

Honest Rogues

In a couple of other instances, Antonio *advised* that the *murga* eliminate a song or at the least obtain the permission of the persons who were sung about. One of the songs which he cited concerned in part four mischief-makers and pranksters in the town: Perico *el Dornillero* (bowlmaker), Pepe *el Mecánico*, José M. *Cojito* ("Gimpy"), and Pepe Casteller, an *albañil* (mason).

The antics of the men in question were often the subject of discussion and jest. Perico the Bowlmaker had been raised in the countryside on the great estate of Jandilla where his forebears had been woodcutters.[6] Like them Perico was a master with an ax. He had cut and prepared mountains of charcoal; each summer he was much sought after as a *corchero* (cork harvester) whose delicate touch never injured the flesh of a tree beneath the bark; and he had enduring fame as one of the last bowlmakers (*dornilleros*) in the region. It was a wonder to see him split a section of a felled tree, use a compass to set the dimensions, and then cut and shape a bowl solely with his ax. In fair weather, he worked under the spindly shade of some quince trees in the orchard which his cousin rented and farmed. When it rained, he would settle in the doorway of a *choza* where there was sufficient light for him to trim and smooth the final touches of the wood with adz and file.

Perico's bowls were highly prized to prepare and to serve *gazpacho* at home and in the fields. Unfortunately, the introduction of cheap plastic kitchenware made the cost of hand-crafted goods seem excessive in comparison. Few could afford his bowls if he charged a fair rate for his work, and Perico felt forced to keep lowering prices. To make matters worse, during extended nego-tiations for a large number of bowls, Perico frequently tossed off too many glasses of wine and as a result he would lose track of the sums. His five children, almost all grown, were often frustrated and angered by his failure to return home with his profits or wages intact.[7]

Pepe the mechanic was a more modern man, a skilled automobile and motorcycle mechanic who had also become a sharp dealer in business. He had been raised in Jerez de la Frontera, a bustling city at the edge of the rolling vineyard region. He was orphaned early in life and had spent long years as an apprentice mechanic barely earning enough to eat. After his marriage to a girl from Medina Sidonia, Pepe moved nearby to Benalup, where the workers turned their first wages into down payments on motorcycles to carry them beyond the nearby dormant fields to distant construction jobs. Pepe quickly realized the relative ease of counting interest on notes compared to manual labor on motors. To help with the work, he acquired apprentices. He bought a piece of land and built a large motor-repair garage. There was a workshop and three bays for cars on the first floor; an apartment went up on the second floor to house his growing family. As business improved, he added rooms, a fireplace, and a solarium to dry clothes. On occasion a used car fell into his hands and he now drove a beat-up Seat automobile of his own.

Although Pepe had left his impoverished past behind, for amusement he was still dependent on a poor man's repertoire of practical jokes. Perhaps that was why Pepe the mechanic frequently chose Perico as a companion on jaunts to investigate taverns distant from the town. On one of their outings far out into the countryside, always on the lookout for an opportunity to tease his friend, Pepe purposely stalled the car. When Perico, at Pepe's request, got out of the car to push, Pepe gunned the engine and drove off without him.

The third man, José M., *Cojito*, had one leg shorter than another. He was a hard worker and always on the lookout for a day's wage. In summer he joined the cork harvest, and in winter he took whatever work came along. In between times, he had a brace of mules which he used to transport sand up from the riverbank of the Barbate to be sold as the mix for cement in construction work. Because of his fondness for wine, he often seemed to be groping his way through a haze. He was unmarried and had no *novia*. Some years before, his sister had been deserted by her *novio* while she was pregnant, and the family scandal, along with his shortened leg, marked him by tavern idlers as someone ripe for ridicule. At times he fell into a deep silence, although when he was extended a friendly greeting he roused himself and became excessively affable.

Pepito Casteller was a slender man of middle height who had an air of reserve and daring. He always wore a slight, friendly smile on his face and, embarrassed by a sharply receding hairline, wore a cap on his head, winter and summer, inside the house and out of doors. Pepito was an *albañil* (mason). He worked during the week on the coast, but he returned every weekend to see his *novia*. Despite this binding commitment, Pepito still liked to go out to a tavern for an evening of drinking. One of his familiar companions, *Cojito*, was a first cousin to his *novia*. Like *Cojito*, Pepito was a man of few words. Behind his steady, slow smile, he could become deeply drunk without anyone being aware of it.

On occasion these men would consume too much churlish Chiclana wine, whose impurities could leave traces of a headache for days afterward. The poison usually struck first with Perico. With each successive glass and in ever-increasing decibels, Perico would declaim his misanthropic opinions of friends and relatives. More dangerous views, such as his contempt for politicians and priests, were delivered in expressive stage whispers.

A *copla* of 1966 includes reference to an outing when the four companions went out to eat chickens at a tavern in the countryside:

We know some others	Conocemos a otros,
already grown up	quizás ya mayorcitos de edad,
who eat all the hens	se comen todas las gallinas
that are raised in our city:	que cría nuestra ciudad.
Pepito the mechanic	El mecánico Pepito
and Pepito Casteller,	y Pepito Casteller
Gimpy from Chimenea,	de Chimenea es el cojito,
and the other one, you know	y el otro
who it is [Perico the bowlmaker].	sabéis quién es;
When the four of them get	cuando los cuatro
together, there is sure	se ajuntan.
to be hell-raising.	segura la juerga está.

Few further details were required since the tale had already made the rounds several times. As the birds were being turned, the men became increasingly drunk. At someone's suggestion, they sat on Perico and tied him up. Next they strung him upside down from the ceiling beam so that he was dangling headfirst over the table. When the chickens arrived, Perico, upside down and just out of reach, was forced to watch his comrades consume all the food, including his share. As an added touch, they then left him to pay the bill. The account served to tease Perico in the tavern during the week, and he found refuge only at the orchard where he carved his bowls.

Frequently Perico could not remember what had occurred. These binges often made Perico the butt of jokes, even taunted to his face with an ugly nickname – Perico *Mierda* (shit) – pinned to him years ago when he lost sphincter control during a prolonged drinking bout. Perico despised the name and the liberties that even the lowliest habitués of the tavern took with him. "If only I had smashed the first one to say it in his teeth, it would have put a stop to it," he said. "After that it was too late. Now any lowlife says it."

His cousin, Manolo Grimaldi, tried to introduce another nickname for him, calling him whenever possible *Cartucho*, a common term for a *duro*, a nickel-size coin Perico usually plunked down emphatically on the bar when he arrived impatient for a glass of wine.[8] It was to no avail. The bowlmaker was the perfect foil for anyone who had just lost an argument or had a bad day or wanted to create a show. Perico's feelings remained tender, but he had no place other than the tavern to socialize and celebrate. In such a small town there was no escape.

Courtship and Other Affairs

Local news and gossip of a more personal sort resounded in the repertoire of Los Llorones. Of their fifty-six songs, twenty concern in one way or another relationships between the sexes. These themes include family conflict, hasty marriage, unwanted pregnancy, illicit sex, and late-blooming romance. Liaisons rumored during the past year, real or imagined, are sometimes merely alluded to and, at other times, reported in full. In most instances, the individuals can be tentatively identified by townspeople. In some examples, knowledge of those involved is certain but is artfully concealed.

The steps of *noviazgo* (courtship) are well established. The introductions and first meetings of the couple occur possibly

during the promenade in the *alameda*, or at a dance, a festival, or a
romería (pilgrimage), or through an introduction by a relative or
friend, or a chance meeting on the street or a country lane. In the
weeks and months following, the young man can be seen at the
doorway or window of the girl's house; a more profound step is
the young man's request to enter the house and, as a result, his
acceptance as a serious suitor. In so far as the family is concerned,
at the heart of the matter is their intent to keep the couple under
observation and to protect the *novia's* virginity and reputation.[9]

Of course it would be a mistake to think that the customs
concerning *noviazgo* were and are inflexible. In one family with
four attractive daughters, only one suitor seeking a more formal
relationship asked permission of the father to enter the house. Two
others began to enter the house to speak to their *novias* without
permission, fearing initially that securing the father's permission
would prematurely fix a match that was still tentative. The suitor
for the fourth daughter remained outside altogether, not that he
was less certain than the others, but because it was already too
crowded inside the three small rooms. (In a similar situation
concerning still introductory ties, another *novia*, Ana, relates: "I
said, 'No. Don't ask permission because if later we quarrel it will
be awkward for you with my father.' So he entered without asking
permission. My father didn't say anything. He knew he was a nice
fellow, and my father was of the same opinion as I – it's better not
to ask permission.")

The passions of young people were often confined to stolen
moments on Sunday strolls in the nearby *campo*. The songs,
however, are anything but rash. Manolo the shoemaker offers only
a discreet hint of what he had seen of one incautious couple during
a walk. Manolo is accompanied by his children, which may help
to account for the prudent abruptness of the song:

I went out one Sunday afternoon	Salí un domingo una tarde
to take a walk with my children.	con mis hijos a pasear.
I took them to the road	Los llevé a la carretera
so they could play.	para que pudieran jugar.
I met a couple	Me encontré una parejita
I was unable to look at.	que no se podía mirar.
The boy was an outsider	El muchacho es forastero
and she was from our town.	y ella de nuestra ciudad.
When we got back to the town	Cuando regresamos al pueblo

I saw them seated at the counter,	los vi sobre el mostrador,
and she was wearing a hat	y ella tenía un gorrito
that made her look like Charlie Chaplin.	me parecía Charló.
Gentlemen of the pueblo,	Señores del pueblo,
we don't want to criticize,	no queremos criticar,
but one sees certain things	pero se ven algunas cosas,
that are impossible to tolerate.	que son imposible poderse aguantar.

In the same discreet spirit the *murga's* potpourri recalls an evening when some children are out gathering chickpeas. They are frightened by a mysterious light in the mission, which turns out to be the glow at the end of a cigarette (*la luz de un cigarro*). The narrative only alludes to the glow and speculates no further:

And we're also going to tell you about those who were frightened	Y también le vamos a contar de aquellos que se asustaron
one night when they went out to gather chickpeas.	una noche que salieron, que iban a coger garbanzos,
They saw a light in the church of Tesorillo	ellos vieron una luz en la iglesia del Tesorillo,
and they thought it was a ghost, according to what the children said.	creyeron que era un fantasma según decían los chiquillos.
And later on it was known that it was the light of a cigarette.	Y luego se declaró que era la luz de un cigarro
But there were some who ran all the way to the houses.	y hubo quien llegó corriendo hasta cerca de los barrios.

Another *copla* (one of the two songs composed by Rafael Cruz known as Rafael Cantador) notes the ever-present carnival singer gathering gossip for carnival songs. The final details, mistaken or not, are clothed in the form of a descriptive euphemism for the heat generated in sex:

In the street Mira al Río"	En la calle mira al río,
a young girl said	decía una muchachita,
one must be careful	hay que tener cuidadito
for a carnival singer might go by	no vaya a pasar un comparsista.
when one slips up,	Cuando una se resbala

though she might be doing nothing.	aunque no esté haciendo nada
I don't know how they manage, but they bring it out in the carnival.	yo no sé cómo se apañan, la sacan en carnaval.
And another girl who was with her	Y otra que estaba con ella
laughed heartedly	se reía a carcajadas.
and told her friend,	y a su amiga le decia,
"I wouldn't care	"a mí no me importa nada,
if I'm sweating.	si que estoy sudando
Another year they sang about me,	el otro año me sacaron,
and it was a funny *copla*,	y era una copla graciosa
for they said that my boyfriend	porque decía que a mi novio
was stirring the hot coals in the brazier."	le meneaba la copa."

The delicious sting of a thorn determines the aftermath of a walk in the country in a *copla* by Antonio Capitas, the construction worker who composed almost half of the songs of Los Llorones.

One Sunday afternoon	Un domingo por la tarde
I ran into two girls.	me encontré con dos chiquillas;
They were taking a walk	iban echando un paseo
down by the road.	allá por la carrerilla.
I learned accidentally	Yo sin querer me enteré
what they were talking about.	de lo que iban charlando,
One of the two was waiting	y era una de las dos
for her boyfriend.	que a su novio está esperando;
She told her friend,	ella le decía a su amiga:
"I tell you the truth,	yo te digo la verdad,
every day that passes	contra más días van pasando
I like him better.	él me gusta mucho más,
He's a very serious person	tiene un carácter muy serio,
but he doesn't show it to me.	pero no me lo demuestra.
The things he tells me	Con las cosas que me dices
sometimes amaze me.	a veces me quedo traspuesta,
When his saint's day comes	cuando llegue el día, su santo
I will present him	yo le voy a regalar
what he always asks for.	lo que tanto me ha pedido,
It will surprise him."	la sorpresa le voy a dar.
The following week	A la semana siguiente
we were told	a nosotros nos dijeron

that she was seen walking	que la habían visto pasar,
by the road.	allá por el llano orero;
She was telling her boyfriend.	ella le decía al novio
"Hurry, it's getting dark."	aligera que es de noche;
They lay down to rest	se pusieron a descansar
by the sign that says "14 km."	en el K. 14,
They reached the new bar	Llegaron a la venta nueva
with their hair in their faces.	con los pelos en la cara,
He drank a beer	y él tomó una cerveza
and she drank a soda pop.	y ella tomó una fanta.
"That's very refreshing,"	Eso es muy refrescante,
the bartender told them.	el ventero le decía.
They looked at each other	Se miraron uno al otro
and the girl laughed.	y la niña se reía.
Some time after this we learned	De aquello nosotros nos enteamos
that she had been struck by a thorn	que se había clavado una espina
and had become swollen.	y a ella le había enconado.
After some days passed	A la temporá de aquello
the boy backed down,	el muchacho echó para atrás
and then that girl	y entonces aquella chiquilla
would not stop crying.	no paraba de llorar;
In her weeping and bitterness	en su llanto y amargura
she could only say	sola ella se declaró
that her weeping was due to	que el llanto era a consecuencia
the surprise that she gave him.	de la sorpresa que dio.

Manolo the shoemaker penned one song of courtship that ends with marriage in sight:

This past summer	Este verano pasado
we overheard a quarrel	escuchamos una pelea,
one night here in the town	una noche aquí en el pueblo
between a young man and an old woman.	un muchacho y una vieja;
She was telling him,	ella le estaba diciendo
"In truth I tell you	de verdad te digo yo,
don't go near my daughter again.	no te acerques más a mi hija,
I ask it as a favor.	te lo pido de favor,
I don't want her to have a boyfriend	no quiero que tenga novio
because she is still too young.	porque todavía es muy chica

And besides, she is being	y a ella la pretende otro
courted by someone else	que el sentío se lo quita ya,
who's going out of his mind.	puesto que le hable
I've already talked to that man	a un hombre
to see if he has some means,	que tengo alguna cosita,
and he who is in love with her,	y ese que la está queriendo
says he has some cash."	dice que tiene perrita,
The boy answers her,	y el muchacho le contesta:
"I have good intentions,	tengo sembrado en mi casa
I have planted at my house	cuatro matos de pimiento,
four pimento plants.	vendiéndolo bien vendido
If I sell them at a good price,	tenemos para empresa,
we'll have enough to get started.	traigo buenos pensamientos,
Since prices are so high,	al precio que están las cosas
we'll gather a little capital.	ajuntaremos un capital.
I have a cow, Luisa,	Tengo una vaca, Luisa;
that my father says is mine,	dice mi padre que es mía
and the day I marry,	y el día que yo me case
I will start a dairy."	montaré una lechería.
When she heard these words	Al oír aquellas palabras
the woman went crazy.	la mujer se volvía loca;
At once she called her daughter:	de seguida llamó a la hija:
"Let's go buy the trousseau."	"Vamos a comprar las cosas."

The singers also reported on a new phenomenon in town: dancing the *yenka*. Four songs explored the varied results of the fad. One described a range of effects: women carrying transistors and dancing in the plaza with baskets, groups of boys who dance so much they lose their hats, a neighbor woman who dreamed she was dancing the *yenka* and fell out of bed, and another about a couple on a motorcyle who wrecked when the driver tried to dance the *yenka* on the top of his cycle. The most touching song about the new fad concerned Antonio Capitas' account of the emotions of a local widow:

This summer I heard	Este verano escuché a una viuda
a widow crying.	llorando de sus penas
She was lamenting	y amargura;
of her grief and bitterness.	se estaba ella lamentando,
She was telling her friend,	le decía a una amiga suya,
"I tell you from the bottom	te digo de corazón,
of my heart that the life	que se me hace imposible

I lead is becoming impossible.
More than four years ago
I was widowed,
and as the days pass
I remember him more.
He liked to dance so much.
He was just like me,
for when I hear the radio
I can't resist.
These modern dances
especially the *yenka*,
when I hear them playing,
I can't stand still.
I'll tell you something more –
a gentleman caller has turned
up.
I might marry him,
even though people might talk.
Though I shouldn't be looking
around,
I'm still a young woman.
They can say what they want,
but I have to enjoy myself."

la vida que traigo yo.
Hace más de cuatro años
que viuda me quedé,
y contra más días van pasando
más me acuerdo yo de él;
le gustaba tanto el baile
le pasaba igual que a mí,
que cuando escucho la radio
no me puedo resistir,
con estos bailes modernos,
en particular la Yenka,
cuando lo escucho tocar
yo no me puedo estar quieta.
También te digo otra cosa
que me ha salido un preten-
diente,
quizás me case con él,
aunque murmuren las gentes,
porque soy una mujer joven

y no debo mirar nada,
y que digan lo que quieran
pero debo disfrutar.

The sexual longings of mature adults, widows and widowers, always drew widespread interest and provided the best opportunity for town pranksters to try their hands at embarrassing couples eager to give marriage a second go-around. Manolo's account of a marriage day is reminiscent of a Maupassant tale of country fun:

This past winter,
gentlemen, pay attention,
a wedding was held
where both of them were
widowed.
They were young enough,
and as it is natural,
they have the right to live
and to enjoy themselves.
The ceremony was over
and they came in to sign
and he went and told his wife,
"Go in and I'll follow."

Este invierno pasado,
señores, pongan atención,
se ha celebrado una boda
que viudos eran los dos.

Ellos se encuentran muy jóvenes
como es cosa natural,
tienen derecho a la vida
y también a disfrutar.
Terminó la ceremonia
y pasaron a firmar,
y él fue y le dijo a su esposa:
Sigue, que yo iré detrás."

On the corner, Alfonso Pérez	Y en la esquina Alfonso Pérez,
a friend, waited for him.	un amigo lo esperó:
"Let's go have a drink,	Vamos a tomar una copa,
at least invite us."	por lo menos invítanos."
He didn't resist	Él no puso resistencia
and he went in the store.	y en la tienda él entró,
One drink followed the other.	una copa y otra copa,
He got a little drunk.	se puso un poco pintan.
What a bad sign that was!	Qué malasombra fue aquello,
A friend came in	un amigo se le presentó,
saying, "At Julio's bar	dijo "en la Venta Julio,
I have a turkey that will feed	tengo yo un pavo pá tós,"
us all."	
He didn't want to go at all	él no quería ni a tiros,
but they ganged up on him	y lo cogieron entre todos;
and got him in a car.	lo montaron en un coche
And to Julio's he went.	y ante Julio se plantó,
When he was eating the turkey,	estando comiendo el pavo
he heard a little cow bell.	un cencerrito escuchó;
It was the joke of a friend	fue una broma de un amigo
who did it in a friendly way.	que por la amistad le dio.
At two in the morning	Las dos de la madrugada
they all returned	ellos volvieron para acá
and he knocked at his door:	y él ha llamado a la puerta.
"Antonio is not here." [his	"Antonio aquí no está."
bride said]	
These are the unfortunate	Esas son cosas malas
things that happened to that	_____, que al muchacho le pasó,
boy.	
He spent his wedding night	La primera noche de novio,
at Julio's.	con Julio la pasó.

Notes

1. Some songs on local affairs carried a playful pinch rather than a reproachful sting. This was the case with the two hunters who rode their motocycle back from hunting sparrows and encountered a bull who tossed them into a stream. To their embarrassment it turned out to be a tame bull well known to most townspeople.

. . . it was the bull of Juan Pareja,	que era el toro Juan Pereja
who was tired of plowing.	que está harto de arar.
He was accustomed	El estaba acostumbrado
to eat by gas light.	a comer con luz de gas,
When he saw the light of the motorcycle,	cuando vio la del motor,
"Here comes the fodder already."	"Ay viene del pienso ya."

2. Don Manuel Muriel Guerra passed away a month after carnival on March 22, 1966. He had been parish priest of Benalup for thirty-two years, beginning in June 1934.
3. See Jerome R. Mintz, *The Anarchists of Casas Viejas*, pp. 42, 110, 285.
4. Isabel R. recalled the reaction to the events in Medina: "We compare Jesús with the mayor of Medina, who was a very good man. They kidnapped him and killed him – shot him in the legs and then in the head. This was during the *Movimiento Nacional* – Franco's uprising]. They killed him because he was good, just like it happened with Jesus. They dragged him through the country roads because he was very good to the poor people of the area. Jesús was also good to the poor, and that's why they killed him."

   For a description of the situation at that time in Benalup, see Mintz, *The Anarchists of Casas Viejas*, pp. 282–7.

   Luis de la Rosa explained the sensitivity to censorship in Trebujena: "Censors rarely had to cross out songs on political themes, since fear prevented lyricists from touching on such topics. Some *murgistas* – among them Eladio and Cristobal, the electrician – had been shot after 1936 for staging Gil Robles' burial or for criticizing the town council, stating the need to clean it [of corrupt officials]." *Breve Historia del Carnaval de Trebujena*, 1992, p. 37.
5. Concerning Trebujena, Luis de la Rosa notes: "The most frequently censored *coplas* used dirty words or made compromising references to people of the town. . ." *Breve Historia del Carnaval de Trebujena*, p. 37.
6. Jandilla lies in the township of Vejer de la Frontera, but Benalup is easily accessible to residents of the estate.
7. In 1987 I released a forty-five minute black-and-white documentary film about Perico, using footage I had shot in 1970–71:

Perico the Bowlmaker. (See "Acknowledgments," footnote 1, for information concerning viewing.)

8. It also is the name of a cartridge for a gun.

9. See J.A. Pitt-Rivers, *The People of the Sierra*, pp. 112–21. See also Richard and Sally Price, "Noviazgo in an Andalusian Pueblo," *Southwestern Journal of Anthropology*, vol. 22 (1966), pp. 302–24.

Chapter 3

Social Problems in the Repertoire of Los Llorones

Los Llorones (the Weepers)

The most critical songs of the *murga* Los Llorones concerned work and land. The images drawn in these songs were often powerful metaphors of the lives of the *campesinos*. Some songs lamented the miserable circumstances of daily life. They railed against individual exploiters and indolent landowners, and they bewailed the failure of the nation – "Beloved Spain" – to redress grievances. Fear of being too pointed in dangerous times, however, tempered specific accusations. During the dictatorship the government and the leadership were immune to direct verbal attack.

The outlook of each group was signaled by its name. The name selected by *"Los Llorones,"* the Weepers, forecast the *murga's* intention to sound heartfelt complaints.

These children have learned by rote the old proverb: "The baby that does not cry does not suckle." And this is the simple truth.	Estos niños han aprendido de memoria este refrán: "El que no llora no mama" y ésa es la pura verdad.

Temporary Workers

During the 1960s, as in all of Spain, the town of Benalup faced a deep and enduring unemployment crisis. Of course, even in the best of times past when the fields were tilled and intensively planted, the *campo* provided no more than six to seven months of seasonal employment for most *campesinos*. Only a very few workers ever held positions as *fijos*, those who worked each day the year around on an estate. The *fijos* accepted low wages in exchange for the security of a yearly contract. Mechanization eliminated still further the number of manual tasks and left the *campesinos* with only odd jobs, weeding or helping at harvest time. With the rise in tourism and a corresponding increase in the price of beef, landowners became dedicated to raising cattle, a practice which required only a few herders and drovers. The area was designated a cattle zone, which made the landowners immune from requirements to plant crops. *Campesinos* were forced to find employment as itinerant construction workers primarily along the Mediterranean coast, or to emigrate elsewhere to the larger cities of Spain or to other countries in Western Europe to toil as fieldworkers or as laborers.

Both Manolo the shoemaker and Antonio the construction worker, the composers for Los Llorones, tackled the themes of unemployment and emigration in their songs. In addition to the frustration over the lack of work, there was anger that those with jobs were being pressured to produce beyond their endurance. Antonio could speak from the point of view of those who had to deal with low-level field bosses:

Chatting one day about their times,	Hablando un día de sus tiempos,
two old men spoke like this:	dos viejos decían así:
"This town has become so unbearable that it is	este pueblo ya se ha puesto
impossible to live here."	que nadie puede vivir,
One said to the other,	le decía uno al otro.
"Before, all the fields were planted.	Ante todo estaba sembrado.
Neither in summer nor winter	Ni en verano ni en invierno
was there a man out of work.	había un hombre parado
You should see the difference.	allí que ve la diferencia,
This all seems unreal.	esto parece un ensueño
For now anyone who works	que ahora todo el que trabaja
has had to have influence.	tiene que ser por empeño,
It's really unbelievable	esto parece mentira,
what has happened.	los parajes que han llegado,
The land is uncultivated and	las tierras todas vacías
all they do is raise cattle.	y sólo crían ganado,
They plant nothing but cotton,	no siembran más que algodón,
and one can't earn anything.	no se gana casi nada;
You have to break your back	hay que romperse los huesos

to earn a day's pay.	para sacar una peona;
Also, at some farms they put	también algunos cortijos
a foreman in charge	te ponen un manijero
to squeeze without conscience	para que apriete sin conciencia
and to keep an eye on his	y fiche a sus compañeros,
fellow workers	
if someone falls behind.	si alguno se queda detrás.
The foremen won't keep quiet	También se van de la lengua
and they inform to the bosses,	con cuento a los operadores,
for they are without shame.	porque no tienen vergüenza,
But that sort of person	y a esa clase de individuo
will also have their day.	también le llega el momento,
For one day, having done this,	que no cabe en ningún lado
they won't fit anywhere.	tener esos pensamientos.

So many men had left to seek work elsewhere that the town's children were pressed into seasonal labor before reaching the proper age. Even the very youngest were hired to weed the fields, or they accompanied the rest of the family to pick cotton. Manolo composed the most biting song of the *murga*, in this instance concerning a family where alcohol had left its mark. It was the heart of the repertoire of Los Llorones, since almost all of the poor shared the pain of hurrying their children to the fields. "It's terrible," one woman confessed, "to have to send your children to work the way I do. I have to wake them up early at 6:30. They're all groggy, and I have to send them out to work. It's terrible."

We, the weepers of Llorones,	Esta murga de Llorones
come to tell you,	les venimos a explicar,
what a woman does	lo que pasa esta señora
to raise her children.	para sus hijos criar;
The father who is a foreman	el padre que es el maestro
has turned to drink,	se ha empicado en el alcohol,
and what he earns in a month,	lo que gana en un mes
he spends in a day.	lo gasta en un día.
"This is my son Juanito,	Este es mi niño Juanito
he is the eldest,	éste es el mayor de todos,
he stayed two shifts working	se me ha quedado dos veces,
in El Aguijón [an estate].	arrecio en el Aguijón,
This other one is Manolito.	este otro es Manolito;
He warms them all [buys coals].	éste los calienta a todos,
"Buy us a new pacifier	"Nos compra un chupe nuevo
or we don't go to pick cotton."	o no vamos al algodón."

This other one is Mariquilla,	Esta otra es Mariquilla,
she is good for nothing.	ésta no sirve para nada.
"You either buy me a little hat	O me compra Ud. un gorrito
or I won't go to school."	o a la escuela no voy más.
Ay see what that poor mother,	Ay que ver esta pobre madre,
has to go through.	lo que tiene que pasar,
Neither by day nor by night	ni de día ni de noche
do they let her rest.	la dejan de descansar.
A turkey that I had,	Un pavo que yo tenía,
Juanito killed it	Juanito me lo mató
to suck on his gobbler [wattle]	para chuparle el moco
since he had lost his pacifier.	porque el chupe lo perdió,
And when they lose the pacifier	y cuando pierden el chupe
they all start to cry.	todos empiezan a llorar,
They start a song	me cogen una canción
that you will now hear:	que ahora la vais a escuchar;
"Ay mama mama,	ay mamá, mamá,
ay mama mama,	ay mamá, mamá,
either buy us a pacifier	o nos compra un chupe
or we won't go any more,	o no vamos más,
or we won't go any more to	o no vas más a cogé algodón.
pick cotton.	
Either buy us a pacifier	O nos compra un chupe
or we will all cry."	o lloramos todos.

The Outmoded Vision of Land Reform

In Andalusia, where land reform had once been a cherished hope of the now defeated Republic, most workers saw the problem of unemployment in moral as well as economic terms. The lack of work and the attendant social misery were thought to be due to the failure of the landowners to abide by a long-standing social contract: the responsibility of the landowning class was to sow crops and thereby provide employment for the benefit of all. This social vision, however, existed only in the minds of the working poor.

Landowners held a different view of their social role. Profit, prestige, security (*tranquilidad*) and leisure were their guiding principles. The soaring price of beef had made grazing cattle preferable to the risks of sowing crops. It was not profitable, most believed, to grow feed crops or to enrich the soil with nitrates or import improved grasses or utilize mechanization to increase production. For most landowners, investment in developing crops seemed as remote an idea as land reform itself. From their point of view, no workers on their land meant social problems were eliminated. There need be no concern about fair wages, health insurance, pensions, education, and living conditions. One hardly had to think of one's fellow man at all.

Some estates, often owned by urban residents who were strangers to farming and herding, were set aside as private hunting preserves and visited only by weekend hunters from the city. This land remained uncultivated tracts of rolling hills and empty pastures the year around, enriched only in some areas by strands of cork trees, and laced with nests of partridges and rabbit burrows. An armed guard was posted throughout the week to prevent the local men from poaching, and to spot game.

> "If you want to kill a good stag you must seek him out. You must go out at night to hear when one calls, because deer cry out during the mating season. So I go to any one of the mountains out there to watch for poachers or if there's a deer. When you hear one, you approach, get a fix on him and look him over. If he looks good, you call the owner to come and make the kill. When they make the kill, they give a bonus, because here hunters give the guard a tip." (Mateo)

Brave Bulls

A few large landowners, such as the Domecqs, used their large estates primarily for raising brave bulls. The Domecq family's primary fortune was in their bodega and vineyards near Jerez de la Frontera, but since the 1920s the Domecq family had also acquired land close to Benalup in the township of Vejer to raise brave bulls as a sign of caste.[1] The primary concern at Jandilla was to raise the *vaca brava*, the breeding animals for the fighting arena.

The country house at Jandilla had no permanent family resident. Jandilla, although more efficient than most properties in the area, was run by absentee landowners who appeared only on weekends. The two symbols of the Domecq family, however, were present at all times: the massive heads of bulls legendary for their courage in the plaza glowered in the entranceway and downstairs rooms; bottles containing the first pressings of the wine from the bodega, and bottled expressly for the family, were in the cupboard. Jandilla was but an hour's drive from Jerez where the family bodega was located, and a wide range of kin gathered at Jandilla on weekends, particularly during the long spring and summer. In a small *plaza de toros*, the heifers would be tested with swirling passes (*verónicas*) and a mock thrust with a sword hidden beneath a small cape (*capote*). Those females (*vacas bravas*) demonstrating the proper mettle were marked to be used in further breeding for the plaza, while the gentler stock were sent to the slaughterhouse.

There were few fences at Jandilla and *campesino* families employed there in scattered settlements had to be careful strolling on the estate not to come between a *vaca brava* and her young. At another site, for their pleasure, family members, guests, and trusted drovers would tilt lances at the bulls from horseback. Bulls were never tried with the cape lest the animals remember the lesson with tragic effect one day in the arena. Since the rules of the bull ring stipulate that a fighting bull be at least four years old, breeders such as the Domecq family were not interested in additional feeding to mature the animals more rapidly, nor (as a consequence) in intensive crop cultivation.

Mechanization

Even when fields were cultivated and sown, many traditional labor-intensive tasks had been curtailed or eliminated by mechanization. Most commonly the ground was tilled by tractors pulling rotary blades, and seed was automatically planted as the earth was turned. Only a few small landowners still broke the earth using the old Roman plow, or sowed seed by hand. At harvest time, in place of a line of men bent at the waist reaping wheat by hand, there were mechanical harvesters and threshing machines. During the 1950s and 1960s, cotton, a relatively new cash crop first introduced into the area around 1920, also provided some weeks of piece work when the cotton blossomed. Cotton was one of the few crops still picked by hand. Pay was by weight, and with so many men away, women and children were the principal workers. Entire families moved, bent over down the rows, picking cotton and depositing it in long burlap sacks which they drew along with them.

Neither in the fields nor in factories in town could workers match the speed of newly introduced machines; nor were crafts-men able to lower the cost of their labor to meet the overwhelming competition from mass-produced products. Cheap factory-made shoes were replacing handsewn shoes even though the latter could better resist the mud and water of the *campo*. With their market reduced, the number of shoemakers sharply diminished and the apprentice system was irretrievably broken. Woodcutters suffered a like fate: the burning of wood into charcoal, once an important local trade, was reduced by widespread use of bottled gas. Synthetic products had replaced the flexible and fire-resistant cork in floors and walls; cork had fallen from favor among vintners and plastic caps now served instead of cork plugs. Even *dornillos* (large wooden bowls used for preparing and serving *gazpacho*) were succeeded by clay pots for use in the fields and by plastic dishes for the home.

The *campesinos* could not turn to their government for understanding or solutions. For decades the Franco regime had ignored the problems with bureaucratic doublespeak. A joke circulating in the 1960s tells the tale:

> Franco is driving down the highway when he sees a man on the side of the road eating grass. He orders the car stopped and he approaches the man. "What are you doing? Don't you know that it's forbidden?"
>
> "Caudillo," replies the man, "I am starving. I have no choice."
>
> "You poor man," Franco sympathizes, "it's a terrible situation." He orders paper and pen and writes a note. "Bring this note to the *ayuntamiento*. They will take care of you."
>
> The poor man thanks Franco and rushes into town. The secretary of the *ayuntamiento* reads the note, signs it, and returns it to the poor man. "You are very fortunate," he says. "The *Guardias* will not bother you. Franco has granted you official permission to eat the grass along the highway."

The End of Land Reform

The problem of land reform, which was at the heart of anarchist unrest during the time of the Republic, had been set aside following Franco's victory. No action to divide or reorganize the land had been taken since the death of the Republic. Following the war, rural Cádiz still bore the stamp of the traditional latifundia – the ownership of estates concentrated in the hands of a few families. In 1930, forty-one men owned 42 percent of the land in the township of Medina Sidonia (which includes Benalup). In the

1960s, forty-eight landowners owned 32,007.6 hectares, or 59 percent, of the land.[2] In some instances, the same landowners had extensive lands in several municipalities, and many of the owners were related to each other by blood or by marriage. It was difficult to calculate how much land each owner possessed in total, since each municipality kept separate records. All but a very few of the large estates were haphazardly managed, with little expenditure of capital or time. In 1962, according to the Primer Censo Agrario de España of that year, 58.2 percent of the approximately 700,000 hectares of land in the province of Cádiz was made up of 488 estates larger than 300 hectares (one hectare is about two and a-half acres). Of these lands, about 100,000 hectares carried nothing more than "spontaneous" growth – clover, weeds, and thistle – and about 150,000 hectares more was forest, a large part of which could have been more productively used. The decade that followed did not improve those figures. There was little incentive for a negligent owner to invest capital in his own land. The lower the official classification of the land, the less tax the landowner was required to pay, and the owner himself declared the value and productive potential of his land.

Some of the landlords had made attempts to sow crops, but often they lacked sufficient means to invest in irrigation and had only limited experience in agriculture. Don Salvador, the deputy mayor, for example, had made various attempts to manage the lands that his in-laws had accumulated, but he was unaccustomed to country life. He could neither do the labor on the land nor administer the property. He owned a beautiful fiery black stallion, but it was his hired hand Manolo who had mastered the horse and proudly rode him between the estate and town. For a time, Don Salvador toyed with the idea of finding someone to administer his family's lands for 10 percent of the profits so that he could live in Cádiz where he would teach and study, but there was no one who had the necessary expertise and experience, and it came to nothing.

Ill luck often accompanied Don Salvador's decisions. From 1962 to 1965 he had had his workers plant cotton, but for three years there had been little rainfall in the spring of the year, and he lacked the means and the luck to overcome the odds. Water from the river was carefully controlled and limited to the use of the great estate of Las Lomas where construction of a dam was underway. Irrigating the land from deep wells required the use of a pump and pipes, which meant a considerable investment of capital. Don Salvador drilled two wells but found little water. In May of 1965, after three years of failure, he rid himself of his agricultural responsibilities: he sold off his herd of over 100 cattle and rented his property to a retired *torero* who wanted land to raise brave bulls.

To a visitor, Don Salvador described his plans to live in Cádiz, and he was unable to stifle a smile at the move that fate had forced on him. He expressed confidence that he could keep himself busy for the month prior to his departure from the town and his break with rural life. He was occupied translating a scientific article on artificial insemination for Don José, the local veterinarian, who believed that with the information he would be able to operate on the scrotum of a bull for the landowners at Las Lomas. It could be a financial windfall for the veterinarian. Out of politeness, the subject changed when Don Salvador's wife entered the room with one request or another. Ignoring her demands – she is partly deaf and doesn't see too well – he noted that he had not been to Cádiz for a month. Speaking almost to himself, he announced that he would have to go to Cádiz, perhaps on Tuesday. Then, hoping to drive her away, in a loud voice overriding his wife's insistent tone, he repeated the description of drawing semen from the bull's scrotum.

Emigration

Beginning in the late 1950s, a rural exodus began to swell: *campesinos* and other rural workers were abandoning the country-side for the nation's cities and for the factories and fields of the more prosperous nations of Western Europe. By the end of 1966, at the height of the emigration, some 600,000 Spanish workers were employed in other West European countries. For several years thereafter, an estimated 100,000 people left Spain each year to work abroad.

The effect of the rural emigration proved to be devastating throughout Spain. In the mountains and high tablelands of the Pyrenees, Castile, and eastern Andalusia, in rugged and poverty-stricken Estremadura and in the hills of Galicia, the exodus left some villages as deserted as in times of plague. Often only the very old and the very young remained behind. In the dry cereal lands of central Spain, sometimes a community's entire patrimony, including the village church, was offered for sale in the classified sections of the Madrid newspapers.

The tone of the songs concerning the rural emigration was not rage but disillusionment. One *copla* of Los Llorones begins innocently but quickly hones its sharp edge:

This village is becoming	Se está poniendo esta aldea
like the capital	a estilo de capital
with the latest dances	con estos bailes de moda
and with Juan Ramón's movie house,	y el cine de Juan Ramón,
modern television sets	televisores modernos
to distract the workers	para distraer los obreros
so they won't think about anything	y que no piensen en nada
that will harm them.	que les perjudique a ellos.
Beloved Spain,	España querida,
what are your thoughts for the worker?	¿qué piensa con el obrero?
If the fields are not sown	Si es que no siembran las tierras
we will all have to go to foreign lands.	tendremos que irnos todos al estranjero.

In the province of Cádiz in western Andalusia, unlike less fortunate regions, the vitality of the communities remained. The land is fertile and the climate congenial. There are wild fruits and vegetables to be harvested in the winter, and rabbits and birds to be trapped in season. While the pueblos were pockmarked by their losses, they were not abandoned. In the nearby coastal cities where tourism was being developed, some of the men found employment as peons and bricklayers at construction sites, while the daughters in the family sought work as chambermaids in the hotels. Andalusian towns could hold out for better times.

Emigration is always painful for those who love their home, as one of the songs of Los Llorones relates:

There are many emigrants	Son muchos los emigrantes
who have left this town,	que han salido de este pueblo,
some for Barcelona	unos para Barcelona
and others for abroad.	y otros para el extranjero;

Others go to Bilbao	otros se van a Bilbao
because they are bored here.	porque aquí están aburridos
And they come back in three days	y se vienen a los tres días
because they're far from their children.	porque están lejos sus hijos.
A couple from here,	Un matrimonio de aquí
newlyweds, left here.	recién casados marcharon,
She didn't like it there	a ella no le agradó aquello
and they came back immediately.	y de seguida regresaron.
She had left happily	Ella iba muy contenta
because she was going to	porque iba
a capital,	a una capital,
and when she got there	y cuando se encontró allí
she wouldn't stop crying.	no paraba de llorar.
She told her husband	Le decía a su marido:
"I don't want to be here.	"aquí no quiero estar yo;
Let's go back to Benalup,	vámonos para Benalup
even if it's as stowaways."	aunque sea de polizón."

When the need for wages pressed its thumb on the scale, however, affection and fond memories usually lost out. As a result, there were misunderstandings recorded that were both sad and comical.

This past summer,	Este verano pasado,
Gentlemen, pay attention,	señores, pongan atención,
with the migration to Valencia;	con la emigración a Valencia
there was great turmoil.	hubo gran Revolución;
We know there are families	ya sabemos que hay familias
there in a very good position.	allí muy bien colocadas
But in turn there have been	pero en cambio ha habido otras
others who have returned here.	que se han venido para acá.
We know of a family,	Conocemos a una familia
all adults,	todos mayores de edad
who sold their little house	que vendieron su casita
and headed over there.	y marcharon para allá.
When they got there	Cuando llegaron allí
they were received poorly.	lo recibieron fatal.
"Why have you come?"	¿Ustedes para qué han venido?
"You have called us."	Tú nos has mandado a llamar.
There were bad feelings there	Allí hubo malas caras
and it was a serious situation.	y grave situación;

When the town found out	el pueblo que se ha enterado
they took up a collection.	ha hecho una subscripción,
The money was soon collected	se recaudó pronto el dinero
with the good will of all.	con la voluntad de todos
And our friend Benitez	y al amigo de Benítez
was sent for them.	por ellos se les mandó.
On his way back,	Cuando venía de vuelta
he called us from Medina,	de Medina nos habló:
"Within a half hour	dentro de una media hora
we will all be there."	estaremos hoy todos.
There were women running around	Hubo mujeres corriendo
getting the meal ready	con la comida arreglada
so when they arrived	para cuando ellos llegaran
they could fill up with food.	bien se pudieran hartar,
When we saw the car arrive	cuando vimos llegar el coche
we all went to welcome it.	todos salimos a la espera
And Benitez came alone	y venía Benítez solo
and showed a letter.	y apuntado en la libreta
Our friend Pedro Solsale	el amigo Pedro Solsale
says that he won't leave.	que dice que se va
Manolo, Juana and Romona	Manolo, Juana, y Ramona
they also say the same.	que también dicen igual
And our friend Juan Gallardo	y el amigo Juan Gallardo
with strongly felt words:	con palabra my asentá
"You give thanks to the town	tú le das las gracias al pueblo
for all their good will,	por toda su voluntad
but we are working	pero estamos trabajando
and so we will not return."	y ya allí no iremos más
We were bothered;	nos encontramos aburridos
we had done it with good will.	lo hicimos con voluntad
As far as collections go,	lo que toca subscribían
we don't think there will be any more.	creemos que no habra más.
– with permission of Antonio Gallardo, a relative.	– permiso de Antonio Gallardo que es familiar.

Las Lomas

In light of the pain and disruption caused by unemployment, it is understandable that on occasion a carnival song would acclaim a landowner who sowed crops on his lands and thereby provided work for the *campesinos*. Most admired among the landowners in the area was Don José Ramón Mora Figueroa, the Marqués of Tamarón, the master of Las Lomas, a large working estate a few kilometers away in the neighboring township of Vejer de la Frontera.

Las Lomas had not always been a model of growth and efficiency.

"The original estate was only five-hundred hectares. In 1941 we had nothing. My father had to buy land from 156 cousins who signed over their share."[3] (Don Ramón Mora Figueroa, eldest son of Don José)

Immediately preceding and following the Civil War, the financial situation of the new Marqués was very precarious. Crucial to Don José's effort to develop his estate was his marriage with Doña Carmen, one of the heirs of the Domecq family, who had extensive holdings in the area.[4]

"Pepito then was very nervous. He had no money. He would steal from his workers a few *pesetas* in pay. He had no money to pay the workers. He would say, 'Come at the end of the month.' And at the end of the month he would say, 'Come next month.' And they would go two months without pay. But then he made his marriage and his alliance with Franco." (José Suárez Orellana, deputy mayor of the town during the Republic.)

With new capital ensured by his marriage, beginning in 1941 and over the next two decades, Don José was able to buy land from relatives who held shares of the property. His purchases of contiguous lands increased the estate to 3,000 hectares. Don José also took over much of the remaining marsh adjacent to his property, the Laguna de la Janda. This further increased his holdings to 9,000 hectares.

New equipment was needed to cultivate and sow the lands, but in 1947 Las Lomas had but a single tractor, and it was in poor condition. Although competition for new tractors and trucks was sharp throughout the world so soon after the Second World War, Don José was able to turn his father's association with the founding of the Falange and his own ties to General Franco to expedite the importation of equipment needed to develop the potential of the estate.

The major source of the strength of Las Lomas, however, was in the master of the estate himself. Tall and imposing in appearance, with a long narrow face and high forehead, Don José looked every inch the grand *señor* of an aristocratic past. Don José was also very much a modern entrepreneur. He formed a company with himself as the sole owner and continued the renovation and development of his agricultural properties. Unlike the other absentee landowners in the region, in order to oversee every aspect of the reorganization of Las Lomas as a modern farm, Don José and Doña Carmen and their two sons lived on the estate. Don José took personal charge of his holdings in ways both imaginative and industrious.

A Working Estate

In 1962 Don José made a major commitment to drain the marsh bordering Las Lomas, the Laguna de la Janda. He brought in technicians and equipment from Holland to recover the land and harness the water for irrigation. One dam finished in 1966 held some five million cubic feet of water. Construction immediately began on a still larger dam that would hold ten times as much water. Raising cattle had initially been the major enterprise at Las Lomas. As the estate grew, the lands became a mix of cattle and crops. By the 1960s, the estate had 3,600 hectares under irrigation and 5,400 hectares set apart for cattle.

At Las Lomas the business of agriculture demanded the same expertise as engineering. Don José hired agronomists to organize the estate and utilize every field in the most proficient way. The estate became a model of efficiency: roads were constructed; the lands were divided into 100 sections and each section was referred to by number; farm tractors were numbered; and machinery and production results were listed in a computer. Although the estate was diverse, with crops and cattle, its major product was hybrid seed. Pure seed was imported from the United States, and hybrid seed was produced and sold throughout Spain.[5]

Las Lomas soon contained within its borders two small villages (120 families in one, 80 in another) and a smaller settlement with nine families. Other permanent workers were spread out throughout the estate. Most of the workers lived in small neat houses built with a single layer of thin red brick. The permanent residents were for the most part agricultural workers, but many others, men and women, were employed in other service areas: the supermarket on the estate, the hotel that is run for visitors, the bar, the bakery, garden, and garage. Their numbers were swelled by professional engineers, medical personnel, and veterinarians, as well as schoolteachers for the children of the staff. Some of the specialists were brought in from other countries.

There was strict control on the estate. Since the estate was completely fenced in, visitors to the farm or to the resident families had to register at the gate set at the end of a double column of eucalyptus trees. The guards made it clear that no one was lost sight of.

The energies and abilities of the workers were maximized. Workers were usually designated as farm laborers, herders, or mechanics, but they could be shifted from one unit in the operation to another, so that in slack times field workers would find themselves in service areas helping in the stores, the mechanical shops, or in general maintenance. If each tractor had a number, so too did each worker. If a worker was assigned as a tractor driver, he would be held responsible that his vehicle was properly cared for and returned to the garage. If something went wrong, the worker was fined. This sometimes created an insupportable burden for the worker.

> "I worked on another *finca* of Mora's in Seville, and they sent me here. They needed someone to drive the tractor that does the excavation work. I came here from Seville in 1950-51. They had only three tractors then; now they have many. All together I worked for him for six years. Then a part in the tractor wheel broke and Don Ramón [Don Jose's son] fined me 2,000 *pesetas*. It wasn't my fault. The part was bad or it was set on improperly. It wasn't as though I had hit something. How could I pay 2,000 *pesetas*? All my salary would go to them. I said: 'I won't pay. I'm leaving.' They said: 'Then go.'"
> (Paco)

Although Las Lomas was a model working estate, it carried reminders of country life in the eighteenth and early nineteenth centuries. There were ample signs of the prerogatives of the nobility seeking sport in their endless leisure time. Las Lomas was stocked with small deer imported from Romania. The deer could bound twenty feet into the air, and so the low stone wall that already surrounded the estate was soon topped by a tall wire-mesh fence. There were hunting parties to shoot the high-flying deer and other game. Each year Franco himself traveled to the estate to shoot hundreds of pigeons in a single day's outing. When the dictator would set out from Madrid, *Guardia Civiles* with sub-machine guns, like a slowly curving row of armed dominoes, would line the highway south to Andalusia.

Don José and his Doña Carmen ruled their lands in paternalistic fashion. Morality and conduct were overseen as carefully as work. Mass was held every Sunday morning and workers were expected to attend. The villages, neatly laid out as models of decorum and order, were carefully supervised by Doña Carmen herself. Each week, usually on Thursday, welcome or not, Doña Carmen would inspect the homes to see if they were clean and if the walls needed to be whitewashed. Each year she awarded a prize of 1,000 *pesetas* or so to the best kept house. Strict governance extended to leisure activities, as well. There was a movie theater on the estate to provide entertainment for the workers but, to avoid the litter usually found in theaters in the towns, workers were forbidden to eat *pipas*, the small sunflower seeds customarily sold in celophane packages, which are spit out with such *brío* by Spanish moviegoers. Worse yet, one had to keep silent during the screening.

Since Don José planted his lands and provided work, most *fijos* tolerated the forced intrusions which the seignorial style brought into their lives. A resident worker who came from a distant town where he had suffered an extended period of unemployment, measured his circumstances by a simple maxim: "My children can eat here."

Some found the atmosphere too restrictive. Demetrius, a shepherd, brought from his post on a smaller outlying property to the main estate at Las Lomas, was told he could not integrate a few animals of his own into the flocks and droves under his care as he had in the past. As a supplement to his meager pay, he had also been permitted to have some fowl and pigs at hand. On Las Lomas he was not allowed to raise anything but flowers: "No chickens – just flowers." Though Demetrius spoke well of his employers and admired the movie theater and the church so close at hand, the many regulations mystified him:

"In Las Lomas if you throw paper on the ground, you are fined, five or ten *duros*. If a window is broken in the house, there's a fine and you have to pay to have the window repaired. They do it so you will be more careful. The woman [Doña Carmen] comes around regularly and looks in here and talks to you, just like this. They always want to know what you're doing or where you're going.

Once I met her and she asked me where I was going. I said: 'To there and there and there.'

She said, 'When will you return to your house?'

I said, 'I don't know.'

She said, 'Why not?'

I said, 'I don't know.'

She said, 'Why not?'

I said, 'Because I have to go here and there and there. I don't know when I will return.'

She said, 'You should know when you're going to return.'

I said, 'I can't because I'm going here and there and there.' It's really odd."

The shepherd was also puzzled that, despite strictures concerning behavior which he considered excessive, some customs concerning the role of women were slighted, particularly when extra hands were needed to weed, cultivate, or harvest. He observed that Andalusian women had never before worked in the fields. Andalusia had retained a Moorish cast, and women remained at home, often going out only to the market or to the church. This region of the latifundia was not like the north, where a husband and wife might labor in their own small plot side by side. The recent rural emigration had swallowed up most of the men, and landowners anxious to protect their crop called on women to take their place. Teams of women from impoverished areas in eastern Andalusia were brought in to do arduous field labor once assigned only to men. Many of them were older women at the edge of their child-bearing years. They were heavily bundled in clothing to protect them from the sun. There were bits of conversation and commentary on passing events, as though they were in their patios at home calling out to neighbors while sweeping or preparing the midday meal. The only man present was the gang foreman. For many Andalusians it was appalling to see women in the fields. The shepherd was shocked by the breakdown of traditional mores:

"In Las Lomas now they put women to work. They take them from
all over. When they're needed there are huge groups of 100 or so
workers. But a woman's place is in the kitchen."[6]

After a period of increasing discomfort, Demetrius left and made
a new agreement to care for the flocks of a landowner with a more
modest estate. He moved to an old stone house in the *campo*,
included animals of his own in the flocks he guarded, and
overcame both his privations and his restriction of movement.

Despite their organization and material advantages, the villages
on the estate of Las Lomas lacked the vitality commonplace in the
simplest and poorest Andalusian towns. Paco, a *fijo* assigned to
the crews clearing brush from the hillsides, could not tolerate the
lack of personal freedom and the poverty of spirit. He preferred
to live in town and bicycle out to Las Lomas each day:

"I wouldn't live there. I live here [in Benalup]. The owners are very
unusual. The kids can't play in the patio. The patios are very small.
They're not allowed in the plaza. There's lots of flowers, but the kids
go from the house to the school and back to the house and they're
not to touch anything. Children have to go out and be free like all
creatures. If anything is touched or broken you're fined. There are
two or three gardeners. There's no rent to pay and no charge for gas
and water. But there's no freedom. Kids have to be free to run around."

Temporary Workers at Las Lomas

With so many other estates kept unproductive, Las Lomas became
the major source of employment in the area. As a result of
irrigation, the number of productive working days greatly
increased. In 1966 the estate employed some 420 *fijos*, workers
employed the year round; in addition, in times of weeding and
harvesting, some 2,000 seasonal workers were hired. As Los
Llorones sang:

He plants all his lands.	El siembra sus tierras todas.
Some seasons he employs	Tiene algunas temporadas
thousands of workers	a veces miles de obreros
and this brings us life.	que mucha vida nos da.
We wish him luck	Nosotros le deseamos
in accomplishing	de que lo pueda lograr
his plan for the swamps	ese plan de los pantanos

so that he can plant	para que siembre
much more.	muchas más.

Seasonal workers living in Benalup saw little of the autocratic life at Las Lomas. When day-workers were needed, they were called to gather at a location on the edge of town. They piled on the buses and trucks that came for them and were driven out to the fields. Don José was, for better or worse, an important part of their daily lives. They shared their luck with him when the crops were high as well as when the fields were a morass of mud and they couldn't work.

With this rainy winter	Con este invierno de agua
that we've had this year,	que este año hemos tenido,
more than a thousand boots	más de mil pares de botas
were sold at one store.	en un comercio han vendido.
I started watching it	Yo me puse a observarlo
because it seemed to me	porque a mí me parecía
instead of cotton pickers	en vez de algodoneros,
there were calvary soldiers.	soldados de caballería.
REFRAIN	ESTRIBILLO
Ay, it is nine o'clock,	Ay que son las nueve,
Ay it is ten,	ay que son las diez,
and it is still raining,	y ya está lloviendo
and one can't pick (cotton),	y no se puede coger,
one can't pick,	no se puede coger.
Ay, the cotton.	Ay el algodón,
It's going to strike three	van a dar las tres
because it's now two.	porque son las dos.
In the Lomas plantation	En la vega de Las Lomas
and also in the Guijón	y tambien en La Guijón.
[an estate].	
Ay you can see the torn boots	Ay se ven las botas rotas,
on every other line.	una línea sí y otra no,
If the boots were to grow,	si las botas se nacieran,
the next year there would be	para otro año sería
the greatest and biggest crop	la cosecha mayor y más grande
that Mora [Don José] gathered	que Mora ha cogío en su vida.
in his life.	

The Uprising of 1933

In the carnival of 1966, the song most requested by the towns-people referred to the tragic uprising that had taken place in the town thirty-three years earlier. In the carnivals held across Spain in 1933, virtually every *murga* included a song concerning the tragic events that had occurred only weeks before in Casas Viejas.

In 1933 during the time of the Republic, Casas Viejas was synonomous with fanatic courage and independence when the town unwittingly became the focus of an aborted anarchist rebellion.[7] The ill-conceived uprising was the result of conflicts between the majority of moderate anarchosyndicalists in the CNT (Confederación Nacional del Trabajo) and a small militant minority (members of the FAI, Federación Anarquista Ibérica, called *faístas*) within the CNT who insisted on pushing the membership into reckless attempts to overturn the state in a single blow. The organizational confusion of the anarchist movement allowed the militants to play a much more influential role in the administrative committees than their numbers and strength warranted. In the uprising planned to take place in January 1933, the major fighting was to occur in the major cities of Spain and was timed to coincide with a railroad strike that would curtail the government's efforts to move troops. The railway strike, however, never took place. The uprising was quickly snuffed out and the leaders were taken prisoner by accident. Diversionary attacks planned in the outlying regions were quickly canceled; however, word failed to reach the small town of Casas Viejas. For a brief moment some in the town gave way to the dream of a revolution that would change the great estates into anarchist collectives. The enthusiasm of the local youthful *faístas* could not be contained. The barracks of the *Guardia Civil* was surrounded and put under seige. During a brief exchange of shots, two guards were mortally wounded.

Casas Viejas quickly became the focus of the entire country. Government reinforcements under the orders of a tyrannical captain of the Republic's Assault Guards arrived to retake the town. The anarchists fled; however, troops met stiff resistance at the hut of an elderly charcoal-maker with the nickname "Seisdedos." The old man's sons and son-in-law had been part of the group that had attacked the barracks, and they now resisted being taken as best they could with their shotguns. The commander of the Assault Guards, Captain Rojas, ordered that the *choza* be set on fire and eight lives were lost in the flames and in the withering rain of bullets. Captain Rojas then took terrible vengeance on the town. He had his troops round up possible suspects and then ordered them to shoot a dozen men. The facts of the case were repressed for several months, but a parliamentary investigation of the massacre resulted in the trial and conviction of the rogue captain. He in turn blamed his superiors for the severity of his orders, including a claim of *"tiros a la barriga"* (shoot them in the belly). Although the allegations remained unproven, the scandal brought down Prime Minister Azaña and his ministers. The events at Casas Viejas and the failure of the government to control anarchist unrest were among the steps leading to the Civil War.

The senseless tragedy had also burned a place in the histories of the families of the small town. In addition to the dead, in subsequent military trials the *campesinos* who had carried arms were sentenced to a year or more in jail. Suspect prisoners had been badly beaten. The year after, in 1934, a *murga* from nearby Alcalá de los Gazules saluted the sacrifice of the people of Casas Viejas:[8]

Casas Viejas: on the great day	Casas Viejas, el gran día
of its revolution	de su revolución,
– tará, tará – ,	– tará, tará –
its weapons in hand,	con las armas en las manos
it overpowered	ya a la burguesía
the bourgeoisie	toda la rindió,
at the shout of "Down	y al grito de "Abajo
with the forces of reaction!"	con la reacción,"
The day has arrived	que ya ha llegado la hora
to put an end	de que se termine
to so much exploitation.	tanta explotación.
What a great example	¡Qué grande este ejemplo
to the nation	para la nación!
this little town	que este pueblecito
has given!	ya lo demostró.
Under the banner	Bajo la bandera
of freedom	de la libertad
they fought for an ideal	lucharon por un ideal
that they knew how to establish.	que supieron implantar.
They were overcome once more	Fueron dominados de nuevo
by the overwhelming forces	por las muchas fuerzas
of reaction.	de la reacción,
They destroyed a humble hut	[que] destruyó una choza humilde

and the libertarian people	y a unos cuantos libertarios
who defended themselves	que se defendían
with great valor.	con mucho valor.

The *copla* identifies some of the victims and those in the government accused of the crime, and it concludes with a prophecy that was to remain largely unfulfilled:

| Those who committed this crime | Si han cometido ese crimen, |
| will pay heavily for it. | bien duro lo pagarán. |

A *copla* sung in the carnival of 1935 in Medina Sidonia, the mother town, continued to stir the memory of the events at Casas Viejas:[9]

Although we arrive singing,	Aunque venimos cantando
each of us in the *coro* of dentists	[en] el coro de dentistas,
carries a sorrow,	todos traemos penas
and not a small one.	y no muy chicas.
Because we are saddened in our souls	Porque sentimos en el alma
for our fallen brothers,	nuestros hermanos caídos
raked by the shots	por las balas que enfilaron
of those miserable bandits.	de aquellos miserables bandidos.
Casas Viejas is mourning;	Casas Viejas enlutada
in white she no longer bedecks herself,	de blanco no [se] viste más,
because the pain that she suffered	porque la pena que hiciste
cannot be erased.	en el pueblo no se borrará.
How many poor mothers	Cuántas pobres madres
cry daily	lloran diariamente
for their poor sons	por sus pobres hijos
unjustly killed!	matados injustamente.
And the ones who bear the guilt go by	Y los culpables de aquello salen
strolling in the pueblo,	paseándose en el pueblo,
showing off	dándose mucho corte
and rejoicing about what happened	y alegrándose de aquello
in the year 1933.	del año mil novecientos treinta y tres.

The following year, 1936, the Civil War began, and many towns throughout Spain suffered a fate similar to that of Casas Viejas. Thirty years after, in the carnival of 1966, Antonio's *copla*, dedicated to the memory of the uprising but actually a plea for clemency from an inhumane and unjust fate, tied the anguish of the past to the present doleful circumstances of life:

Casas Viejas is in the memory of our nation	Casas Viejas está en la memoria dentro de nuestra nación
and engraved in the history of the Spanish people.	y grabado está en la historia de todo el pueblo español.
We feel grief in all our hearts	Sentimos un dolor tan fuerte en todos los corazones
that such a noble town has fallen behind other regions.	que siendo un pueblo tan noble se evacúe a otras regiones.
We ask clemency so that there will be humaneness	Clemencia pedimos de que haya humanidad
that the lands be cultivated and the terrible unemployment end.	que se cultiven las tierras y el paro tan grande se levantará.

Notes

1. Jandilla had been purchased by Don Juan Pedro Domecq y Núñez de Villavicencio in 1928. On his death he willed it to his six sons (who subsequently sold shares to each other).
2. This situation was not unique; at that time in the adjacent township of Alcalá de los Gazules, twenty-seven owners controlled 27,128 hectares, or 58 percent, of the land, comparable to 1930 when 64.50 percent of the land was owned by 31 men.
3. The Marqués of Tamarón, the father of Don José, had died 1931–1932, leaving his son the title but little else. In 1941 Don José Ramón Mora Figueroa des Allimes purchased the primary estate from his uncle and began to add to it through purchases from other relatives. The estate Las Lomas was formerly called Laguna de Janda. It was the result of joining various smaller *fincas* and pieces of land. The estate had been purchased in 1900

by Don José de Mora Figueroa y Danza, the Marqués de Tamarón. When Don José died in 1910, the estate passed to his widow Francisca Ferrer y Rabech and their eleven sons (named Mora Figueroa y Ferrer). The breakdown of some of the large estates can be attributed in part to the Napoleonic Code which established that at least one-third of an inheritance would be divided equally among the heirs.

4. The Domecq family held the great estate of Ahijón in the adjacent township of Alcalá de los Gazules. The daughter of Don Juan Pedro Domecq y Núñez de Villavicencio, Doña Carmen, the wife of Don José Ramón Mora Figueroa, held half of the estate in her own right. As we have already seen, Doña Carmen's brothers owned the estate of Jandilla in the township of Vejer de la Frontera, and they also held the nearby estate of Espartina.

5. The company became associated with the largest international companies in the world. Ties to the Domecq family led to associations with the Hiram Walker liquor company, Canada Dry, and Coca Cola, for whom they served as distributor in Spain. Don Jose's two sons served to cement these alliances, with young Ramón in the employ of Hiram Walker. Both sons attended universities in the United States.

6. A vestige of the old civility is retained: women brought in to cultivate the land work in teams separate from the men. The only man among them would be the foreman.

7. See Jerome R. Mintz, *The Anarchists of Casas Viejas*, especially chapters 12–15.

8. The complete text of the *copla* is given in Mintz, *The Anarchists of Casas Viejas*, pp. 240–1.

9. A similar tragedy had occurred in Medina Sidonia itself in 1932 when, during a demonstration, *Guardia Civiles* fired at workers without warning. One worker was killed and two were wounded. A *copla* retelling the events was sung in the carnival in Medina Sidonia in 1933. See Mintz, *The Anarchists of Casas Viejas*, pp. 168–9.

Chapter 4

The Rivalry

The Competition between Los Llorones and Los Turistas del Figuras

A sum of money from the local municipality had been set aside for prizes for the singing groups of 1966. The organizers of the festival, who also served as the jury, intended to award prizes to the group with the best songs, taking into account the popular response of the audience. Since many of the subjects treated in the songs were the same, direct comparisons of the artistry of the groups and the merit of the songs seemed to be possible. The reaction of the audience of townspeople was simple to record. In 1966, however, the issue soon became whether the decision of the jury was compromised by ties to the social structure of the pueblo and by the judges' prior expectations.

Los Llorones and Los Turistas del Figuras, the two adult bands of strolling singers in Benalup in 1966, presented totally different images, antithetical in style and point of view.[1] The two groups were distinct in terms of work experience, education, and class. In the social scale of the town, the players of Los Turistas were considered to be a cut above Los Llorones. The Llorones were *campesinos*, field hands. Few had attended school of any sort, and they could read and write with difficulty. Unemployed most of the year, they suffered the brunt of the region's economic and social failings. In carnival their simple costumes reflected their meager purse. The composers were a shoemaker and two fieldworkers. Their talents, however, should not be underestimated.

In contrast, the singers of Los Turistas were for the most part skilled construction workers, principally masons. Their number also included construction foremen and a bank clerk. They all could read and write, and they also had the use of a tape recorder to help them master the lyrics. The leader of Los Turistas in the streets was a construction foreman and fledgling entrepreneur with close ties to Nicolás Vela. The composer was a schoolteacher.

Los Turistas del Figuras, costumed as foreigners on holiday, reflected the great change overtaking Spain: the presence in the Mediterranean resort towns of the growing number of tourists from abroad, particularly from Germany, England, and the Scandinavian countries. The new visitors were providing a much needed boost to the economy. The construction of new hotels and chalets was bringing fresh money into the country, encouraging investment, and providing work for the men of the region. At the same time, however, the influx of so many foreigners flooded the region with novel customs and fashions. Older Spanish women visiting the beach clad in long, often black, dresses seemed outnumbered and out of place among the visitors from the north in their scanty bikinis. The construction workers, once back in their hometowns, could tag these strangers (with their walking shorts, brightly colored shirts, and odd-shaped hats) ripe for ridicule in the carnival.

Shoemaker and Schoolteacher

The natural rivalry between the two groups, marked by slight but real social and class differences, was mirrored by contrasts in the talent, style, and personality of the two principal songwriters. Manolo Lago of Los Llorones and Angel Guillén Benítez of Los Turistas shared many beliefs in common: both were native to the town, widely known and well-liked; and both were serious in manner and intent on expressing their opinions in their songs. Their most obvious distinctions were social class, personal background, and convictions. Manolo Lago, the lyricist of Los Llorones, was a shoemaker, usually considered among the lowliest of the artisans in terms of income and social standing, ranked on a par with the *campesinos*. In contrast, Angel Guillén Benítez, the lyricist of Los Turistas del Figuras, was a *maestro* (schoolteacher), who by dint of profession and education belonged to the middle class. *Maestros* were licensed by the State and bid for their assignments from a national list on the basis of seniority. Of necessity most teachers began their careers in small towns and as their seniority increased they would move on to assignments considered more desirable in the larger towns and cities. Angel Guillén, however, a son of Benalup, had strong ties to the community.

Angel Guillén, then in his early thirties, was only a few years older than Manolo. He was a slender, self-effacing person. During carnival, unlike his counterpart, Manolo, Angel Guillén did not lead the group himself and usually did not participate in the singing in the street. Although clearly sympathetic to the problems of the *campesinos*, he was not a fieldworker. His social background was modest. Angel's father had had a bar on Medina street and for a time had a taxi as well, but he passed away when Angel was young. In order to gain an education, Angel enrolled in the seminary and studied to be a priest. The seminary was not an uncommon passage for a poor boy eager for schooling. Before taking his priestly vows, however, Angel left his religious studies and became a schoolteacher. As events proved, he had more interest in the few days of carnival than in the forty days of Lent.

Points of View

Angel Guillén had close friends among the *campesinos* and workers of the town. But, first as a seminary student living away and later as a schoolteacher in residence, he was somewhat removed from the *campesinos* in terms of daily life. Perhaps as a result, his lyrics lacked the sharp edge of bitter personal experience. The songs sung by Los Turistas expressed sympathy with the *campesinos*, but they appeared as bystanders *watching* but not participating in their struggle. Of course, dressed as tourists they could not even appear to suffer from fatigue. They were observers of the *campesino's* daily trials:

From Las Lomas and other *cortijos*	Vienen desde Las Lomas y otros cortijos
men on bicycles return from work.	hombres en bicicleta de trabajar
On days when the wind blows from the straits	Y el día que hace levante pá que le cuento
need I tell you the cotton and sand made peddling hard;	harto algodón y cemento darle al pedá
when they reach home they're exhausted.	cuando llegan a casa van agotados.

The accounts of Los Turistas del Figuras seemed pale in comparison with the laments of Los Llorones, in part because they lacked the detail and individuality expressed in the songs of the *campesinos*. Seen through the eyes of Los Turistas del Figuras, the pain of emigration seemed distant and failed to evoke deep emotion. Again it is some distant group, *they*, who are suffering, and not *we*.

They go abroad looking for a better situation	Se van al extranjero buscando ambiente
or to other regions of the nation,	o a otras regiones de la nación
and we all understand how they regret it,	y todos comprendemos cuanto lo sienten
for we see their hearts weeping.	pues llorando los vemos de corazón.
It's a shame that this occurs in Andalusia,	Es pena que esto ocurra en Andalucía
which is the richest region in the whole country,	que es la región más rica de tó el país
but the fault lies in cattle-raising which is what matters most	pero la culpa es de la ganadería que es lo que priva "pa" los amos de aqui.
to the landowners around here. If these proprietors would create new sources of wealth,	Si estos ricos propietarios crearan fuentes de riqueza no era emigrar necesario
it would not be necessary to emigrate because there would be no more poverty.	porque ya no habría pobreza.
We, the turistas, your great admirers,	A nosotros los turistas tus grandes admiradores
are deeply grieved, Andalusia,	nos da una pena enorme Andalucía
that your people are leaving your dwellings,	de que de ti se marchen tus moradores
but as they leave this paradise to go to foreign lands we are certain they will carry	al dejar este paraíso para irse a tierra extraña te llevarán metida estamos seguros
you deep within them.	en todo lo más hondo de sus entrañas.

Los Turistas del Figuras criticized the failure of the landowners to sow their lands, but the attack lacked the fire of Los Llorones who face disaster and who cry that *"we"* will be forced to leave:

If the fields are not sown we will all have to go to foreign lands.	Si es que no siembran las tierras tendremos que irnos todos al estranjero.

There is emotion and irony in the account told by Los Llorones of the emigrants who declined to return to Benalup (chapter three, page 53). A good family has left for Valencia, and the town learns they have been treated badly. Their old neighbors raise money to send Benítez the taxi driver and while he is en route they prepare a welcoming banquet of food. But Benítez' taxi arrives empty and, in the account of Los Llorones, he carries only the message that employment outweighs older ties:

"You give thanks to the town for all their good will, but we are working and so will not return."	Tú le das las gracias al pueblo por toda su voluntad pero estamos trabajando y ya allí no iremos más.

Compare the depth and speed of the almost cinemagraphic account of Los Llorones, with shots of the joys of home, family, and friends flashing from Benalup to Valencia, to the curt *cuplé* below of Los Turistas del Figuras. In the Turista version, emotion seems to be held in abeyance, and the disappointment and irony of the scene have vanished.

When the fools left when they left (bis), they had some difficulties, according to what they said. We collected money to go for them. To pick them up Benitez went in the Mercedes, and they almost hit him because none of them wanted to return.	Los tortas fritas cuando se fueron cuando se fueron (bis) pasaron fatiguitas según dijeron. Reunimos el dinero para ir por ellos a recogerlos con el Mercedes se fué Benitez y por poco le pegan porque ninguno quería venirse.

In the song spun out by Los Llorones relating the prank played on the family of the supposed lottery winner, emphasis was placed on the self-interest of the banker who left the family without a return ride home after learning the disappointing news that the family were still paupers. There is a recognizable gulf created by coin and class. (See chapter two, page 27.) When all is said and done, "one is worth as much as one has" (*tanto tienes, tanto vales*). In contrast, in the brief and elliptical narrative sung by Los Turistas del Figuras, the moral ground is unexplored. The shameful action of the banker escapes notice, the social irony is lost, and the bitterness of the workers is left unexpressed.

When the Moreno boy said he had	Cuando el niño el Moreno dijo
the winning ticket,	tenerla el boleto acertado con la reserva,
oh, what happiness!	¡Ay qué alegría!
They brought him in a Land Rover,	en un Land-Rover se lo trajeron
but it was a lie	pero era mentira
and they had to crawl home.	y andando en gata p'allá se fueron.

It was clear that the lyrics of Los Llorones had won the empathy of most of the townspeople. The majority of the listeners were *campesinos* like themselves, and in spite of their lesser education and simpler costumes, the songs of Los Llorones had the cutting edge. Los Turistas del Figuras were fun to watch, but their songs were second in the hearts of the public.

Style

Differences in class between the singers in the two groups were sharpened by their contrasting organization and style. In their songs, Los Llorones refer to themselves as a *murga*, a traditional band of street singers. Los Turistas del Figuras was a *chirigota*, a more pointedly comical and madcap chorus. In the capital, it is accepted that the aim of the *chirigotero* lies close to burlesque and ridicule.[2] In Benalup, however, most carnival players made little distinction between *murgas* and *chirigotas*. Jesús Máñez, for example, observed: "A *murga* and a *chirigota* are the same. They both are comical. [Only] the *comparsa* is distinguished by its seriousness from those two."[3]

According to the official regulations of the Cádiz *concurso*, *chirigotas* must number between seven and twelve singers in order to compete. They may include a maximum of two guitars for accompaniment (in addition to the bass and snare drums) plus the ubiquitous cane whistle (or a plastic kazoo). They may, but are not required to, sing part-harmonies.[4] In contrast to this specific description, *murgas* are never listed at all in the bulletin. In order to find an adequate characterization of *murgas*, it is necessary to refer to Luis de la Rosa's *Breve Historia del Carnaval de Trebujena*. He distinguishes the *murga* from other *agrupaciones* and notes their relative simplicity with regard to music, accompaniment, and dress:

> The *murga* does not resemble other groups like the *comparsa, chirigota,* or *charanga*. It is an association with an indeterminate number of members, both children and adults, and it sings *coplillas* [little verses or couplets] without distinguishing harmonies. . .Its satirical lyrics dwell on well-known events that happened during the year. . .The *murgas* do not use string instruments. Their music is very rhythmic, dominated by the bass drum, the snare drum, and the cymbals. One of their most outstanding aspects is that it does not care about the costume, favoring the use of the mask. . .Another characteristic of the *murgas* is the character of the *maestro* – the person in charge of directing who carries a booklet with the *letrillas* (lyrics) and a baton. . .to mark the beat.[5]

Some of the composers and singers in Benalup apparently saw similar distinctions between the two types, *murga* and *chirigota*. On the surface at least, Los Turistas del Figuras seemed to be more flamboyant and more imaginative than Los Llorones. Their costumes, walking shorts and wildly colored shirts and hats, mimicked the new tourist dress style. As they sang their songs, these *chirigoteros* stepped to a complex set of movements, reflecting new peculiar patterns that had been added to the more controlled Spanish ambiance. While keeping to the intricate pattern of the group as a whole, each of the players of Los Turistas sported a distinctive rhythmic walk of his own. They were a comical chorus of singers and dancers gliding and strutting their way up the street like a New Orleans jazz band at a funeral.

Differences between the two groups were emphasized by the particular genre of songs each performed. Los Llorones sang *coplas* with a varied number of lines. Some songs ran ten lines, others twenty-six, thirty, and some even fifty lines. It is difficult to tell with absolute certainty how many lines Manolo and the other composers of Los Llorones intended for each song. Apparently with little notion of what it meant to render spoken verse in written form, they had copied down their *coplas* in prose paragraphs without indicating line breaks of any sort.[6]

The poetic forms employed by Angel Guillén of Los Turistas del Figuras consisted of *pasodobles* and *cuplés*. *Pasodobles* are narrative or evocative songs which generally offer a focused account of an event or a set of circumstances. The songs are flexible in length but they usually run from twenty to twenty-five lines. Themes in *pasodobles* can be serious, melodramatic, ironic, comic, and risqué, and they serve as well for *piropos*, compliments (*piropo*) to a city or town, or to a woman. *Pasodobles* performed by *chirigotas* are frequently more fast-paced than renditions by *murgas* and *comparsas*.

Because of their snap and brevity, *cuplés* are the specialty of the *chirigotas*. The *cuplé* lends itself to comedy. The swift lines usually turn on a joke and often deliver the most risqué and spiciest lines of carnival songs. The traditional *popourri* (medley) is composed of a string of short, pointed *cuplés*.

Unlike Manolo's varied renditions of verse in prose, Angel tried to fulfill every formulaic expectation. He was an exacting schoolmaster. He composed ten *pasodobles* and twenty *cuplés*. Each *pasodoble* consisted of exactly twenty lines. With the exception of one *cuplé* of four lines, each *cuplé* was eight lines in length (with the second line repeated). Like the street bands of the city, the men of Los Turistas had printed their lyrics in a set of two little pamphlets which they sold on a street for one *duro* (a nickel).

During the days of carnival, the two bands of singers strolled the streets and sang in the packed bars. Despite the greater skill and assurance of Los Turistas del Figuras, the lyrics of their songs did not catch on as well with the townspeople as those of Los Llorones. It was said that the music and style of Los Turistas were copied from a group in the capital. Los Turistas del Figuras had the advantage in costume, precision, style and performance, but their *pasodobles* were thin and lacked detail, and the musical tempo of their *cuplés* was too concise to present themes requiring a longer line or a more complex narrative. No single line of Los Turistas del Figuras could capture the power of the simple cry of Los Llorones: *"El que no llora no mama"* (The baby that does not cry does not suckle) or the wail of children brought to the fields to work before their time:

Ay mama mama,	Ay mamá, mamá,
ay mama mama,	ay mamá, mamá,
either buy us a pacifier	o nos compra un chupe
or we won't go any more,	o no vamos más,
or we won't go any more to	o no vas más a cogé algodón.
pick cotton.	

In contrast, serious themes posited by Los Turistas del Figuras seemed undermined by their comic air and the quick pace of the *cuplé*. Possibly because the costumes of the singers identified them as foreigners, they were further set apart from their Andalusian audience.

Independence

If the Turistas' lyricist, Angel Guillén, failed to convey the deepest sentiments of the *campesinos*, he championed another theme that would increase in importance over the coming years: independence from Medina Sidonia. Although they were part of the same township, Medina and Benalup were actually nineteen kilometers apart. From Angel's perspective, most of Benalup's problems would be settled if the town won its freedom from the mother town and controlled its own *término*, with the power to collect and spend tax monies. This would translate into a greater number of streets lit at night, the main street paved in the poor barrio of El Tajo, and repairs to the little-used but important road to the cemetery. Other resentments had built up over the inconvenience of going to court, or settle other official matters in Medina, which meant lengthy car or bus trips to the mother town.

My beloved Benalup	Benalup de mis amores
if your children would unite	si tus hijos se unieran
there would be nothing,	no habría cosa por difícil
no matter how difficult,	

that they could not get for you:	que pa ti no consiguieran,
the first thing would be	lo primero sería verte
to see you self-governing,	gobernarte por ti sola
free from that ruinous Medina,	libre de esa Medina ya ruinosa
which keeps the prerogatives of	que conserva los fueros
a noblewoman and allows herself	de gran señora
the luxury of having a town	para permitirse el lujo
under her rule.	de tener un pueblo abajo.

In contrast, Manolo and the other writers of Los Llorones never mentioned independence. Most *campesinos* moved in a completely different direction. For them government of any sort had proven to be oppressive and unnecessary. The *campesinos* would best be served by no government at all.

In similar fashion, in support of local religious loyalties, Los Turistas del Figuras sang of the need for the town to choose its own patron saint (rather than cheer for the *patrona* of Medina Sidonia). This religious symbol of local loyalty was of interest primarily to the few who attended the Mass. In the following *pasodoble*, religious loyalty was tied to home rule – the desire for independence in land and governance:

In our sincere opinion,	Nosotros opinamos sinceramente
from among the most revered saints,	santos de mayor devoción,
the patron saint of a town springs spontaneously	que la patrona de una población brota del pueblo
from the people.	espontáneamente entre ellos.
Therefore, it is an unparalleled absurdity to try	Por eso es un absurdo incomparable que quieran
to impose her by coercion.	imponerla por coacción
In spite of being worthy of veneration, we will not give her	pues a pesar de ser algo venerable no la celebraremos
heart-felt celebration.	de corazón
. . .	. . .
We hope on the Day of the Virgin	Que el día de [María de] la Paz no aumente
our logical quarrel does not become more severe, although it	nuestra lógica pendencia aunque ésta durará naturalmente
will naturally last as long as	mientras no consigamos
we don't get our independence.	la independencia.

It sounded logical and loyal to favor independence. Proponents would argue that only good could come of it. Of course the difficult part was to convince Medina that granting independence to Benalup should be accompanied by relinquishing some of the mother town's cherished land so that the smaller town would have tax resources. Medina appeared to agree to allow its erring child, Benalup, to strike out on its own, but with little more than the clothes on its back.

The Competition

The competition for the local carnival prizes meant more than simply enjoying the honor of the occasion. The money was an important consideration for men on the economic margin of life. First prize was 1,000 *pesetas*, second was 600 *pesetas*, third was 250 *pesetas*, and fourth was 150 *pesetas*. Manolo was certain that his lyrics were the best and that they were the most appreciated by the townspeople. The situation was especially awkward since Angel Guillén, the lyricist of Los Turistas del Figuras, was listed as one of the judges. No one had anticipated any problem since everyone expected that Los Turistas del Figuras would clearly stand above the rest, but the judges were tripped up by the difference between their expectations and the truth of what they had heard. Now they had to weigh more carefully the artistic merit and the social reality of the songs of both groups. Their decision came as a surprise to everyone: a draw. All the groups were determined to be equal and each group received 500 *pesetas*. In the end, in the eyes of many, the judges had faltered.

Most of the members of Los Llorones accepted the verdict gracefully. They were satisfied with the *pesetas* that they received, since they had never before won anything. First and foremost, each member of the group had cleared 1,000 *pesetas*, including the money earned by passing the hat in Benalup and in the nearby town of Barbate, and by the special contributions for songs especially composed to honor someone. The 500 *pesetas* from the carnival judges helped a little to round out the sum.

Manolo, however, could not accept a tie. He was bitter over the failure of the judges to render a just decision:

"Our *murga* was the most popular, and we were cheated out of first prize. The schoolmaster was one of the judges, and he was also the author of the lyrics of Los Turistas del Figuras. Their group had always won before. They all knew how to read. They were clerks and bricklayers. They were considered middle-class, with foremen among them. One has a fabric store; he has a new apartment that's fixed up. Our group was comprised of men along in years. They were all agricultural workers except for me.

When the others left the movie house they couldn't look at me. They didn't shake hands. They didn't say anything. I thought: '*Vaya usted con Dios.*'"

Contention over the carnival prizes lingered like a vague headache. Some months later Manolo composed a new *copla* for the carnival to be held the following year in 1967. He sang of the injustice that he felt: *Copla para el año próximo* (Song for the coming year):

Last year we criticized	El otro año criticamos
the movie house in this city,	al cine de esta cindad
and we criticized	y nosotros criticamos
the carnival itself.	las cosas del carnaval.
Last year the groups were:	Y el otro año salieron
the Maletillas (the Aficionados)	un coro de Maletillas,
the Algodoneros (the Cotton-	y el coro de Algodoneros,
pickers), the Llorones (the	
Weepers), the Turistas.	Los Llorones, Los Turistas.
The Llorones all illiterate,	Los Llorones, todos incultos,
the Turistas all quite literate.	los Turistas, cultos todos.
Since they are advanced	Como están muy adelantados
they learn with a tape recorder.	salen con magnetofón.
They were confident	Ellos iban coufiados
of a local triumph.	en su triunfo local,
But the *murga* of Llorones	y la murga los Llorones
turned the tables on them.	les pegó la revolcá.
When they sang their first *copla*	Cantan su primera copla
the judging committee was	la Junta se (des)concertó
taken aback.	
They were telling each other,	Se decían uno al otro.
"They've taken the prize from us."	"Ya el premio nos lo quitó."
They [the judges] thought fast	El momento lo pensaron
and without further consider-ation,	y sin reparar en nada

to avoid losing face,	para no quedar debajo [?]
they called it a draw.	dieron premio a tós igual.
The leader of the Llorones	Y el maestro los Llorones
said with indignation,	decía con indignación:
"If we have deserved it,	"si lo hemos merecido,
why has it been taken from us?"	i por qué a mi me se quitó?"
And I said to them, "Gentlemen,	Yo les digo, "yo señores,
I don't want to start trouble,	yo no quiero molestar,
but one must know how to lose,	pero hay que saber perder
if one also expects to win."	pá cuando se pueda ganar."

Preparations for the Carnival of 1967

In the months following the carnival of 1966, Manolo continued to compose on the theme that he considered to be central to the life of the community: the failure of the landowners to plant crops and the consequent lack of work. Even the more onerous tasks such as weeding were being eliminated by insecticides sprayed over the fields from crop-dusting airplanes.

In lean seasons *campesinos* had always turned to the natural harvest of the countryside in order to survive. Gathering snails and wild fruits and vegetables supplemented their own diet, and they could be sold to middlemen for stores and restaurants in the city. Combing the countryside for prickly pears, wild asparagus, and golden thistle, and turning over rocks for land snails were commonplace activities for the young and the unemployed. But these intermittent and uncertain tasks could scarcely support the needs of a family. Poaching for birds and rabbits added meat to the table and could bring the equivalent of a good day's wage, but culling game without permission was risky. It could result in a stiff fine and the loss of one's traps as well. The worker himself was caught in a series of snares. Manolo described the narrowing chances to escape:

With so much progress	Con tantísimos adelantos
that one sees nowadays,	que se están viendo hoy en día
the poor, the workers,	a los pobres, los obreros
find their lives more bitter.	les están amargando la vida.
With this new ingredient [insecticide]	Con el ingrediente nuevo
that they have brought for the cotton,	que han traído pá el algodón,

at the same time that the cotton is planted	a la par que van sembrando
everything else is killed.	eso lo va quemando todo.
Not a single weed grows	No nace una mata de hierba,
and there is no work.	no se puede trabajar,
And if any weeds grow	y si alguna mata nace
they dust them from a plane.	en avión escardan ya.
Today the workers stand on the corner,	Los obreros en la esquina
today everyone is unemployed,	hoy están todos parados
looking at each other	mirándose el uno al otro
because they have no work.	porque no tienen trabajo.
Wild asparagus and thistle	Espárragos y tagarninas
don't have a chance to grow.	no se dejan de criar
Wherever one grows there are	donde quiera que una nace,
twenty knives to cut it.	tiene 20 cuchillas.
If you get desperate	Si alguno se desespera
and go rabbit hunting,	y en buscar un conejo va,
since everything is a preserve	como todo está cotado
you trespass on private property	atropellan a propiedad
and if the *Guardia Civil*	y si es que te pilla el guarda
catches you, you'll land in jail immediately	de seguida está en el cuartel
or you'll be before the judge in Medina	o en el juzgado de Medina
or the one in Vejer.	o si no en el de Vejer.
They'll make a case against you, as might be expected,	Te forman la represión como es cosa natural,
and when you return home,	y cuando vuelves a tu casa
there will be a fine following you.	la muleta viene detrás.
The worker gets desperate –	El obrero desespera
he doesn't know what to do	no sabe qué hacer
"If I don't earn enough to eat	"Si no gano para comer;
how am I going to pay a fine?"	como multa voy a pagar."
We should not criticize	De muestra querida
our beloved land,	no debemos criticar
but if there's no work	pero si no hay más trabajo
I believe we are going to emigrate.	creo que vamos a emigrar.

Manolo grumbled that he was not going to lead the *murga* again because of "complications": he would have to criticize all the people, all of the judges, and it was better not to put himself in bad with everyone.

As it turned out, Manolo never had the opportunity to sing the *coplas* he composed for the carnival of 1967. The midwinter carnival (the *fiesta típica*) was canceled. Most significantly, the time of the festival was changed to the springtime, a season thought better suited to promote tourism. In February 1966, Los Llorones had sung in tune with the capital.

This festival is celebrated	Esta fiesta se celebra
today in our capital.	hoy en nuestra capital.
We celebrate it too.	Nosotros la celebramos
	también:
We want to do the same.	queremos ser igual.

In 1967, however, the carnival singers of Benalup considered May to be an unusual and inappropriate time of the year to celebrate carnival, and they refused to participate. Capital officials could not be moved. By the following year, May 1968, the composers and singers from Benalup felt compelled to accept the calendar change demanded or give up carnival altogether. They prepared to shift their attention to the new season when, unexpectedly, they were warned against initiating any carnival activities at all. All attention was to be focused on the program in the capital. Carnival would once again be banned from the towns, but this time for commercial rather than political reasons. One of the local singers related how he had received the news:

"I was working on the *finca* [estate] below, and I was called to the barracks of the *Guardia Civil* to hear an order sent by the governor general of the province prohibiting carnival. The sergeant said that if he hears me sound on the drum, he would throw everyone in jail. I had to sign the order. I always obey the law. If we had gone out in February, no one would have said anything, but we waited until May to be like Cádiz, and carnival was forbidden everywhere except in Cádiz." (Enrique)

The winter carnival did not reappear in Benalup until 1978, which turned out to be a watershed year signaling the return of democracy under a constitutional monarchy.

Notes

1. The name Los Turistas del Figuras refers to a well-known series of Paleolithic line drawings in a cave in the countryside a few kilometers from the town, La Cueva del Tajo de las Figuras. The cave has fallen for the most part and only a steep cave shelter remains. The drawings are partly exposed to the elements and careless use and are rapidly fading. Nonetheless, the drawings are the most notable in the area. The cave is a national shrine and a local goatherd is usually on duty with a rope to help visitors ascend and retreat from the steep slope leading to the cave shelter.

2. Ricardo Villa, one of the leading figures of the carnival in the capital, describes: "In the *chirigota* we do it the other way around – what everyone takes seriously we love to mock. I wrote a *copla* about the parliament for a *chirigota* once. I called members of parliament [*parlamentarios*] chatterboxes [*parlanchines*] and weirdos [*estrafalarios*], and in the *copla* I had them dressed in regional costumes: Felipe Gonzalez [the prime minister], who is from Andalusia, wore an Andalusian hat; Fraga, from Galicia, had a Galician cap; a congressman from Madrid wore a derby hat, and another from the Basque country wore a *chapela*, a typical Basque beret. We were being ironic about parliament, which is supposed to be a serious matter. This is what *chirigotas* do: they satirize, make fun of people and things."

   R. Solís Llorente describes the actions of the *chirigota* in the capital: "The *copla* is sung while the *chirigota* is stationary, and it is accompanied with arm movements and gestures – these are the salt and pepper that season the lyrics. The gesture is often more expressive than the lyrics. . .When the *coplas* are over, the *chirigota* moves on, and at this point the rhythm acquires its own personality. This rhythm does have peculiar character-istics of its own, and the *comparsistas* who know the rhythm insert it in between *coplas* like a sauce that unifies and spices their repertoire." R. Solís Llorente, *Coros y Chirigotas, Carnaval en Cádiz*, p. 20.

3. Support for this tie early in the century can be found in varied references to *chirigotas* in Cádiz with *murga* made part of their name: "The Murga del Siglo XX" (1901) and "Murga Moruna de Suárez" (1927). A. Ramos Santana, *Historia del Carnaval de Cádiz*, pp. 94–5.

4. See *Bases para el concurso oficial de agrupaciones* (Cádiz: Fundación Gaditana del Carnaval, 2nd ed., 1989), p. 6.

5. Luis de la Rosa, *Breve Historia del Carnaval de Trebujena*, pp. 54–5. Support for the view that use of variant terms for the singing groups may be based on rural and urban ties, can be found in the discussion of Carnaval in the illustrated encyclopedia *Cádiz y su Provincia* (Sevilla: Ediciones Gever, 4 vols., 1985), vol. 4, pp. 159–62. The rural carnival, typified by the carnival of Trebujena, is said to be defined in great measure by the *murgas*; elsewhere in the encyclopedia article, the term *agrupaciones* is used for groups in the urban carnival. The citations concerning urban and rural manifestations, however, span activities in different centuries without distinction.

6. The design of the poetry is very flexible. As Solís Llorente notes: "The rhymes of the carnival lyrics are highly arbitrary, since they are not written to be sung, but are born at the beat of the music and then transcribed. When necessary – for example when the idea does not fit the length of the verse – the rhythm is tampered with, or the poet leaves some words out. Sometimes, he changes the ending of a word to help the rhyme. These freedoms increase the comic overtones of the songs." Solís Llorente, *Coros y Chirigotas, Carnaval en Cádiz*, p. 24. Ellipses in the lyrics are easily understood by the Andalusian audience who are accustomed to eliminating endings in common speech. Most commonly, *pá* is used for para, and *tó* for todo.

Chapter 5

A Country Poet

A Shoemaker Poet

Esteban Moreno, a shoemaker, lived across the road from the agricultural settlement of San José de Malcocinado (four kilometers from Benalup).[1] During the day he improvised with scraps of leather and rubber to repair worn shoes and boots; in the evening he frequented a tavern near the settlement to exchange conversation and help to empty the keg of Chiclana wine. On occasional evenings on request, he would recite some of his narrative poems for the *campesino* patrons. Esteban Moreno was a poet-entertainer, well-known locally and celebrated for his talent.

Carnival was prohibited for almost three decades of Esteban Moreno's lifetime. During that time, however, Esteban continued to entertain his neighbors and fellow workers. Unlike the composers for carnival, no one ever prepared music to inspire Esteban's poetry. He composed as he worked – the beat for his verses were established as he pounded nails, the words composed as he sewed and trimmed leather. The words were never written down, and Estevan was the only one who knew and could recite them.

When carnival was restored in the 1960s to Benalup and other rural towns in the province, it was evident that composers like Esteban Moreno had helped to maintain an Andalusian poetic tradition. His performances had also kept the *campesino* audience in place, eager and waiting for a new generation of artists to mature. If we consider some of the songs for which poets like Esteban Moreno won local fame, we will taste the starter dough of rural poetry and carnival songs.

A Remnant of the Republic

San José de Malcocinado had been organized in 1934 as a co-operative farm for forty families by the agrarian reform program of the Spanish Republic. In this instance no lands had been expropriated. The 3,000 *fanegas* set aside had been used earlier as a horse farm for the army, and so it was government land that was turned over to the settlement.[2] The farm included tracts for plowing, common pasture for grazing, and a large wooded area which government engineers set aside for stands of pine trees to be planted for future sale as telephone poles. These cooperatives were thought to herald a new future for impoverished *campesinos*. Unlike the collectives planned by the anarchists, however, the settlers of the cooperatives could never claim the land as their own. In the socialist scheme, the land would always belong to the government (to prevent resale and incorporation by the well-to-do); the settlers were paid a modest salary as an advance against the future profit from the sale of their common crops, animals, and timber. Of the twenty cooperatives organized in the province of Cádiz by the socialists during 1932 to 1936, only Malcocinado survived the defeat of the Republic. Since the land had belonged to the army, there was no private owner to return the land to, and it continued as a curious anomaly under the dictatorship.

Esteban Moreno was not one of the *campesino* settlers chosen to be a pioneer by the social engineers of the Republic. Since the town of Benalup had a surplus of shoemakers struggling to earn a wage, Esteban had moved close to Malcocinado in search of customers living in the cooperative and in the narrow band of *chozas* and houses clustered along the public highway.

Esteban was regarded with affection among a wide circle of workers, friends and relatives. He had married young but never had children, and his social life was in the public domain. His only vice was drinking too deeply the wines of Chiclana, a failing shared by many talented but discouraged men. As his lyrics noted:

A master shoe-maker,	Un maestro zapatero,
who lived in a hut,	que en una choza vivía,
swallowed a rat	se le metió por la boca
the other night. [some laughter]	una rata el otro día.
Due to the racket which broke out	Al escándalo que hubo

his neighbors came	acudieron los vecinos,
and they induced the rat out [of his stomach]	y le sacaron la rata
by means of a half liter of wine.	con medio litro de vino.
[some laughter]	
[When] the man came to his senses,	El hombre reaccionó,
he said in his folly:	y dijo con desatino:
"Let them introduce some more rats inside me	"¡Que se me metan más ratas
so that they can bring me more wine!"	para que me traigan más vino!"
[some laughter]	

Narratives often feature aficionados of the grape. There was the drunkard who, rescued from a fall into a well, tearfully made out his will. To his wife he left his donkey, and to his daughter his goat, and to all his other heirs "the ribs of an umbrella." He concluded his emotional farewell with the wish for continued sanctified contact between the living and the departed:

"I am going to the other world,	"Yo me marcho al otro mundo,
because that is my destiny,	porque sería mi destino.
and on All Saints Day	y el Día de los Difuntos
send me a liter of wine."	me mandan un litro de vino."
[roar of laughter]	

Tavern Times

As always the people made their own entertainment both in the *campo* and in town. In past times in winter during plowing and sowing, the *campesinos* would spend their nights in *gañanías* (straw bunk houses) far from the town. In the evenings they would visit the oldest and wisest workers to hear an exchange of folktales and fables which provided a history of past times and often included some verses on contemporary matters.[3]

Aside from the fields and the church, the tavern (and particularly the country tavern) was the only place where men could collect without exciting notice. During the dictatorship, any gathering was regarded with distrust by the authorities (the legal limit was nineteen without a specific writ of permission, but any number would arouse suspicion). The country taverns, strung out near the edges of towns and settlements, were oases of sociability where men exchanged conversation and played dominoes, cards, checkers, and on occasion chess. Taverns were rude places without running water and at night dependent on the dim light of kerosene lamps. On occasion there was singing as well as tale-telling, especially during the Christmas holidays and at fair time in the summer, when visitors would pass through from other towns and settlements. Invariably an aficionado of cante flamenco would appear, such as stout Madera of Alcalá de los Gazules, and after a flicker of encouragement, he would strike up a song.[4] This would often be followed by a dramatic turn by a local singer. A vocal combat would ensue, often ending only when one of the two singers, hoarse and exhausted, would fall silent.

The tavern was Esteban Moreno's theater. Esteban savored performing almost as much as he did drinking and composing, and nights after work, the audience for his verses were his fellow patrons. As he recited his poems, usually on request and when only his admirers were gathered in the dim light of the kerosene lamps, only the sharp crack of laughter interrupted the sound of his voice.

Tales of the Cooperative

The cooperative itself was an inspiration for the poet. For the most part the Franco government was at a loss how to oversee the socialist enterprise. Their great problem concerned how to demonstrate their managerial skills and at the same time dismantle the cooperative and get it off their hands.

The most memorable account concerning the cooperative was the grand day in 1949 when the members of the community were given the opportunity by the Franco government to decide whether to continue as a cooperative or to divide the land and goods. After seventeen years of bickering about whose contribution was greatest, who worked the hardest, and whose family was largest and the most deserving, the majority of the families elected to divide the lands and the herds. The government retained ownership and rented plots, with each settler working apart, raising his own crop and arranging care for his own animals. As Esteban Moreno recalled:

What a great day it was	¡Qué grande fue aquel día
when they divided up the pigs	que repartieron los cochinos
in Las Yeguadas!	en Las Yeguadas!
There was one who didn't sleep	Hubo quien no cogió el sueño
for at least a week.	en por lo menos una semana.
So great was his surprise	Tan grande fue la sorpresa
that he said at that time,	que él dijo en aquella hora,
"I'm the owner of a pig	"Soy propietario de un cerdo
with a weight of seven arrobas."	con tope de siete arrobas."
[175 lbs.]	
I'll always remember	Siempre lo tendré presente
the day of the division,	el día en que se repartió,
for it was a comical affair	que aquello fue un caso de risa
for all those who were there.	para todo el que lo presenció.
All the agrarians were running,	Todos los agrarios corriendo
looking for ropes and screws,	buscando soga y tornillos,
and others cried out very loudly,	y otros gritaban muy fuerte:
"Grab one for me, little boy!"	"¡Cógeme uno, chiquillo!"
The children also ran	Los niños también corrían
to witness the division,	a presenciar el reparto,
And now and then some would say,	y de cuando en cuando decían,
"Long live the Agrarian Institute!"	"¡Viva el Instituto Agrario!"
The women were half-crazed	Las mujeres medias locas
opening doors and windows,	abrían puertas y ventanas
and one old lady was so overjoyed	y una vieja de la alegría
That she pooped in her bed.	hasta se cagó en la cama.
That night in their house	Aquella noche en su casa
a couple said:	un matrimonio decía:
"Our old age will be	"Vamos a tener una vejez
better than I thought	mejor de lo que yo creía
because when they make us all equal	porque cuando ya nos pongan a todos iguales
they will have another distribution	harán un nuevo reparto
so that we can go on.	para poder continuar.
They will give us land and cattle	Nos darán tierra y ganado,
and grain to sow	grano para sembrar,
and a few little *pesetas*	y unas cuantas pesetillas
so we can manage.	para podernos manejar.
If things go well	Si las cosas vienen bien
and the times favor us	y el tiempo nos favorece

for the coming year,	para el año venidero
we can breathe heartily.	podremos respirar fuerte.
Then I will be able to say:	Entonces podré decir:
'For the health of my children,	Por la salud de mis hijos,
with my labor	entré aquí de jornalero,
everything is mine, thank God.'	y gracias a Dios todo es mío.
And if things turn out otherwise,	Si viniera lo contrario,
I shall tell my companion:	le diré a mi compañera:
'I'm smothered by debts,	'A mí me ahogan las trampas.
so screw whomever I owe!'"	¡Que se joda el que le debo!'"
"Don't kid yourself,"	"No te hagas ilusiones,"
said the woman to her husband,	Le dijo la mujer a su esposo,
"because our end here will be	"Que aquí el final de nosotros
when we throw ourselves	será tirarnos a un pozo."[5]
down a well."	

Esteban Moreno ended his poem on a comic but somber note. He had long before lost any illusions either that cooperative labor would see rural workers equal and happy or that a distribution would make them farmers rich in land, grain, and cattle. Nonetheless, it was sad to see the death of social experiments that had once been undertaken with high hopes.

New Plans

The division of the plots and the work did not resolve all of the organizational issues of San José de Malcocinado. Esteban recorded one of the great ironies of government modernization that soon followed: converting pig pens into small cottages:

Last night I had a dream,	Anoche tuve un ensueño,
and it was a beautiful dream.	y un ensueño precioso.
It should be nice to tell it	Será digno de contarlo
since it was so nice and beautiful.	por agradable y hermoso.
I dreamed that there were no more pig pens at Las Yeguadas.[6]	Soñé que no había en la yeguada los corrales de los cochinos.
They had been changed over to the housing of the neighborhood families.	Los habían destinado para viviendas para casas de vecinos.
Since I am so curious	Yo como soy tan curioso

I took a little walk	fui echando un paseíto
around the corral.	por la nave del corral.
Then the next morning,	A la mañana siguiente,
one could see	entonces se pudo apreciar
that what I had dreamed about	lo que yo había soñado
was already a reality.	ya era una realidad.
The next day	Al otro día siguiente
one could see a group of neighbors,	se veía un grupo de vecinos,
the majority of them	la mayoría de ellos
from the "Suspiro" neighborhood.	del Barrio del Suspiro.
Some of them were felling walls,	Unos cayendo tabiques,
others were removing pig pens,	otros quitando zahurdas,
and an old lady, in the pine grove,	y una vieja, en el pinar,
was shaking off some fleas.	sacudiéndose las pulgas.
[some laughter]	

The same events were also seen from the point of view of the animals involved:

The day they gave away	El día que repartieron
the pigs' corral.	el corral de los cochinos.
You will see what happened	Veréis lo que le pasó
to a female pig and to a baby pig.	a una puerca y a un gorrino.
Since it was so cold,	Como hacía tanto frío,
they went to the corral,	marcharon para el corral,
and the baby pig, shivering,	y gorrino, tiritando,
told his mother:	le decía a su mamá:
"Tell me who is the guilty one	"dime quién ha sido el culpable
so that we are losing the corral."	que nos quiten el corral."
And the mother answered	Y la madre le decía
to her "boy" Saturnino:	a su niño Saturnino:
"We have no other choice	"no nos queda más remedio
but to sleep under a pine tree.	que dormir debajo de un pino.
We shall file a protest	Haremos una protesta
with the farmhouse council,	a la junta del cortijo,
so that they build a [new] corral	para que hagan un corral
before it gets much colder.	antes de que vengan los fríos.
If they don't do it,	Si es que no nos lo hacen,
we shall have to perish;	tendremos que perecer;

| [and] the pig raiser will have to go | tendrá que ir el puerquero |
| to work at Las Lomas." | a Las Lomas a trabajar." |

Guardia Civiles and Municipales

While Esteban recited, a careful vigil was kept for a patrol of the *Guardia Civil*, the rural police force. After ridiculing the fiasco concerning digging out stumps with tractors, the listeners break in: "Look out and see if the *Guardia Civil* is coming [laughter]. . .. Bring me another glass. . ..Let's hear a longer one."

No one wanted to be taken by surprise relating a controversial joke or singing a suspect lyric. Esteban had good reason to be wary of coming to the attention of the authorities. In 1933, at the time of the anarchist uprising in Casas Viejas, Esteban had been arrested for carrying an old shotgun and had served more than a year in jail in Cádiz. Not that he was ever an *obrero consciente* (dedicated anarchist) or had any special knowledge or interest in anarchism or socialism. Esteban Moreno was a poet, and not a leader or an intellectual. He had joined the uprising the way almost everyone else had, to show his support for his fellow workers.

On occasion Esteban would choose a municipal policeman to serve as the subject of a verse. While his comical verses seem innocent enough, mocking a veteran of Franco's army who became a city policeman, had a bad marriage, and was a cuckold, could be seen as another shout of protest:

I am a native of Alcalá,	Soy natural de Alcalá,
baptized in Algeciras,	bautizado en Algeciras,
I was drafted in Casas Viejas,	entré en quinta en Casas Viejas,
and they fitted me out in Medina.	y me tallaron en Medina.
I started the service in Seville,	Hice el servicio en Sevilla,
when the Civil War started,	cuando saltó el movimiento,
and they gave a couple of slaps there,	y allí me dieron dos tortas,
which made me a sergeant.	que me hicieron sargento.
From there I joined the legion,[7]	De allí pasé a la legión.
and because of a beautiful involvement	por un empeño muy hermoso,
and merit in war,	y por mérito de guerra,
I was confined to the stockade.	ingresé en el calabozo.

After serving seven months,	Al cumplir los siete meses,
I was set free.	me echaron en libertad.
I had a sweetheart in Tarifa,	Tuve una novia en Tarifa,
and I was married in Gibraltar.	y me casé en Gibraltar.
I put in an application,	Eché la solicitud,
to become a municipal	pá guardia municipal,
policeman,	
and I used to hear the people	y oía decir entre la gente,
say,	
"That woman is already in	"ya está la mujer arreglada:
quite a fix:	
with ten *pesetas* as his pay	con diez pesetas de paga,
and he is so fond of alcohol,	y él que le gusta el alcohol,
it won't take very long,	no tardará mucho tiempo,
before he gets himself assigned	que se apunte al comedor.
to the mess hall."	
In fact, it was true that,	Fectivamente[8] fue cierto
during my honeymoon,	que tóa mi luna de miel,
I spent the whole time begging	la pasé cogiendo rancho,
for leftovers,	
at the entrance to the barracks.	en la puerta de un cuartel.
until they realized	Hasta que se dieron cuenta,
that I was a newly wed,	que era yo recién-casado
and [then] blows began to	y me llovían las tortas
pour over me	
from the officers and the	de los jefes y los soldados.
soldiers.	
After nine months	Al complir los nueve meses
my wife became sick,	mi mujer se puso mala,
and she had to give birth	y tuvo que dar a luz
because otherwise she would	porque si no reventaba.
burst.	
I became very happy	Yo me puse muy contento
because I liked the idea of	por el amor de ser padre,
being a father,	
but afterwards I realized	y luego me vine a enterar
that it was the mayor's son.	que era hijo del alcalde.
[laughter from the audience]	
I left my wife	Me aparté de mi mujer
as it was the natural thing to do,	como era natural,
and I married for a second time	y me casé de segunda
about which I am going to	que ahora se la voy a explicar:
explain:	
her left eye is missing,	es tuerta del ojo izquierdo,

slightly hunchbacked,	un poquito jorobada,
she suffers a little from asthma,	padese un poco de asma,
and her legs are all crooked.	u las piernas escacharradas.
The meals that she prepares for me,	Las comidas que me guisa,
have neither oil or salt.	no tienen aceite ni sal.
She is a model for a wife	Es un modelo de esposa
for the man who knows how to appreciate [her].	para el que lo sepa preciar.
The other day she sewed me	El otro día me pegó
a button on the fly of my trousers,	un botón en la portañucla,
[laughter from the audience]	y me meé en los calzones
and I had to pee in my underwear because she sewed the two fabrics together.	porque cogió las dos telas.
[roar of laughter from the audience]	
She was a widow of a barber who died in Palmones,	Fue viuda de un barbero que murió el marío en Palmones
and in order to bury him they had to cut off his sexual organs.	y para darle sepultura le cortaron los pitones.
[roar of laughter from the audience]	
About my new marriage my story ends,	De mi nuevo casamiento termina mi relación
and if anybody doubts it let him marry like I did.	y el que no quiera creerlo que se case como yo.
[laughter from the audience]	

Concupiscence

In common with carnival songwriters, Esteban Moreno's repertoire included many references to lustful activities, such as the short poem citing the "stars" a young wife had won from encounters with the men of the regiment at Pavía:

A girl said one day	Le dijo una niña un día
to her boyfriend, Rafael,	a su novio, Rafael,
"When you marry me,	"cuando te cases conmigo,
you will become a colonel."	vas a ascender a coronel."

It has been four months since   Ya hizo cuatro meses que
the wedding took place,   se echaron las bendiciones,
and one day he feels a lump   y un día se tienta un bulto
protruding from his pants.   por encima de los calzones.
  [some laughter]
He became very worried,   El se puso muy apurado,
he would look at it and say,   se lo miraba decía,
"these must be the stars   "éstas serán las estrellas
[medals]
from the Regiment of Pavia."   del Regimiento Pavía."
  [laughter]

Another short poem concerned a young girl who liked to visit
the youthful medical practitioner to receive her "injections":

There was a young girl who   Una niña que le hablaba
was friendly
with a young male nurse,   a un muchacho practicante,
so that whenever she fell ill   el día que caía mala
she had medical help instantly.   tenía cura en un instante.
  [some laughter]
As soon as the young man was   No fue llamado el muchacho
called
he arrived right away.   que de seguida llegó,
"Where do you want me, my   "¿adónde quieres, hija mía,
dear,
to give you the shot?"   que te ponga la injección?"
"Put it on my lower belly,"   Pónmela en el viente bajo,"
she said with deep emotion,   le dijo con sentimiento,
"so in case the needle breaks,   por si se rompe la aguja,
something may remain inside   que me quede algo dentro."
me."
  [more laughter]

Mastery in Marriage

Some of Esteban's recitations point to age-old problems of couples
sharing bed, hearth, and hardship. His own wife Consuela was a
sweet and accommodating woman, all too patient with his
affection for the grape. Esteban's account of country marriage,
however, appears to have been inspired by the same wry irony
that depicts the domestic quarrels and entanglements that survive
in traditional fabliaux. In the fabliaux, a contrary personality was

considered a commonplace cause of contention between the sexes, as some of the country people recalled.

> "There was a woman who was always contradicting her husband. The husband would say to her, 'This is straight,' and she would say, 'No, no, no. It's hooked.' And again, 'No, no, no. It's hooked.' So he grabbed her and threw her in the well. And while she was drowning, sinking under the water for the last time, she stuck her arm up with her finger bent like a hook. And so she ended, drowned like a rat." (Paco)

Or another:

> "Once there was a couple in the country who had to go to town. They had a mare and a stallion, and the man said to his wife: 'You go on the mare and I'll go on the stallion.'
> And she said to him: 'No, I'll go on the stallion.'
> The husband said to her: 'If you go on the stallion, you'll fall in the river.' She said to him: 'Let me fall. I'll go on the stallion.'
> They rode to town and when they were crossing the river the stallion became frightened by the current and she fell in the river. The husband continued on to town and notified the authorities that his wife had fallen in the river. The officials went to look for her downstream, but the husband said: 'No, no, no. Look for her upstream. She always goes against the current.'" (Paco)

After a recitation or two, the audience would be whetted for more: "Let's have another one. Another good one, c'mon." Someone would recall an old song or another tale. They were much like Chaucer's pilgrims on the road to Canterbury, sharing tales not on horseback but in the stationary bark of the tavern. One of Esteban's poems was reminiscent of one told by the much-married Wife of Bath, revealing what women wanted most from men – mastery in marriage. "This is dedicated to women," he said.

Every woman, when she marries,	La mujer, cuando se casa,
has the great desire	todas tienen el capricho
to subject her man,	de dominar a los hombres,
and to rid him of all vices.	y quitarles todos los vicios.
The first thing is wine,	Lo primero es el vino,
the second tobacco,	lo segundo el tabaco,
the third is advice	lo tercero le aconcejan

to work without rest.
If the man is a little docile,
the woman becomes stronger,
and after three days of marriage,
what he desires is death.

If the mother-in-law is at
their home,
and their characters are not
compatible,
the son-in-law loathes the
mother-in-law
and the mother-in-law despises
the son-in-law.

If they burden themselves with
a large family,
and the income is not much,
on the best day of the year
the man throws himself in a
well.
The woman becomes a widow
with a houseful of children,
and from time to time she sighs,
"What an insult from my
husband!
My only consolation is
that on the day that I married
him,
I neither loved him much
nor could he stand me."
Upon hearing those words
says the mother, "Dolores,
I also killed your father
through nagging."

"Mama, what nerve have you,"
answered the daughter,
"to say that about my father,
regardless of my love for him?"
"C'mon, you fool, you know
that we women
want to have the right
to subjugate our men,

que trabajen sin descanso.
Si el hombre es un poco dócil,
la mujer se hace fuerte
y a los tres días de casados,
lo que apetece es la muerte.

Si la suegra está en la casa,

y no se llevan los genios,

ni el yerno puede ver a la
suegra,
ni la suegra puede ver al yerno.

Si se carga de familia,

y los haberes son cortos,
el mejor día del año
se tira aquel hombre a un pozo.

La mujer queda viuda
con una casa de hijos,
y en cuando en cuando suspira,
"¡qué herejía de mi marido!

La conformidad que tengo
que el día que me casé,

ni yo lo quería mucho,
ni él me podía ver."
Al oír aquellas palaleras
dice la madre, "Dolores,
yo también maté a tu padre
a fuerza de irritaciones."

"Mamá, tiene usted valor,"
le contestaba la hija,
"decir eso de mi padre,
¿con lo que yo lo quería?"
"Anda, tonta, tú sabes que las
mujeres
queremos tener derecho
de dominar a los hombres,

even if our necks are wrung.
When he [your father] courted me,
everybody used to tell me
that I was going to be unhappy
if I ever became married.
In fact, it was true that,
since the day in which we married,
I spent nearly a year
enjoying the honeymoon,
  [some laughter]
until the time came
when the money ran out,
which was an inheritance which
I received after my mother-in-law's death.
  [some laughter]

As long as we had money
we got along very well;
when we didn't have any more,
we could not stand each other.
There came the arguments,
quarrels, and foolishness,
and we slept every night
with an empty stomach.
  [some laughter]
I told him one day to go to work,
and he answered me by saying:
'That's very cool of you!
If I don't work during the summer,
  [laughter]
am I going to work during the winter?'

The days went by like that,
until there came a time,
when a long illness
took hold of his body.
I went to the city hall
to take out a poor man's pass,
in order that I could

aunque perdamos el pescuezo.
Cuando él me pretendió,

todo el mundo me decía,
que iba a ser una degraciada,
si me casaba algún día.
Efectivamente, fue cierto que,
desde el día en que me casé,

se llevó cerca de un año.
pasando luna de miel,

hasta que llegó el momento
en que se agotaron las "perras,"
que fue una herencia que tuve
por la muerte de mi suegra.

Mientras tuvimos dinero
nos llevábamos muy bien;
cuando ya se terminaron,
no nos podíamos ver.
Entraron las discusiones,
disgustos y tonterías,
y dormíamos todas las noches
con la barriga vacía.

Lo mandé un día a trabajar,
y me contestó diciendo:
"¿estás tú fresca?
No trabajo en el verano,

¿voy a trabajar en el invierno?"

"Así pasaron los días,
hasta que llegó un momento,
que una larga enfermedad
se apoderó de su cuerpo.
Yo marché al Ayuntamiento
a sacar un volante de pobre,
para que las medicinas

get free medicines.	me las pasaran de balde.
I would give him a spoonful,	Le daba una cucharada,
and he would become irritated,	y le entraba una irritación,
and after twenty days	y al cumplir los veinte días
my poor man died.	el pobre se me murió.
It is said that death has quite an influence,	Dicen que la muerte impone,
and I affirm it to be true,	y yo lo apruebo que es cierto,
because I began to love him	porque creí de quererle
when I saw him dead.	cuando lo tenía muerto.
I recognize my fault;	Yo reconozco mi falta,
I say it from the bottom of my heart,	lo digo de corazón,
because in the whole world there is no woman worse than me.	porque en el mundo no hay mujer más mala que yo.
That's why I advise	Por eso doy un consejo
any woman with a husband:	a la que tenga marido:
may she kill him through nagging	que lo mate a irritaciones
just like I have killed mine."	como yo he matado al mío."
[roar of laughter]	

A Personal Touch

Esteban Moreno's personal views are not too difficult to discern. His verse was a direct expression of his views and experiences. Irritated at repairing shoddy factory-made boots sold at a new discount store, the old-fashioned (and impoverished) artisan snipped:

They also sell high boots	También venden botas altas
for married women and single girls,	para casadas y solteras,
which when kept in a box,	que guardadas en un cajón,
do not wear out their soles.	no se les rompen las suelas.

One verse complained of the number of women encouraged by welfare money to have additional children:

Since they established the subsidy	Desde que en toda la España

[child support] throughout Spain,	se estableció el subsidio,
all women wanted to have a baby every week.	querían tener las mujeres todas las semanas un niño.
Only because of their greedy desire to obtain the pension,	Sólo por el interés de coger dicha pensión,
and later, when they get it,	y luego, cuando la cogen,
it doesn't even last them to buy soap.	no le alcanza para el jabón.
If the husband, unfortunately,	Si el marido, por desgracia,
spends it in alcohol [drinking],	lo distribuye en alcohol,
the next day his wife	al otro día está su esposa
is in quite a mood.	para pedirle un favor. [slang]
The kids asking for food,	Los niños pidiendo pan,
the woman without even hemp sandals,	la mujer sin alpargatas,
and the husband in the tavern [saying],	y el marido en la taberna,
"Pour me a drink with a snack!"	"echa una copa con tapa!"
After this is all over,	Pues cuando ya pasa esto,
he comes home with a sick stomach,	llega a su casa estragado,
and he asks his wife,	y le pregunta a su esposa,
"What have you [all] eaten for lunch?"	"ustedes ¿qué han almorzado?"
"The savings which you left from the last subsidy."	"Los ahorros que dejaste del subsidio pasado."

There are many other verses not included here. Some are so specific to the place that they are difficult for outsiders to understand or appreciate, although unlike the meals prepared by an awful wife, Esteban's fare is always rich in oil and salt. Details of daily life include belly pains, asthma, lice and bedbugs. The low comedy usually involves sex or flatulence, or increasing age and wrinkled penes. Characters often worry not only over their daily bread but also about the insurance covering their burial.

Ties that Bind

Despite the division of the lands into separate plots, San José de Malcocinado continued its separate life with elements of a quasi-cooperative, particularly concerning the remaining common lands.

The pine trees had proven to be an unhappy choice to plant on their wooded lot. Matured, they were virtually worthless since concrete had replaced wood as the construction material of choice for telephone poles. The settlement had then wisely decided to seed flower beds instead of pine trees. The flowers would be sold to shops and restaurants in the cities. The venture proved to be not only a commercial success, but it became an important source of employment for the young women of the settlement.

For decades Esteban Moreno had charted an independent course with his own verse. With the revival of carnival, however, the old poet found himself composing on some of the same matters taken up by those preparing librettos for their *murgas*. While Esteban had no *murga* to write for, in 1966 he too found inspiring the false report of a lottery winner.

One fifteenth of March	El día quince de marzo
will always be remembered,	en memoria quedará,
because of the scandal that took place	el escándalo que hubo
because of a lucky number [number game].	con la "quiniela preñá."
The people from Las Lomas	Los vicinos de las lomas
did not sleep that night,	no durmieron aquella noche,
because a boy from the neighborhood	porque un muchacho de allí
had picked "the fourteen" [winning teams].[9]	había acertado "los catorce".
A representative of the Bank	Un corresponsal del Banco
arrived at Las Lomas:	en las lomas se plantó
"Here is my car,	"aquí tenéis a mi coche,
which is at your disposal."	que está a su disposición."
The lucky couple	Salieron para Benalup
departed for Benalup,	el matrimonio agraciado,
because they wanted to celebrate	porque querían celebrar
"the fourteen" which they had won.	"los catorce" resultados.
They ate their breakfast	Tomaron el desayuno
with lots of "Colacao"[10]	a base de "Colacao"
and it did not take a half-hour	y no tardó media hora
before they were all mad at each other.	que estaban tós disgustados.
The news was already spreading	Ya corría la noticia
that it was all a joke,	que todo era una broma,

and in a small hand-drawn cart	y en un carrillo de mano
they returned to Las Lomas.	regresaron a las lomas.
Once they were at home	Una vez puesto en su casa
they had to drink some linden tea,	tuvieron que tomar tila,
in order to correct	para poder corregir
the belly pains.	los dolores de barriga.
[some laughter]	
The father took a stick,	El padre cogió una estaca,
and said, "Exaggerator,	y dijo, "exagerado,
I will give you	yo sí que te habia acertado
'the lucky fourteen'."	los catorce resultados."
[a beating with the stick]	
"Don't harm your son,"	"No maltrates a tu hijo,"
his wife kept saying.	le decía la mujer,
"Since the goats [are loose]	"que los chivos
others will eat them."	otros se los van a comer."
"I had already planned",	"Yo que tenía pensado,
the husband replied, "to take it easy permanently,	de echárme la permanente,
and now I cannot buy	y ahora no puedo comprar
even a half liter of oil."	ni medio litro de aceite."
"We were very unfortunate,"	"Tuvimos muy mala suerte,"
she said to her husband,	ella le dijo al marido,
"we didn't even get a refund	"que no tuvo ni el reintegro
for your son's *'quiniela'* [ticket]."	la 'quiniela' de tu hijo."

In its length Esteban's account of the practical joke matches those written for Los Llorones and Los Turistas del Figura in the carnival. Only the focus sets it apart: rather than an account of the lax morals of a banker seen by Manolo the shoemaker (chapter 2, p. 27), or the hapless joke depicted by Angel Guillén the school-teacher (chapter 4, p. 72), Esteban dwells on the pathetic and hopeless expectations of a generation that had suffered more than its lot of hardship. The ill-fated family were now deprived even of a half-liter of olive oil and a refund for a losing ticket.

Notes

1. See J. Mintz, *The Anarchists of Casas Viejas*, pp. 279–82, 285, 310–11.
2. The government was more than willing to surrender the land, since the sandy soil had proven to be an unhealthy element for the digestion of the breeding mares.
3. See Mintz, *The Anarchists of Casas Viejas*, pp. 49–50; 50–61.
4. Typically, a *campesino* like Madera of Alcalá de los Gazules would risk riding his small motorcycle on the rocky road to Benalup for a visit to a local bar or two. Madera was a short man, little more than five feet, but he was not a small man, being almost as broad in the chest as he was in height. One could say that Madera of Alcalá was one of the greatest singers (and, without depreciating anyone else, perhaps the very greatest) in the region, including Benalup, Medina, Conil, and Vejer de la Frontera. He was a welcome visitor to any tavern.
5. The poem is also printed in Mintz, *The Anarchists of Casas Viejas*, pp. 310–11.
6. This is another name for San José de Malcocinado and refers back to the period when mares were bred there for the army.
7. The Spanish Legion of the Spanish Sahara.
8. Fectivamente = efectivamente.
9. A prize is given each week to those who pick the 14 winning soccer teams.
10. Brand name for a chocolate type of powder mix.

Chapter 6

Old and New Voices

Odyssey

During the early 1970s, in response to diminished agricultural activities, the *campesinos* continued to leave the pueblo in search of employment. Some emigrated permanently to other parts of Spain, particularly Valencia and Barcelona, where there was industry; others signed contracts for terms of temporary work abroad. Money sent by husbands and sons working in Germany, France, Holland, or Switzerland kept many families afloat. During the year the families of the emigrant workers were kept together by the women and the grandparents, but in December the men returned for the Christmas holidays. Some of the men, who were mostly between the ages of twenty to forty, had been lost to the town for years. They arrived by bus with cardboard suitcases and boxes of toys. Excited children ran through the streets with their presents: one had a huge life-size doll that drew the attention of onlookers. The local storekeepers, too, were happy that the men had returned with money in their pockets. The pharmacist even sold a luxury item, a bottle of aftershave lotion. A worker just returned from abroad ordered a whole chicken from the butcher. The purchase visibly startled the women with lesser means waiting in line to purchase a quarter of a chicken or a skimpy strip of beef to add to a chickpea stew for an entire family.

For two or three weeks, while the men were home, the streets were filled with young faces, and Benalup seemed to be fully alive again. Workers in Benalup customarily congregate along the main street in front of the cafés and by the *alameda*, once the site of the shape-up where foremen chose hands for field work. Wearing suits and jackets like men of leisure, the newly returned men stood out from local *campesinos* and workers. Well-wishers and passersby stopped to exchange greetings and news.

Juan, the son of Pepe Bulla (Pepe in a Hurry), had spent his first five months in Germany. Now he was playing cards with his friends in Alfonso's café on the main street opposite the church. His oldest son, Pepe, age eleven, stood at his shoulder watching him. The men exchanged tales and jokes of life in Germany. In one factory some Spaniards were said to have battled with a group of German workers. The police were called, but the Spanish workers would not give in. Then the German chief of police jumped on the table. "Friends!" he cried. "It is good to see you so united. If you had been as united in Spain as you are today, you would not be here."

When the game broke up Juan walked up the hill to his home.

"For eleven years I worked on the estate of Las Lomas. The first year I walked it. I went eleven kilometers on foot each way. Afterward I bought a bicycle, and finally I got a small motorcycle. When I did not earn enough, I had to owe to the store until I could sell something that we raised – a pig or a turkey. I have owed up to 7,000, even 8,000 *pesetas*. In the winter when one earns less, one gets into a trap. In the summer, since one earns more, well, then one pays off one's debts.

"A fellow who had just come back from Germany told me about it and how much he earned. The wages were good. I decided to go. I'm thirty-six years old. We have ten children. The oldest is fourteen, a girl. No one works in the family but me. Before, we didn't eat half the things we eat now because I didn't earn enough. Since I earn more, my family can buy other things to eat – good meat, fish. If there's a good lettuce. . ..

"I've been working in Germany near Hanover for five months, digging trenches for sewer pipes. We go from town to town. When we finish one, we go to another. It's a boring life. Bitter. What is there to do when you're alone? Your family is here. You can't speak the language. We live in a rooming house arranged for by the company. We pay for it, so many marks a month. We each earn four and a-half marks an hour. We make our own meals. There are four of us in the room."

Some families abandoned their towns and joined their men in a new land. For Juan's wife, however, it was impossible:

"If I didn't have so many children, I would go to Germany with my husband. But you can't go with so many children. When Juan comes back, we will go to Barcelona and I'll stay there. There's more opportunity for the children to find work in the factories, and there's more chance for education. I have mixed feelings about going, because I was raised here. And my mother is here. She's over seventy. But I'll come back to see her. I have family in Barcelona: my other in-laws, my husband's family, my cousins."[1]

Some of the returning men had already decided not to leave again. A few had accumulated modest savings from their wages which they planned to use to break the cycle of hard labor and unemployment. Pepe Colmena, who had worked as a waiter in London, rented space to open a bar which quickly became a center for the younger men. After over a decade in Holland where he had soldered metal frames for gates and windows, Paco and his wife returned to Benalup to open a fish stand in the market. His daughter was now eight years old and they wanted to raise her in Spain. "Holland is nice" he said, "but you always feel like a foreigner. I had seen a bit of the world and wanted to go home."

There were also men who had returned with empty pockets and few ideas. Antonio S. had been in Germany for five years with little to show for it; nevertheless, he insisted that he had come back to stay:

"I sent home five thousand *pesetas* a month for forty-eight months, but I spent 3,000 *pesetas* a month myself in Cologne and came home with nothing. The money I sent to the family was enough for food, but not enough to buy clothes; I won't go out again. I'm too old, forty-two. It's not good to be without your family. I've decided to stay here. If we starve, we do it together."

A Forecast of the Future

The need for temporary workers at Las Lomas had varied with the seasons and with the crop sown. In 1968 a world-wide shortage of sugar existed due to the United States embargo on purchasing Cuban sugar. In order to take advantage of the rising price of sugar, the administrators of Las Lomas began to switch from cotton to planting sugar beets (*remolacha*). Sugar beets had advantages over cotton, other than the market price. Unlike cotton which had to be hand-picked, the hardy sugar beets could be ripped from the soil by a grappling iron attached to tractors. It required only a few workers to heft the uprooted beets onto waiting trucks or, as methods improved, to toss them onto a moving belt. Crops such as sorghum, grown for fodder to meet the needs of the increasing herds of cattle, also superseded cotton. A large workforce of seasonal laborers was suddenly unnecessary. In 1966, 2,000 workers had been required to pick cotton. As sugar beets and other crops gradually replaced cotton as the crop of choice, the number of day-workers dropped. By 1973 the number of temporary workers needed in the sugarbeet harvest had fallen to a mere 200.

Modern agricultural methods had brought about a revolution of its own in the countryside, as Don Ramón Mora Figueroa, the principal administrator and the eldest son of Don José, explained:

> "There has been a tremendous change in efficiency and productivity here. The development has come about in four stages: first, the draining of the marsh; second, the irrigation of the land; third, the building of roads; fourth, the drainage of the land. The drainage of the land is the most important. Instead of having 200 days a year when we could not farm – if we could limit that to fifty days, you can see what a difference in productivity that would make.

> "Mechanization means reduction of the labor force and, at the same time, an increase in the number of days those men remaining can work. The productivity of each man has increased and, at the same time, there has been a reduction of the men needed. Training has improved; education has improved. The last two years have seen a big change. The next five years will see an even greater change. Leadership has improved. Middle management supervision is better. We have brought in people from the outside. One man was general manager for a sugar beet plant in Malaga. We were able to make it attractive enough for him to move here. Better understanding between middle and upper managers and laborers is important."

Campesino and landowner could agree on the virtues of intensive use of the land. Their conception of the purposes of agricultural production contrasted. How different was the view of the sophisticated managers at Las Lomas, as they studied production figures and the most efficient use of the labor force, from the worker who still looked to the landowners for consideration and care. How distant were they both from the now defunct visions of the anarchists and the socialists who had struggled there a generation before to work the land in common and to share in its harvest. A new purpose had succeeded.

Don Ramón, elegantly dressed in riding clothes, his legs crossed, reclined on a leather couch. The exodus of the rural workers was in his mind as he commented on the need to tie the *campesinos* to the land with sophisticated and heretofore unknown schemes of enticement and indenture:

> "There's no reason why the worker is not able to earn enough here. He has to be in a critical position to want to leave. He must be kept busy so he will not look outside. We must increase their efficiency. We build a movie theater, increase their pay, arrange time for them to go to the beach. They don't save money and, instead, look for ways to spend money. We must provide those ways. Now many have cars. They buy a car and pay it off. That's the kind of saving I like to see. We have to be careful that they can spend money. They do not like to save. They like to go to the city to spend money. We have to provide ways for them to spend. Buy a house in advance. Buy a car on credit. Over 100 here now have private cars. There are over 250 televisions and refrigerators. One is forced to create outlets for them to spend money. If not they want to go to the city where it is easy to spend money. If they're happy they would never go to Germany. They go to Germany because they're seasonal workers. It's a sad thing."

Itinerant Workers

As the tourist industry expanded, many local men enlisted as itinerant construction workers in developments mushrooming along the Mediterranean. Since the job sites were too far from Benalup to commute each day, during the week workers either paid for a berth to sleep somewhere nearby or else arranged makeshift bunks in the basement of the building under construction. They set up portable stoves there to prepare their morning coffee and most of their daily meals. Every Saturday evening the workers returned home to Benalup. They would spend Sunday at home, and well before dawn on Monday morning, take the bus or catch a ride back to their temporary quarters at the job site.

For the men who had been *campesinos*, there were correlations to be made between field labor and construction work. Their bunks in the basement were similar to accommodations in past times in *gañanías* (straw bunk houses) in the *campo*, although the basement was not as comfortable nor as clean, and no meals were provided by the "house." There were reminders too of the exploitive system of paying field laborers *a destajo* (piecework, or contract labor). In an effort to speed up agricultural work, landowners would bypass wage agreements and pay a team of *campesinos* a fee to sow or weed a particular field. The system assured shoddy results as well as unfair distribution of work and wages. In construction trades, the masons discovered that they were not paid by the hour, but instead received a fee set by the foreman for each task. A mason earned so much to build a doorway or a window or a wall, regardless of the time he took.

Construction work had a singular advantage: the men acquired skills which were quickly applied to improve their own housing in Benalup. Men who learned to build houses of stone blocks and bricks had ready cause to replace *chozas* made of thatch, mud, and stone. There was a flurry of activity on virtually every street and lane as workers saved for bricks and cement and over time built, rebuilt, or added onto their homes.

The higher wages earned in construction attracted *campesinos* and artisans with a variety of skills and experience. Manolo the shoemaker abandoned his craft and became a peon. Like other newly enlisted unskilled and semiskilled laborers, he hauled lumber and tools to set up and secure each floor as the building ascended, and he carried bricks and mixed cement for the more experienced bricklayers. The new hardships of heavy work, extended travel, and long stays away from home quickly affected Manolo's appearance. He lost weight. His body became as lean and hard as his hands. His face suddenly aged when the dentist, who came once a week to Benalup to pull teeth, extracted molars from each side of his jaw.

The lure of better wages tempted the two shoemakers who had worked with Manolo to follow his lead. Although both men were in their thirties, were married and had children, they abandoned their craft and began the arduous metamorphosis from artisans to itinerant construction workers.

One of the partners of the shop that had employed them passed away. The remaining partner, Juan L., an older man who had retired from the arduous labor of hand-sewing shoes many years before, went through a curious transformation of his own related to changes in the economy. The new wages, the monies sent home from abroad, the tourist presence, and foreign investment greatly increased the amount of money in circulation. There was also growing inflation and competition for savings and investment.

Recognizing an opportunity, Juan L. offered to keep the money of townspeople at a higher rate of interest than that offered at the recently opened branch banks. He would invest the money wisely, keep the interest high, turn a good profit for himself, and keep the capital safely on hand for the depositors. He had many takers, attracted primarily by the high interest he preferred. To all appearances the wily old shoemaker appeared to have mastered modern business practices as he had learned to tame leather with thread, glue, hammer, and nails. He certainly seemed to be prosperous. To show off his stock of leather boots and shoes that Manolo and the others had laid up for him, he rebuilt his shoestore with a glass front window instead of stone and mud walls. The rooms of his own house were refurbished with new furniture and *objets d'art*. The sad truth would be discovered only a decade later when he failed to meet a depositor's request for his capital investment. The townspeople learned that their petty banker had covered their interest payments with new deposits. The failure of the business coincided with the sudden death of the shoemaker. Unfortunately, he had not earned a *peseta*. All their money had gone for glass, furnishings, and a short-lived high style.

Angel Guillén, the local schoolteacher who was the composer for Los Turistas, also made a serious change in his life. Since he was an experienced teacher with several years to his credit in the national system, he was able to bid on a teaching post in the capital, Cádiz. Angel was concerned with increasing educational and employment opportunities for his three sons. Benalup still lacked a high school, and there were insufficient teachers to cover all of the children at the primary grades. Since Cádiz was less than seventy kilometers away, Angel could still return frequently to Benalup to see his family and his friends. Each year he continued to write *coplas* for the carnival singers of Benalup.

Times of Change

From 1967 to 1977 the *fiesta típica*, the fledgling carnival, was celebrated in Cádiz in the springtime. The winter celebration did not resume in Cádiz until 1977. The only town that dared to maintain the traditional date was Trebujena. In Benalup there was an occasional *fiesta típica* held in the spring, as in 1974 when an anemic festival was mounted, but no one considered it to be the same. One *copla* of the 1974 festival, however, was memorable for honoring President Kennedy, assassinated a decade earlier, for holding values important to men with little means. As El Melliso sang:

He was Christian and charitable,	Cristiano y caritativo
a man of good heart,	y hombre de buen corazón
who always shared his wealth	que su paga entre los pobres
with the poor.	él siempre la repartió.

It concluded with a terrible forecast for Oswald, the killer:

Assasin and wretch	Asesino miserable
you do not have the pardon of	no tiene perdón de Dios.
God.	

Kennedy was only forty-six years of age when he met his death in 1963. Participants in the carnival of 1974 may have wondered if the poet was holding his breath waiting for Franco, then age eighty-two, to pass from the scene. If so, the vigil ended a year later in November 1975 when the Spanish head of state expired from natural causes. Franco still retained loyal supporters; however, unlike Kennedy, he had no champions among the carnival singers.

Broad social and political change swiftly followed the death of the dictator. The establishment of a new government was deftly managed by another man in uniform, King Juan Carlos I, who had been recognized by Franco nine years earlier as his future successor as king and chief of state. In 1976 the new king appointed as head of Spain's government a moderate Francoist, Adolfo Suárez González, who subsequently won a term as prime minister in the elections of 1977. Suárez negotiated the approval of universal suffrage and the legalization of opposition political parties, including the PCE (Partido Comunista Español).

Winter carnival fortuitously reappeared in Benalup in 1978, anticipating by a few months the passage of the new national constitution ensuring democracy under a constitutional monarchy.[2] Some early reactions in song to the anticipated democracy were skeptical and tongue-in-cheek. The following *cuplé* from the Benalup carnival of 1978, several months before the consitution was accepted, questioned the mystique of the much discussed but illusive ideal of democracy. After all, after four decades who could recall what it was?

One day we heard some old men	Sobre la democracia,
discussing democracy.	escuchamos un día
There was an uproar akin to a thousand demons.	unos cuantos viejetes que discutían.
Some said it was a suppository	Allí tenían un lío de mil demonios.
and others said it was a pill against insomnia.	Unos decían que era un supositorio
In order to resolve the question,	y otros que unas pastillas contra insomnio.
they went to ask a man who	Pá salir de dudas van a preguntar
had been councilman for forty years.	a uno que llevaba cuarenta años de concejal.
And he told them that democracy	Y les dijo que la democracia
is the mayor's sister-in-law who lives in France.	es una cuñá que tiene el alcalde viviendo en Francia.
(Los Segaores, 1978)	

The constitution of 1978 formally established Spain as a constitutional monarchy. Prime Minister Suárez now had to face a range of daunting problems, including an economic recession. The nation now consisted of seventeen regional communities with limited autonomy, and several, most notably Catalonia and the Basque region, demanded complete autonomy. Basque terrorism to achieve that end presented a serious threat to order. With most state bureaucrats still in place, the machinery of government could not keep pace with the need for innovation and modernization. Economic conditions in Andalusia took longer to reflect the effects of the new spirit of the nation. Andalusia lagged far behind Catalonia and Valencia in industrialization and growth and continued to lose population to those regions.

In time the emigration of Andalusians would nourish a wider renewal of carnival. The *gaditano* settlement in Barcelona became the center of carnival in the north. In a few years *comparsas* from Barcelona and Cádiz would be exchanging visits to entertain and to pass the hat.

The *Guardia Civil*

During this period of transition, the role of the army and the *Guardia Civil* were observed with trepidation. The *Guardia Civil*, patrolling in pairs, kept vigil in rural areas. The corps had a dual reputation throughout their history. They were considered to be incorruptible on matters that plagued most police forces, and they were also feared for their rule of harsh interrogation and swift punishment.[3] Rural crime was rare. Two major concerns of the *Guardias* were protecting the estates from poaching and controlling the smuggling of contraband goods, both illegal (but at times important) means of survival for rural people.

Following the Civil War, when conditions in town and country-side were at their nadir, desperate *campesinos* risked a long trek through the mountains to Gibraltar and a still more perilous return with necessities to sell: tobacco, coffee, flour, bread, medicine, cloth, and even thread. If they were stopped, they could expect severe punishment as the *Guardias* sought a confession and the location of their store of goods. The quick end to infractions in the mountains might be *ley de fugas*, shot while trying to escape, with the corpse carried to town slung over the back of a mule. Accounts of brutal treatment by *Guardias* left a memory of pain and suffering in many *campesino* families.

> María: "My father was a *contrabandista* [smuggler]. Someone informed on him. I still remember how they came to the door and he was taken out with his brother. He didn't die from a shot, but *carabineros* wanted him to tell where he had hidden his tobacco. My uncle was single and wasn't worried, but my father couldn't go to prison. He had five children to feed, and he was thinking of them. They ran him all through the countryside, through rivers to make him show them. He didn't die from a shot, but they killed him another way. When he returned he went into the hospital and died there. My uncle died as well. My mother was left with five children, including a baby of eleven months."

> Juan: "The corporal of the *Guardia Civil* who was stationed here some time ago said in the bakery: 'I'm a peaceful man, but I like to kill gypsies more than eat chicken.' He shot a gypsy in the shoulder and the gypsy said, 'May your favorite child fall sick.' By coincidence the corporal's daughter fell ill and became paralytic. The gypsy and his wife left town."

Mari: A woman left her house for a few minutes and someone entered and stole a radio and a watch. The *Guardias* brought the garbageman's son in and slapped him. We heard later that it was said he had been seen to ride by several times for no reason. There were donkey prints near the door. They understood he is not quite all there in the head. The *Guardia* slaps you in the face or hits you in the behind with the horn of a cow."

The residual ill feelings salted bitter tales and jokes:

Manolo G.: "Franco was driving on the highway and the bridge was out. There was a *Guardia Civil* and a worker, and they both ran to warn the car that the bridge was out. And Franco said to them, 'You have saved my life. What can I give to you? Ask me anything that you like.' And he said to the worker: 'Because you are a worker and he is a *Guardia*, whatever I give to you I'll have to give double to the *Guardia*.' And the worker thought for a moment and said: 'Put out one of my eyes.'"

In spite of the rural exodus, the *Guardia Civil* was still a force to be reckoned with. In their *cuarteles* (barracks), the *Guardia* maintained a log on troublemakers, former soldiers of the Republic, and suspected radicals, and they kept themselves informed on ordinary citizens as well.[4]

"In Curro's bar the *Guardia* asked Juan [who was moving to join his children in Marbella] the date of his wife's birth. Juan said he didn't know but he would bring it up to the *cuartel*. The *Guardia* said, 'No, leave it at the bar.'
This is control. They have a slip on everyone. Some say you have to inform the *Guardia* if you move. Juan says you are not obligated to do so but many do. The *Guardia* often ask where the families are after they've gone. They ask a relative." (Pedro)

There were signs, however, of a new mood in the south. In the late 1970s the spell the *Guardia Civil* had kept over rural life seemed to be shaken. The rural exodus, tourism, and industrial development had brought about deep structural changes. The death of the dictator Franco in 1975, the formation of a new government, and in 1978, the promise of a national constitution, heralded a freer civil and social order.

The *campesinos* had never lost their courage, and now they were regaining their voice after forty years of silence. In the carnival of

1978, a *murga*, Los Volaos, recorded a conversation between Manuel Gallardo, a carnival composer and singer, and two *Guardia Civiles*. The mischievous Gallardo, small and slight, was better known by the nickname *el Chispa* (the Spark) because of his darting quickness.

Last Saturday in the public walk	El sábado en la Alameda
"el Chispa" was singing	estaba el Chispa cantando
when he was approached by a pair of *Guardia Civiles*	se le acercó la pareja
who said he was being a nuisance. . .	le dijo está molestando. . .
"Show me your papers	Enséñame los papeles
to see if you have identification."	si está bien documentado.
"Show me yours,	Enséñame tú la tuya
to make sure you aren't disguised."	no vaya a estar disfrazado. . .
And the *Guardia* said to him,	Y el Guardia le decía
"You know me.	tú me conoces a mí
I've lived here seven years.	que llevo aquí siete años
I am a *Guardia Civil*."	y soy Guardia Civil.
The lad said to him	El muchacho le decía
with a little bit of insight,	con un poquito de vista
"I've lived here 31 [years]	yo llevo aquí 31
and they call me 'el Chispa."	y a mí me llaman el Chispa.
(Los Volaos, 1978)	

Manolo Lago in 1979

The carnival of 1979 preceded the national election by a few days. Ash Wednesday, signaling the start of Lent, fell on February 28; the election took place on March 1. For the carnival of 1979, Manolo Lago, the former shoemaker, picked up his pen again and composed the lyrics for the *murga*, Los Confiteros (The Candymakers).

Manolo Lago's *coplas* for the Los Confiteros of 1979 ran the gamut of town news: the purchase of a new ambulance, the opening of a discotheque whose dark corners attracted the young people, a dispute between two barbers and Gallinito that ended with a razor slash, a hit-and-run car accident, the theft of a television set from a bar and a futile chase after the thief, and the arrival of a new lady doctor instantly beloved by the townspeople.

There were also songs of criticism, such as the lack of consideration for the bones of the interred when the old cemetery was bulldozed to make a small park. Chastized as well were the gossips hanging around the town hall, and the undemocratic way a decision was made to hang a sign, *Asamblea Local* (Local Assembly), on the new ambulance as if it were the private property of the four men involved. One song recounted the adventures of three men on a tear, the same mischievous celebrants (including Perico and Chimenea) sung about thirteen years earlier. They went to a tavern to enjoy a stew along with their wine and, as usual, were carried away with the musical clink of glasses. In the morning they awoke tied to each other by one leg, a circumstance discovered when one of the men tried to reach the bathroom to urinate.

Manolo also offered a tongue in cheek salute to the town doctor, retiring after forty years of service. For those who knew the doctor or had endured his ministrations, it was a masterpiece of innuendo.

As we all know	El día 15 de Septiembre
On September 15	como lo sabemos todos
a doctor spoke to us	aquí en la casa del pueblo
here in our meeting room.	nos dio una charla un doctor.
He spoke about Spain,	El nos habló de la España
and a few other things,	y de algunas cosas más
and about the town's hygiene,	y de la higiene del pueblo
which was his topic in reality.	que era su tema en verdad.
Some went to listen to him	Algunos fueron a escucharlo
with the sole intention in mind	con una intención nada más
of seeing the doctor	esperando que sus nervios
have a nervous breakdown.	lo hicieran fracasar.
But that was not to be, gentlemen.	Pero no fue así señores
He spoke with certainty	con acento nos habló
for he demonstrated	como hombre muy instruido
his fine medical training.	su carrera demonstró.
Afterwards, there were opinions,	Después están las opiniones
which is something natural.	es cosa muy natural
Some said he had been a good doctor,	unos que han sido un buen doctor
others that he had never done anything.	otros que no ha hecho nada
He always took	En todos los casos graves
the tough cases	él siempre los ha acertado
but he always has avoided	pero a las cosas corrientes

the routine ones.	él siempre le ha dado de lado.
As expected, his character is always	Es debido, a su carácter
concerned with profit.	siempre con la economía
To prescribe three injections	para mandar tres inyecciones
you must see him three times.	lo tiene que ver tres días.
Gentlemen, it is said,	Pero es triste señores
that for forty years in our town	que siendo tan buen doctor
ha has been such a good doctor	40 años en el pueblo
and we have never honored him.	y no merece un honor.
Others have done much less,	Otros han hecho muchos menos,
some have done harm.	algunos perjudicaron
Nevertheless, in our town	y sin embargo en el pueblo
we have plaques engraved with their names.	tienen sus placas grabadas.

Views Local and National

Manolo had developed clear ideas on how to shape his art. To his distaste, he found that national news often supplanted local matters in current carnival songs.

"Today it's different than in the past. Now they use material from outside the town. I draw on the town. Whatever it is, it's mine. It belongs to me. It may not be as good as yours, but it's mine. I write about local events. I don't like the lettering on the ambulance. It was bought for the entire town and it's used that way, but the lettering is for four big shots – *señoritos*. I didn't say anything before because they'd say I'm crazy. I waited until carnival to express my criticism. That's what carnival is for, right? I don't write smutty songs or little light-hearted ditties. I deal with matters I want to criticize."

Manolo had also come full circle concerning prize money. Thirteen years earlier, he had been furious that his *murga* had been denied the full prize and had to share it with other groups. Participation in the carnival over the years had tempered his views:

"We don't give a prize anymore for the best group. It was my idea to divide the money equally that would be earned from the [concert at the] theater, because it's a shame to invest all that money and then the major share goes to just one group. I said we should give a trophy instead of money. I proposed it to the commission – that's one representative from each group and three outsiders. And they agreed.

Most of the money comes from the [performance at the] theater. We get a little profit from the pamphlets, but very little, and just a bit from the advertisements in the pamphlets."

Rural Problems

Manolo Lago continued to express the puzzlement and pain of the displaced agricultural workers of the town:

I don't know what's the matter with modern life.	No sé lo que está pasando con esta vida moderna
Half of the crops are being left in the fields.	que están dejando en el campo la mitad de las cosechas.
It seems that the children and the adults are in accord to pick the crop in one day although they lose about half of it.	Parecen que están de acuerdo el chico y el grande ya para recogerlo en un día aunque pierdan la mitad.
Everything is being automated, and no jobs are being replaced.	Todo a base de maquinaria y no reparan en nada
Life is miserable for the poor workers.	para los pobres obreros está la vida fatal.
I don't know what has happened,	No sé lo que habrá ocurrido
but it does cost money when half of the chickpeas are spilled on the ground.	porque eso vale dinero que la mitad los garbanzos vayan en el suelo.
For three days the workers worked well after midnight.	Y los obreros tres días dándose las madrugadas
Today they can't pick them because there is a dispute.	hoy no se puede coger porque hay bronqueá.
Then they inform the workers that they won't work late anymore	Entonces le comunican no hay que levantarse más
because the chickpeas are already inside the warehouse.	porque dentro del almacén los garbanzos están.
Gentlemen, it was all a lie, one may call it exploitation, for the poor workers will not be called back.	Señores tó fue un engaño se le puede llamar abusar para que los pobres no fueran ni siquiera a rebuscar.
Gentlemen, that's the way life is in our town today.	Señores así está la vida hoy nuestra ciudad
Just with family aid a town cannot endure.[5]	sólo con la marcha verde un pueblo no puede aguantar.

There was now increased assistance for the unemployed, but the aid remained uneven and uncertain. Unfortunately, on occasion the governor, in desperate straits to run the government, withdrew aid in a seemingly capricious way that left poor families baffled and without food. With the arrival of democracy, however, protest could move beyond *coplas* into action in the street. As Manolo Lago recounts in the following *pasodoble* (by Los Confiteros), the year before, on June 20, 1978, there were demonstrations throughout Andalusia:

On June 20,	El día 20 de Junio
as you can remember,	ustedes recordarán
there was a manifestation	hubo una manifestación
by the people to protest.	del pueblo para reclamar.
All the Andalusian towns	Todos los pueblos andaluces
got together	en contacto se pusieron
so the community lay-offs	que el paro comunitario
would not affect the workers.	no les venía a los obreros.
The government made an offer	El gobierno hizo una oferta
of about half,	y llegaba la mitad
so the workers continued	y trabajan los obreros
for a half-week more.	media semana más.
The workers got together	Se pusieron en contacto
and took to the streets.	y por la calle salió
They achieved something,	por fin algo conseguimos
although it wasn't everything.	aunque no lo fuera todo.
It was very unfair,	Aquello estuvo muy injusto
for some of the workers	por alguno los obreros
who protested the most	que son los que más reclaman
found themselves on the street corner.	y en la esquina se estuvieron.
I, who went along with others,	Yo que iba acompañado
did nothing but look	no hacía más que mirar
at the older workers	a esas personas mayores
whose faces reflected their suffering.	con la cara muy "asufrá."
Down their cheeks ran	Por sus mejillas corría
tears of pain and sorrow.	gotas de llanto y dolor
One could see through it the sadness	y se les veía la tristeza
that they had known.	que en otra ocasion pasó.
The uneducated are afraid that	La incultura tiene miedo
they can't achieve any more.	no puedo alcanzar mas nada

But things have changed,	pero está cambiado
and so they should be happy.	se debían de alegrar.
We can't eat our freedom	Con libertad no se come
nor maintain a household,	ni se mantiene una casa,
if the government doesn't give	si el gobierno no le da
every worker a job,	a cada obrero una plaza
We, the Amarraos, say	los Amarraos le decimos
to all of the senate,	a toditos los del Senado
"What's the use of so much freedom	pá qué tanta libertad
when what we really need is a job?"	si lo que hace falta es trabajo.
(Los Amarrados, 1979)	

Hurried calls to the capital by local officials had finally resulted in the release of the funds and the end of the strike.

The Elections of 1979

The arrival of democracy brought with it a sense of euphoria. Freedom was a tangible dish to taste and enjoy. It could be smelled in the air and tasted in the bread. Church and state were now separated, and subjects long forbidden could now be discussed. New laws concerning divorce and abortion would soon be on the table.[6] Everyone was suddenly talking. Free discussion became as tasty as dessert. Open conversation was a reawakened national obsession.

The first national election under the new constitution in 1979 bore witness to the great changes taking place. For the first time since the Republic, there was a wide range of parties opting for representation. In Andalusia the most significant parties included the UCD (the Unión de Centro Democrático – the Christian Democratic Party, a catchall for a dozen centralist parties), the PSOE (Partido Socialista Obrero Español – The Spanish Socialist Workers' Party), the PCE (Partido Comunista Español – The Spanish Communist Party), and finally the smaller regional PSA (Partido Socialista de Andalucía).

The three major parties brought speakers to present their case to the voters in the largest room at the Casa de Cultura. The Socialists clearly outnumbered all others, although the front row sheltered a few committed supporters of the UCD. Everyone

expected fireworks; however, the speakers were far more circum-
spect than their spirited audience. Not one speaker offered a
program for his party. They spent their time criticizing the others.
Little was expected of the Communist speaker who was from
nearby Medina. His clothing was threadbare, particularly compared with the well-groomed representative of the UCD. He
proved to be the most effective spokesman of the three, however,
boasting of his party's continual opposition to Franco and of the
number of comrades who had been imprisoned.

The meeting was a mirror image of the campaigns held
nationwide. The leftist parties were afraid to spell out their
programs for fear of losing votes. They spoke of unemployment
but not of land reform. They were also reluctant, in the unlikely
event of victory, of making promises that they would not be able
to keep. As Antonio, a young mason and one of the local leaders
of the socialist PSOE, who was running for a seat on the town
council, explained:

> "The PSOE can't express their real program, or they would frighten
> everyone away. They are for land reform, with collective farms run
> by the government. They are for public education and opposed to a
> school system administered by the Church. They favor laws per-
> mitting divorce and the right of a woman to choose to have an abortion
> under certain circumstances. I'm worried we might win. The economic
> situation is very bad."

Discussion in the street in front of Pepe's Bar was less guarded.
When the pharmacist stopped to greet an acquaintance, Antonio
seized the opportunity to accuse him of tearing down the posters
of the PSOE. "Ridiculous!" the pharmacist said. "Don't accuse me!"
Antonio became still more rancorous: "We've had forty years of
dictatorship and now this!" It was a popular refrain, and it
attracted still more attention. The storekeeper by the fountain
joined the fray on the pharmacist's side, but Antonio's circle of
supporters increased. One of the workers buttonholed the storekeeper and shouted: "Keep out of it. Don't touch Antonio." The
pharmacist kept cool and the passions subsided. Later Antonio
admitted that he knew the pharmacist had not personally ripped
down the posters, but that someone from his party surely had done
so.

There was another dispute in front of the market where G. hawked vegetables. He had left the stand in charge of his wife, and he was in the street shouting into the face of a *Guardia Civil*. Such a sight was unimaginable just weeks before. One could almost see the fine hair in the *Guardia's* nose vibrate with the volume, but he made no move with his hands to chastise, rebuke, or even question G.'s fury. How had this rage and daring been hidden for so long?

The results came as no surprise. In Benalup, support ran roughly three to one in favor the PSOE. (Local official results gave the PSOE 1350 votes, the UCD 451, the PCE 77, and the PSA 68 votes.) In the country as a whole, however, the center coalition and the UCD continued to dominate the political scene, and Premier Adolfo Suárez González was able to create a minority government.[7]

One song in 1979 (by a composer other than Manolo) was a forecast of future social and political change. Although it would not be until 1982 that Felipe González, the leader of the PSOE, would begin his tenure as prime minister of the country, the following *cuplé*, recalling a campaign visit, makes it clear that he was already anointed by the desperate workers of the countryside:[8]

No one here imagined,	Nadie aquí imaginaba
that on Sunday morning,	que nos iba a visitar,
that very popular man	un domingo por la mañana
was going to pay us a visit.	ese hombre tan popular.
At dawn	A las claritas del día
you could not walk the streets,	ya no se podía ni andar,
because so many people were out to	de tanta gente que había
shake his hand.	para su mano estrechar.
In our Casa del Pueblo	En nuestra Casa del Pueblo
you couldn't fit in one more person;	ya no se cabía más,
most everyone was overcome with emotion.	la gente emocionada
Someone kissed him,	uno un beso le dio,
and when Felipe spoke	y cuando Felipe hablaba
one person passed out.	creo que uno se desmayó.
(Diego Mateo, Los Dormilones, 1979)	

The Failed Coup

Had the police and military been so quickly brought to heel? There was concern and fear that the most devout followers of the dead dictator could not be controlled for long. On February 23, 1981, *Guardia Civil* Lieutenant Colonel Antonio Tejero, at the head of a troop of 200 men, their guns firing, charged into the Cortes, the legislative assembly. They made the startled cabinet officers and 350 deputies their prisoners. After the first frantic shots, only former prime minister Adolfo Suárez González, who had resigned his office the previous month, and one or two others, remained upright in their seats. The Cortés was held captive for eighteen hours. Tejero surrendered only when Juan Carlos, the king, remained steadfast to the new democratic constitution and the army remained loyal to the king.

In Benalup, Jesús Máñez gleefully composed a carnival *pasodoble* on the failed coup:

We'll never forget	Nunca se nos olvidará
what took place on February 23rd.	lo que sucedió el veintitres de febrero.
Guardias civiles led by Tejero stormed into the Congress	El Palacio del Congreso y aquellos Civiles al frente de Tejero.
shooting.	Entraron pegando tiros:
"I'm in command here.	--Aquí mando yo
Nobody move."	que nadie se mueva.
All the restrooms in the Congress were clogged by the diarrhea.	Todos los váteres que allí había fueron atascaos por las cagaleras.
Tejero, with his twisted mustache,	Tejero con su bigote
was showing his balls.	todo retorcío, echando cojones.
"If anybody moves,	--Al primero que se mueva
I'll blow his brains out!	le vuelo los sesos
You bunch of tit-suckers!"	¡Mancha de mamones!
Thank God it didn't last long	Menos mal que duró poco
and the guy with the mustache surrendered soon.	y pronto se rindiera el tío del bigote.
He's tried it twice already,	Dos veces que lo ha intentao
and he failed on both occasions, the prick!	ha fracasao el tío carajote.
(Los Hijos de la Ramona, 1982)	

Despite the victory of the fledgling democracy, the sudden uprising was proof that the civilian population and the new government had to remain wary of the police and military.

Just as troubling to the *campesinos* was the failure of the new government to remedy unemployment and to resolve problems of inadequate and haphazard assistance.

What a shame for the masses	¡Qué vergüenza para un pueblo
to depend on charity –	depender de una limosna,
to wait every Monday to see	esperar todos los lunes
what they will give us.	si es que nos la van a dar!
Shame on the leaders too,	Y los dirigentes,
because they stay tranquil	que se quedan tan tranquilos
even those weeks	cada semana
when they give us nothing.	que no hacen caridad.
And the working class	Y la clase obrera
must bear it,	debe conformarse,
because if they rebel,	pues si se rebela,
the government will respond	responde el gobierno
by unleashing the full weight	descargando el peso
of its power.	de su autoridad.
We see millions being spent	cómo los millones se van gastando
to no good purpose,	sin producto ninguno,
and we are impotent	y nosotros estamos impotentes
and powerless to react.	sin poder reaccionar.
And the señoritos	Y los señoritos
continue with their estates,	siguen en su finca,
with lands for private hunting	para coto ganado solar
and for their cattle,	mientras que los pobres
while we, the poor, burn,	nos vamos quemando
and nothing is left to us	y sólo nos queda
but to groan.	más que lamentar.
Today with my fellow singers	Hoy yo quiero
I want to lament and express	desde mi comparsa
the general mood	para el lamento y sentir popular,
and to give vent to my feelings	desahogarme
and shout to the wind	y gritar a los vientos,
with all my strength:	con toda mi fuerza:
"I want to work!"	¡Quiero trabajar!

Democracy provided no magic charm for success. The inept blunderings of newly elected local officials led to comic turns in government affairs: three mayors were in and out of office in Benalup in a matter of months. The townspeople, initially hopeful and supportive, finally lost their patience. Angel Guillén noted: "Since the inception of the new town council we've had three mayors. People put their hopes in the new council, democratically elected, but it didn't work out, because the truth is the people don't approve of the way the councilmen behaved." Even the sympathetic eye of Angel Guillén couldn't resist a wink in a brief *cuplé* which ties bureaucratic incompetence to the town's failure to receive its share of *la marcha verde* (benefits for jobless fieldworkers).

We all put our hopes	Todos pusimos nuestras esperanzas
in the new town council,	en este nuevo ayuntamiento;
but oh – do they play tricks	pero vaya si tiene castaña
and pull the wool over our eyes!	la faena que nos están haciendo.
These people want to squabble	Estas gentes tienen vocación
day in and day out.	por formar tó los días un follón.
As regards the "green advance,"	A cuenta la "marcha verde,"
see the tangle they've made.	no vea la que liaron,
Even a brave bull	no se ponían de acuerdo
couldn't make them agree.	ni delante de un toro bravo.
To top it off,	Para colmo de desgracia
everybody in Medina keeps mum,	en Medina todos callan,
except for a few birds of prey.	sólo algunos que forman
"No, no, that can't be!"	unas buenas pajarracas.
– "Quiet!"	--¡Que no puede ser coño, que no puede ser!
	--¡Que te calles, coño!
– "Who's the mayor?"	--y ¿alcalde que?
"Take it easy, Vicente,	--'Tate tranquilo, Vicente,
we've already had three."	que ya van tres.

In September, 1983, when the governor of the province again withheld supplemental family assistance, the *campesinos* of Benalup held a sit-down strike in the middle of the roadway leading past the town. The *Guardia Civiles* were present in numbers, but they avoided any contact with the workers. The *Guardias* and their officers were more interested in negotiation than in asserting their authority. A single misplaced blow in a town as notorious in Spanish history as Casas Viejas would have far-reaching consequences. Several ultimatums to the workers slipped by without any action. Persistent calls to the capital finally resulted in the release of the funds and the end of the strike. There was no violence on either side.[9]

Ironically, the victory revealed faultlines of tyranny and dogmatism among the workers. Following their success in the streets, the workers held a meeting at the Casa de Cultura that soon turned into a bitter argument. The group's most militant leaders suddenly declared that only those who had joined in the strike should be given an allocation from the relief funds being sent down. This would demonstrate that those who failed to show courage and join with the others would be denied aid. There was a roar of surprise and protest. To some it was a sudden recall to the zealotry that had led to disaster in earlier times. A few old-timers reminded everyone in the crowded meeting room of the pain of 1933. Some workers, they argued, were too traumatized by the violence of the past and the long reign of oppression to have openly protested. The matter was quickly put to rest.

Ubrique

The old ways of the *Guardia Civil* seemed to be changing. At the same time the common people were better able to resist tyrannies that were once routine. Nonetheless, the authority of the *Guardia Civil* was deeply entrenched in the towns and countryside, and local injustices were uprooted gingerly. A carnival song in 1989 from Ubrique, an isolated mountain town in the northeastern region of the province, helps to illustrate that the wheel had turned, but oh, how slowly.

The mountains surrounding Ubrique are hospitable to little more than goats and wild game. In troubled times of the past, the high rugged countryside shielded bandits and *contrabandistas* (smugglers) who plied the trade route from Ronda and the sea to the cities and towns of the interior. Bitter memories of matching wits and arms with the mounted *Guardia Civiles* still cling to the mountainsides. Today, however, away from the sweeping vistas, vertical landscape, and an obscure and romantic history, Ubrique is a factory town with almost all of the workers dedicated to the manufacture of leather goods. Ubrique is a mountain sweatshop where workers cut and sew wallets, gloves, and jackets. They are tightly united by class and occupation as well as their propinquity.

During fair time in the summer of 1988, an overflow crowd entering the stands of the local bullfight arena threatened the safety of the stadium. Some in the crowd were being pushed by those behind. To establish order the sergeant of the *Guardia Civil* decided to set an example. He arbitrarily picked out one of the workers, a man named Ceferino, and slapped him several times. In this new age, however, the workers made public their anger in the Ubrique carnival the following year when the *chirigota*, "Los Toreros Tuertos" (the One-Eyed Bullfighters) sang a *cuplé* condemning the incident. The group also alerted the newspaper in the capital, the *Diario de Cádiz*, which carried the story of their protest throughout the province.

We went to the bullfights in fairtime	En feria fuimos a los toros
to learn to have a taste for it.	para coger afición
The stands started to sag	la plaza empezó a doblarse
due to overpopulation.	por la superpoblación.
The management made an enormous	Fallo que tuvo la empresa
and irresponsible mistake:	temerario y garrafal
in order to make more money,	que por recoger dinero
they neglected security.	pasó de seguridad.
But Ceferino was the one	Pero el que peor lo tuvo
who had the worst time of all;	fue el pobre de Ceferino
humiliated in such a fashion	humillado de esa forma
by an idiot sergeant.	por un sargento cretino.
And if that guy doesn't change,	Y como este tío no cambie
we know what to do:	ya sabemos lo que hacer
we'll send him with Pinochet	para repartir galletas
to slap people.[10]	lo mandaremos con Pinochet.

The *copla* and the unwanted publicity offended the sergeant of the *Guardia Civil*. The sergeant excused his actions at the stadium saying: "In my line of work I have to do this." He summoned the men to the *cuartel*, charging them with ridiculing the institution of the *Guardia Civil*, but the men refused to appear, asserting that they were laughing at one individual policeman, not at the institution. For their part, the One-Eyed Bullfighters basked in the notoriety. For the moment, at least, the workers were united and the *Guardia Civiles* were in check.

Angel Guillén

As the times changed, Angel Guillén, the schoolteacher, remained
alert to the need for independence for Benalup, convinced it was
the key to a better life for the people and a more modern town. In
1979 he tied the superior position of Medina to economic as well
as local political problems. In his eyes Medina was the great
oppressor. For some, Benalup was now tied to the much larger
struggle for regional autonomy. The drive for independence had
always plagued Spain in the northern Basque and Catalonian
regions, but now the idea was beginning to cut deeper in Andalusia
as well.

Unemployment and misery	El paro y la miseria
is what Medina has given you.	es lo que te da Medina
My town, I see you unhappy	pueblo mío te veo sin alegría.
and they forgot, they forgot to sow	Y se olvidó el sembrar
the fields that are not as productive as before.	el campo que ya no produce igual
The laborer has to emigrate.	el labrador tuvo que emigrar
What sorrow, Lord, help us.	que dolor Señor alivia este mal.
My beloved Andalusia,	Mi Andalucía esta tierra mía
get out of your lethargy	despierta de tu letargo
and struggle for your autonomy.	y lucha por tu autonomía.
(Los Presidiarios)	

The song that many remember Angel for, however, was one that
concerned not independence but the scandal involving tainted
cooking oil. In 1981 doctors in the Madrid area observed the
sudden appearance of what appeared to be a mysterious disease.
The cause was discovered to be toxic syndrome brought on by
ingesting poisoned cooking oil. It was discovered that the so-called
cooking oil sold door to door by street vendors was rapeseed oil
treated with aniline, a poisonous and colorless oil liquid derived
from benzene and used in dyes. The oil, intended for industrial
use, was mixed with olive oil and sold door to door principally in
Madrid but also in eleven of Spain's fifty-two provinces. Up to
650 people died and 20,000 were maimed or otherwise painfully
affected. Patient complaints centered on lung and respiratory
problems, skin rashes, spasms, and wasting of the limbs. It was
devastating to public trust, for the villains had stolen into the

homes and hearths of the victims. In the new democracy such scandals could not be hidden. Angel Guillén thought his *pasodoble* on the subject was the song that the people liked most that year, and it is a fitting monument to his years of composing for his town carnival:

> "It's a critique, an account of all the problems that occurred. It blames the egotism of those businessmen so interested in making money they stop at nothing. In brief, we ask for justice in the name of the dead, and of all those scarred by the disease."

How many tears have been shed!	¡Cuántas lágrimas han
How many young people felled!	sido vertidas, cuánta juventud tronchada,
How many dreams broken!	cuántas bellas ilusiones rotas,
How many families wrecked!	y familias destrozadas!
Innocent children	Niños inocentes que
have lost their mothers,	a sus madres pierden,
broken-hearted mothers	madres sin consuelo que
have lost their sons.	pierden a sus hijos.
Boyfriends are left without their sweethearts,	Novios que sin novia quedan,
and wives without their husbands.	y mujeres sin marido.
The sick struggle without hope.	Enfermos desesperados que luchan sin fe
Tomorrow they might be counted	porque entre los muertos
among the dead.	mañana puede estar él.
As for the few who elude the death	Y los pocos que se salvan
that lies in wait for them	de esta muerte que les acecha
and pursues them cruelly. . .	y les persigue con crueldad,
Ah, wretched ones, what a pity, forever scarred	¡pobrecillos, qué desgracia!, para siempre quedan marcados
by this terrible disease!	por la terrible enfermedad.
This infamous deed, gentlemen,	Esta es, señores, la obra infame,
without exaggeration,	y no exagero,
is the work of swine	de unos canallas obsesionados
obsessed by money.	por el dinero.
Oh heartless merchants!	Contra ti claman, ¡ay comerciante
The dead and the crippled	desaprensivo!,

cry out against you.

It is an evil act
to sow destruction and fear

among the people. . .

to think only of oneself
and nothing of others.
"Let there be justice!"
all Spain shouts,
"and let us feed the oil
to those predators."
(Las Primaveras, 1982)

todos esos muertos y esos lisiados
que has producido.
Porque éste es un hecho de mucha maldad,
sembrar en el pueblo ruina y terror
por pensar en sí
y no en los demás.
¡Que se haga justicia,
pide toda España,
y le den aceite
a esas alimañas!

The verdict in the case, rendered in May 1989 after a hearing lasting fifteen months, fell far short of what the public desired. Of the thirty-seven persons tried, three principals in the case were given extended jail sentences of ten, twelve, and twenty years; ten others were given short sentences; and twenty-four of the accused were acquitted. Survivors, some permanently deformed and crippled, wept openly, while others cursed the judges and threw rocks at the riot police.

The Death of Angel Guillén

Angel Guillén died in 1988, the year before the verdict of the contaminated oil was reached. Although Angel kept up his attack against Medina and for the independence of Benalup until the last, he failed to see Benalup achieve the goal of independence. On March 20, 1991, Benalup was declared an independent township. Unfortunately for Benalup, its inauguration was not crowned with ample terrain. The original extension of the township of Medina Sidonia was 54,475 hectares. After the division, Medina Sidonia retained 48,540 hectares; Benalup ended up with 5,935 hectares.[11] Benalup dropped "de Sidonia" from its name to erase any trace of its former dependence.[12]

In the carnival following Angel's death, Santo, a good friend, fellow teacher and *coplista*, and for a brief time the socialist mayor of Benalup, saluted him with a *pasodoble* in which Angel speaks from paradise to his fellow townsmen. Angel bids farewell to the barrios, the streets, the rivers and valleys, and at the same time urges them to continue the struggle for independence from Medina.

. . .	. . .
Sing with all your heart	que de corazon le cantes
to the things in my land.	a las cosas de mi tierra
Sing to all the barrios in town,	cántale a todos sus barrios
Ay! streets, squares, and	¡Ay! calles, plazas y alamedas
boulevards.	
Sing to my Barbate river,	Cántale a mi río Barbate
bronze snake that surrounds	serpiente de bronce que te
you.	rodea.
Sing to this green valley,	Cántale a ese verde valle
and to its lovely flowers.	y a sus lindas flores.
And to our mountains [sierra].	Y a nuestra sierra.
Sing to the old Janda,[13]	Cántale a la antigua Janda
lost paradise. Tell her: "What a	paraiso perdido. Dile, ¡¡Que
pity!"	Pena!!
Don't forget the spout,	No te olvides del cañuelo
because I still have loving	que aun recuerdo a esos
memories	chiquillos
of those children whom I	que eduque yo con cariño.
educated.	
And demand, with all your	Y pide con todas tus fuerzas
strength,	
our Independence,	nuestra Independencia a gritos
because Casas Viejas is alive.	que Casas Viejas está vivo.
I'm leaving. . . I'm leaving. . .	Me marcho ya. . . Me marcho
	ya. . .
I leave you composing little	Te dejo componiendo coplillas
verses.	
From heaven this angel	desde el cielo se despide
comparsista	compañeros
says good-bye to you all.	este ángel comparsista.
(Comparsa Local, 1989)	

Angel's untimely death meant that his voice would not be heard in carnival on new plagues to the town, which according to other composers would be the influx of hashish and heroin from Morocco, the ubiquitous presence of slot machines and, beyond the pueblo, hunger in the Third World and the rising toll of infant deaths. They would miss, as well, what would surely have been a sure-handed comic account of the woman who introduced the novel fashion of making love in a bus.

Notes

1. During 1969 and 1970 I shot two documentary films on the effects of the rural exodus in Benalup. One film, "Pepe's Family," concerned the family just described: Juan, Carmen, and the grandfather, Pepe. The film, 41 minutes long, is in black and white The second film, "The Shoemaker," concerns a shoemaker who is forced to close up his shop and join his children and his wife in a newly developing tourist town on the Mediterranean. (See "Acknowlegments," note 1, for information concerning viewing and distribution.)

2. It is necessary to recall that from 1967 to 1977 in the capital, carnival was celebrated only in the springtime; and in most rural towns during this period (except for Trebujena in mid-winters from 1967 to 1974), there was but sporadic carnival activity.

   There is a curious parallel in the temporary decline of carnival in latter day Cuba as the result of a change in the calendar from winter to spring. In 1970, in order to ensure the presence of the work force necessary for the winter sugar cane harvest, the government of Fidel Castro commanded that carnival be celebrated in July. Interest in the festival sharply declined. In 1990 the festival was completely canceled as the result of a new period of austerity following the end of aid from the Soviet Union. In 1996, after an absence of twenty-six years, carnival was celebrated in Havana once again at its own time preceding Lent.

3. The semimilitary organization had been founded in 1844 to combat bandits who then plagued the highways and rural areas. In order to discourage corruption and favoritism, they were never posted to their native towns. To maintain a social distance between themselves and the townspeople, they lived in a *cuartel* (barracks) with their families. They proved to be efficient and

honest in clearing out banditry. They were, however, the strict
servants of the state, the wealthy landowners, and the middle
class, and their role in keeping order expanded with changing
social conditions.

> With the rise of anarchism in the second half of the nineteenth
> century, the Guard was used increasingly to break up peasant
> demonstrations and to prevent or break strikes. It was a frequent
> practice for the Guard to fire point-blank at strikers, and the
> Ministry of the Interior invariably protected the anonymity of the
> marksmen if it could not entirely suppress the news. If for the
> landlords the Guard was indeed *La Benemérita*, for the landless
> peasants it was an army of occupation composed of 25,000 well-
> armed servants of the rich. (Gabriel Jackson, *The Spanish Republic
> and the Civil War, 1931–1939*, Princeton, N.J.: Princeton University
> Press, 1965, p.68.)

The *Guardia Civil* was reorganized and united with the *cara-
bineros* (customs guards) in 1940. As before they patrolled the
countryside in pairs, fulfilling their original summons, to wipe
out banditry and end an epidemic of kidnapping, and also to
root out any Republican and anarchist remnants hiding in the
mountains.

4. The towns had municipal policemen of their own, who had
   little to do except keep an eye out for suspicious strangers who
   might appear in the town after hours. Many of the *municipales*
   were men who had been wounded in the war (on Franco's side
   – veterans of the Republic were not eligible for such benefits),
   and so it was commonplace to encounter municipal policemen
   with severe physical handicaps. But there was no violence to
   speak of in the small towns, and criminal matters were brought
   to the attention of the *Guardia Civiles*.

5. "*La marcha verde*" (the green advance) was the name given to
   weekly aid provided to unemployed fieldworkers in the 1970s
   and 1980s. Workers were given two or three days' pay each
   week according to the amount of money available to the local
   government. Some weeks they were paid for three days and
   some weeks for only one day, and some weeks they received
   no aid at all. Many local workers charged that administrators
   in Medina kept most of the aid for their own workers and
   funneled little on to Benalup. Others attributed the organizational problems to the governor's office. Of course the lack of

funds was also related to nationwide problems of limited economic growth and widespread unemployment.

The appellation "la marcha verde" originated with the Spanish colony in Morocco at the edge of the Sahara desert which earlier had been popularly baptized with this name.

6. In 1981 a long-awaited law permitted divorce, and two years later abortion was legalized in a limited number of situations.

7. The UCD commanded 35 percent of the vote, gaining 167 of the 350 congressional seats. The PSOE won 29 percent of the vote and 121 seats. The Communist Party took two seats with 10 percent of the vote, and the regional party from Andalusia gained five seats.

8. In 1982 Felipe González, forty years of age, the leader of the PSOE, won election and settled in for a long stay in power (until March 1996) as leader of the 350-seat parliament. The years of his greatest success, 1986 to 1991, coincided with Spain's entry into the European Community, massive foreign investment, and the fastest growth of any European country. The great issues of the Civil War generation, concerning ownership of the land and the distribution of wealth, were now bypassed by the surging economy of the postwar age. Crucial questions concerned development, investment, and the creation of new industries and new high-paying jobs. Additional challenges included providing unemployment insurance, minimal medical care, and social security for the work force. The devaluation of the *peseta* in 1992 brought Spanish economists back to reality.

9. Newspaper accounts that violence had occurred are incorrect. I was present and observed the events.

10. A *"galleta"* (a biscuit or cookie) is often used as a colloquial equivalent for a "blow" or a "slap in the face." The suggestion here is that such a sergeant could be employed by a regime such as Augusto Pinochet's in Chile to torture people.

11. *Boletín Oficial de la Junta de Andalucía*, no. 22, 26 March 1991, *decreto* 63/1991.

12. According to residents of Medina Sidonia, the animosity was limited to the smaller town, as one resident described: "Benalup has always been very hostile towards Medina, but this sentiment was not reciprocated by the larger town. The *Benalupenos* used to see Medina as powerful and oppressive and regarded their independence as a shaking off of their yoke.

On the other hand, the town of Medina sighed with relief at Benalup's secession, as Benalup, a poor, needy town, was quite an albatross around Medina's neck."

The population size of Medina Sidonia was listed as 11,700 and that of Benalup as 5,000.

13. The lagoon being drained for agricultural use by Las Lomas.

Chapter 7

Sexual Targets

Carnival Comedy

Carnival is identified with varieties of sexual licentiousness. In every carnival there are flashes of unsettling sexual comedy. It is at its mildest during the public festivities and parades; there are some couples strolling who have exchanged clothing so that the man is dressed as a bride and the woman as the groom; a band of singers will often include a man mockingly attired as a woman. At times the comedy stretches for new highs or lows. The *chirigota*, *Los Kokorokos* [The Cock-a-doodle-doos], in the Benalup carnival of 1982 included three men in their sixties dressed flauntingly as women. To further confound their sexual identities, each of the rouged and incongruously costumed men also had strung under his skirts a brightly colored corncob shaped and painted as a phallus. Following each round of songs, the androgynously dressed dancers would lash their hips and lift their skirts to reveal their wildly bobbing sex organs. Although it was a scene to short-circuit most other social gatherings, the carnival performances took place in a serene circle of townspeople, men, women with babes in arms, and children (including the elderly dancers' own families), all curious but unruffled by the comical sexual turnabout.

The change of costumes and sexual personality sometimes may develop a scenario all its own: in one *comparsa* in Benalup in 1982, Los Primaveras, the refusal of a young man (nicknamed el Topo, the mole) to put on a woman's dress stuffed with cotton breasts, caused him to break with his friends and leave the *comparsa*. El Topo had been pressured by his *novia* not to participate, and his departure became the theme of the *comparsa's* refrain, repeated to his embarrassment after every song:

And the Mole, who was already in costume,	Y el Topo que era un careta
split from the *comparsa*	se rajó de la comparsa
because he wouldn't wear tits.	por no ponerse la teta.

Four years earlier, in 1978, a *murga* called Los Volaos offered an inspired dramatic presentation for a sexual misalliance best known to isolated young shepherds in the countryside: bestial intercourse. The *murga* was led by Jesús Máñez, an energetic mason who was at the time the funniest carnival comic in Benalup, with lyrics written by Pepe Colmena, whose bar was a center for carnival activities. Each chorus concluded with a shout: ¡*Burra a la vista!* (I see a *burra* on the horizon!) to indicate that the isolated country lad finds sexual relief at hand.

| BURRA AHOY!! | ¡¡BURRA A LA VISTA!! |

When the groups took turns presenting samples of their repertoires on the stage of the movie theater, Jesús Máñez, seemingly carried away by his infatuation, strode to center stage, unrolled a sheaf of tattered papers and began to read passionate love poems to his unidentified sweetheart. In the midst of his recitation, his fellow *murgistas* heightened the romantic scene by stampeding his ostensible sweetheart, a skittish and perplexed country *burra*, down the center aisle of the theater. The Andalusian audience collapsed in laughter. It was the sort of scene that would have brought down the house at *A Midsummer Night's Dream* at the Globe theatre or delighted listeners of a rendering of Apuleius' *The Golden Ass*. The remaining days of the carnival, Jesús Máñez continued his assault on animal affairs by reading his poems from rooftops and rock walls in various barrios in town.

There are occasional accounts of misplaced sexual targets, as seen in medical treatment required following a careless visit to a homosexual in Badalejos, a small settlement of houses on the highway a few kilometers from Benalup:

There is in Badalejos,	Tenemos en los Badalejos,
gentlemen, a lioness;	señores, a una leona,
they made his rear look like	que le pusieron el trasero
the ass of a female monkey.	como el culo de una mona.
He grabbed some guys,	Cogió a unos cuantos muchachos,

gentlemen, and in one instant	señores, y en un instante
made their trunks swollen	les puso a todos la trompa
like that of an elephant.	como la de un elefante.
They came to Casas Viejas	Vinieron a Casas Viejas
to show it to the doctor,	a enseñársela al doctor,
and the doctor said to them:	y el doctor le decía:
"What do I see here!"	¡qué es lo que estoy viendo yo!
"What kind of broken-down tramps	¿Qué clase Rompechapines
have you been with,	es donde habeis "estao",
and what kind of women	y qué clase de mujeres
have gotten you in this fix?"	es la que se habeis "cargao"?
One of the guys	Uno de aquellos muchachos
answered him hesitantly:	le dijo entrecortao":
"Juani of Badalejos (twice)	La Juani la del Badalejos (Dos Veces)
is the one who stuck it to us."	es la que nos la ha "pegao".

The chorus then thoughtfully adds:

Be careful screwing,	Cuidado al desconejar,
Mañez told us tenderly,	nos dijo Máñez muy tierno
that you don't trip	no vayáis a tropezar
and plant your dick in the sand.	y en la arena hinquéis los cuer. . .

(Los Volaos, 1978)

Gossip among Men

Carnival songs can be read to reveal sexual crosscurrents in Andalusian society. There is, however, one serious caveat: it is critical to realize that carnival songs are composed and sung almost exclusively by men – and these are rambunctious men of the workplace, the street, and the tavern. A glance at the themes of carnival songs over twenty-five years in Benalup confirms this circumstance of male authorship. Many serious songs concern matters that gnaw at the heart of every man: work, unemployment, emigration. A still larger number of songs aim at sexual targets from a man's point of view.

During the year composers have been watching their fellow creatures stretch and strut. Most attention is accorded those who have reached the age of sexual experience and who skirt along the edge of courtship and marriage. It is the season of life that most frequently produces incidents, plot, and motives which ripen into the songs of carnival.

> "Before carnival the young men go around and pick up the news – the gossip about a woman who got pregnant or about a girl who ran off with her boyfriend. That sort of thing. . .This is a boring town. . .a small town, that's all." (Pedro el Relojero [watchmaker])

Mateo, who composes each year for the carnival, is a guard on an estate outside the pueblo. The estate he patrols provides him with a stone house on a distant hillside where he lives with his wife and three teenage daughters. Although he is far from town, the singers of his *comparsa* keep him informed as to news so that his songs will catch the interest of the crowds and set the pueblo to laughter:

> ". . .Whatever is raunchy, things that are spicy. . .things that happen to young people, between sweethearts and the like."

Some circumstances have a natural punch line easy to translate into song:

> "María was very hot and always had her hands on her boyfriend – talking and touching him. María is to blame for her pregnancy. The boyfriend looked much more modest – embarrassed. María was shameless since this was an ugly matter. She had told everyone that she was going to the doctor because she ate an ice cream pop and it stopped her menstruation. Now the joke is that she's the girl with the hot ice cream pop *(la chica del palo caliente)*." (Antonia)

Church records of earlier generations indicate that approximately one third of the young women were some months pregnant at the time of their marriage.[1] When pregnancy or birth control appear as themes in the songs, it is usually not to consider the social ramifications but to record another young maiden tripped up – a subject for mirth in carnival songs composed and sung by men.

At the doctor's office	A la casa del médico fue
was a young woman.	una joven toda sofocada
She was feeling uptight	se le había cortado el período

because her period was late.
While the doctor examined her,
she offered her opinion:
"This might be fright,

because a few days ago

I saw a dead man."
"I'll be frank with you.
I doubt that very much,
because from what I see,
you're pregnant in and out.
And it's not from a dead man,
but from one who's quick."

(one of the chorus yells): And
how quick!

(refrain): How pretty are the
flowers
when spring arrives!
Yet prettier are you, sweetheart,
when you're next to me!

A young man at work
with his girl wore a rubber
to keep the stork from arriving
ahead of schedule.
Once he went in too far
and left his rubber behind.
"Now you've done me in!
Alas, my true love!
Now I'll end up pregnant.
What rotten luck!
The day the baby is born,
there'll be a grand party,
because your dearest child
will come out wrapped in a
sock."
(Los Primaveras, 1981)

desde hacía ya varias semanas.
Y mientras la examina el doctor
ella quiso darle su opinión.
Esto que me pasa a mí yo creo
que puede ser
(por)que el otro día yo vi un
muerto.
Vaya susto que me pegué.
Lo dudo mucho, señora,
le digo de forma franca,
porque por lo que yo veo
está preñada hasta las trancas.
Y eso por lo que adivino
no ha sido de un muerto, sino
de un vivo.
(Una persona): ¡Y bien vivo!

(estribillo): ¡Qué bonitas están
las flores
al llegar la primavera!
Más bonita está tu niña
cuando te tengo a mi vera.

El muchacho que se trajinaba
a su novia con la funda puesta
porque no quería que llegara
la cigüeña antes de la cuenta.
Un día le metió un apretón
y la funda adentro se quedó.
 ---Bien que has metido la pata,
chiquillo del alma mía,
ahora me quedo preñada,
¡vaya desgracia la mía!
El día que nazca el niño
se formará un gran festín,
Porque el niño de tu alma
saldrá metido en un calcetín.

Eros

If carnival is seen as a time of sexual liberty when erotic thoughts
are given free rein, the content of the fantasy depends almost
exclusively on male libidinous energy. The arc of love soars
upward and then tumbles into matters more piquant and racy or
perhaps more mundane.

Some guy with a lot of gall	Un tío con mucha cara
gave his father-in-law a surprise:	a su suegro le espetó
"I've come to ask you for your daughter	vengo a pedirle el conejo
Concepcion's pussy [rabbit]."	de su hija Concepción.
"You must mean her hand,"	La mano querrás decir
the father-in-law seriously replied.	le digo el suegro muy serio.
"I'm asking for her pussy,"	Yo le pido a usted el conejo,
the daring guy said,	el tío carota dijo,
"I've had her hand for so long I	porque de la mano tengo
have calluses on my sex."	hasta callos en el "pi. . ."
(Juglares, 1980)	

Most commonly, the songs with sexual themes reveal how foolish
and foolhardy we are from *noviazgo* (courtship) to old age. Songs
selected over a wide span of years from Benalup show that ridicule
is the common currency of the songwriters. Some songs tell of
couples tripped up by their passion and forced to wed. Some reveal
affairs between those married to others. It comes as no surprise
that a favorite *cuplé* theme is to salute the failed erection – that
moment when passion flounders and pride seems at its nadir.
Erections are a major source of humor, from songs expressing the
conceit of youth to the worries of those with declining powers,
either from age or a betrayed lover's curse. In the following *cuplés*
the poets use various euphemisms for the male sexual organ: spear
(*lanza*), saber (*sable*), macaroni (*macarron*), but these only hint at
the range of names used for penis and vagina, depending on the
reference to piercing strength, ferocity, condition, or, concerning
the vagina, the shape and suggestion of fire and succulence.[2]

Some women in this town	Hay mujeres en este pueblo
are very lascivious and gossipy,	muy cachondas y criticonas

and among them we have the group	y entre ellas está la partida
of those who discuss weddings.	de las mironas de bodas.
There is a group of these women	Hay grupo en este sentido
who enjoy a hell of a lot	que disfrutan una "jartá"
reviewing the physiques	repasando de cuerpo entero
of all the men that are getting married.	a tó el que se va a casar.
One day a husband of one of these critics	Un día a una criticona
woke her up saying:	el marío así le despertó:
"With all this wedding tumult	con la leche de tanta boda
you get all horny,	tú te pones toda morá
and here I am, like Don Quijote,	y yo como D. Quijote todo
all teeth, and with my spear ready."	canino y la lanza armá.
(Cosacos, 1981)	

I don't know the motive	Yo no sé por qué motivo
nor the reason	ni tampoco la razón
why girls nowadays are	las niñas de hoy en día
such hypocrites.	lo caraduras que son.
They go around with guys	Se van con los niños
in cars day and night.	montadas en los coches
Can you imagine the places	ya puede ser de día
they go to?	lo mismo que de noche.
Because they know well enough that their fathers	Ustedes imagináis al sitio que ellas van
won't punish them.	porque ya saben de sobra
I punish them	que papá no castiga ya.
with a saber we have	Castigo les daba yo
under our nightshirt.	con el sable que tenemos
(Dormilones, 1979)	debajo del camisón.

Fransisca from the mountains	Francisca la de la peña
went to the doctor very worried,	fue a la doctora muy preocupada
complaining of some pains	quejándose de unos males
that she could not stand.	que la señora no soportaba
She went to the pharmacy	fue a recoger a la farmacia
to pick up all the things	todas las cosas que le mandaban
prescribed for her,	
and when she got home	y cuando llegó a su casa
the medicines had been changed.	las medicinas estaban cambiadas

It so happens that at the pharmacy	resulta que en la farmacia
they made a serious error.	habían formado el gran pestiño
They gave her some pills	le dieron unas pastillas
that are used for birth control	que son "pa" no tener niños
"Why should I take them?"	"pa" que las voy a tomar
she said very frankly.	dijo con mucha franqueza
For my dear Diego	si a mi Diego de mi alma
never straightens up his macaroni.	el macarrón no se le endereza.
(Segaores, 1979)	

In this town, gentlemen,	En este pueblo señores
we have all types.	hay de tó
Young men who can't find girlfriends,	jovenes que no ligan
not even on special occasions.	ni en ocasión
Yet, we have here,	sin embargo tenemos
a great womanizer,	aquí un ligón
who is past eighty but can get it up.	que pasa de los 80 y se le upa el porretón.
One must see his weapon,	Hay que ver mi arma
I have never seen any	como tu la tiene
quite like it,	no he visto ninguna
so thick and long.	tan gorda ni tan larga
"With that," said the gypsy, "You	con esa hechura dijo la gitana
can reach the top of your sister's backbone."	se la mete en la rabaílla del toto a tu hermana.
(Confiteros, 1979)	

Given this limited perspective, it is inevitable that questions concerning the loss of affection are given short shrift. For some poets, solutions are simple-minded, whether the subject is a man or a woman:

We are going to say something to modern girls.	Algunas niñas de hoy le vamó a decir una cosa
If your boyfriends leave you don't lose your head.	que si la dejan los novios que no pierdan la cabeza.
We know this girl whose boyfriend	Conocemos una chica
intended to dump her,	que el novio la iba a dejar,

and she swallowed a bottle of pills,	se tragó un tarro de pastillas
and we almost lost her.	si por poco va p´allá.
She became lethargic,	Le entró un letargo muy grande
and her blood pressure went down.	se le bajó la tensión
She was taken to Cádiz	se la llevaron a Cádiz, gracias a Dios se salvó.
and was saved, thank God.	A algunas mamás
We say to mothers	Le vamos a decir
to hide the key	que escondan la llave
to the medicine cabinet,	de su botiquín
or at least give these girls a vibrator,	si no que le pongan un consolador,
so they can scratch when it itches	que arrasca si pica
and cool off.	y alivia el calor.
(Los Amarrados, 1981)	

For men the solution is even more blunt. One *cuplé* drolly mocks the director of the group who lost control of himself after dancing with a girl.

He went to the river	dice que se fue "pal" río
and screwed a burra.	y una burra se "cargó."

Democracy

Little is sacred to the composers of carnival erotica. After the end of the dictatorship the new democratic reforms were quickly swept up into popular currents involving comedy and sexuality. Any misstep, any sign of diversity in custom and behavior, whether it was related to growing tourism or any other factor, could be attributed to this new democracy. One *pasodoble* in Benalup in 1979, one year after the constitution was passed in the Cortes, begins:

We have democracy	Tenemos democracia
and we also have	y ya tenemos
ladies without underslips	en cualquier sitio vemos
anywhere you go. . ..	hembras sin faldas
(Triunfo Andaluz, 1979)	

Democracy as a forcible influence changing town life, became part
of common speech, often serving as an introduction to events:

With the new democracy,	Con la nueva democracia
you will see what has happened,	veréis lo que ha sucedido,
a young man went for a walk along	un muchacho con su ligue,
the river with his latest conquest.	fueron a dar una vuelta al río.

After a tumble in a ditch, the girl's mother arrives at the pharmacy
and tells the druggist to "give her an injection," but the young
man protests:

"Good heavens, madam,	"Señora válgame Dios
don't give any more injections,	no poner más injecciones
as I have already given her one."	que ya se la he puesto yo."
(Los Volaos, Benalup, 1978)	

Another *cuplé* in 1979 linked the new democracy to a homosexual
encounter spied in the woods:

We have democracy.	Estamos en la democracia
Don't be astonished	no se vayan a espantar
about the story I am about	del caso que ahora mismo
to tell.	nosotros vamos a contar.
They said they saw them,	Se dicen que lo pillaron
hidden in a prickly pear patch.	escondidos en un tunal,
One was naked,	uno se encontraba en pompa
and the other was behind him.	y el otro estaba detrás;
What they were doing,	lo que ellos estaban haciendo
you already can imagine.	ya se lo pueden imaginar.
Whether this should be allowed,	Si es que eso está permitido
we shall remain silent.	ya nos vamos a callar,
But for God's sake,	pero por Dios no ponerse
don't do it where you can be seen.	donde los puedan pillar.
(Los Dormilones, 1979)	

La Cencerrada[3] (The Ringing of Cowbells)

While an occasional song celebrates marital bliss, the carnival singers return to form when they consider latecomers to love. Mockery is commonly directed at the match of older couples, particularly of widows and widowers beyond the customary courting age or of couples of disparate ages. It is an occasion for the *cencerrada*, the ringing of cowbells in the front yard of aging newlyweds. What once may have derived from a variety of protective folkloric devices (to separate the living from the dead, and past spouses from present mates) is now simply a means of mockery. The lyrics are sharply focused: the same preoccupation with erections that affected the young men still remain as the centerpiece of the humor for the songwriters.

In Benalup in 1979, several comic *cuplés* greeted the wedding of an eighty-year-old man and a younger woman of gypsy ancestry. Of three of the versions included here, one is fairly straightforward, a second includes comic imagery, and a third turns on folklore and reputed gypsy folklore, at that.

Méndez' Wedding:	La boda de Méndez
last year	Tuvimos una boda
we had a wedding	el año pasado
which has been	que todo el pueblo
the talk of the town.	mucho ha comentado.
With great hopes,	Con mucha ilusión
Méndez got married	el Méndez se casa
when he was well over eighty.	ya más que ochentón.
He made Balilla	El Balilla hizo
the priest and godfather	de cura y padrino
and as for the rest	como sería todo
I can already imagine.	yo ya me imagino.
But the best part	Pero lo mejor
was that night	fue aquella niche
making love.	haciendo el amor.
She was willing to do anything	Ella se prestaba a todo
so that he might give her the goods,	por si él afloja la guita
but to no avail.	pero no lo consiguió
And she told the old man	y con sus castas
take your nuts and go to hell.	al viejo mandó.
(Pueblo, 1979)	

The town heard	Una noticia graciosa
the funny news.	el pueblo entero escuchó
In the Balilla store	que en la tienda del Balilla
someone found love.	había surgido el amor.
Méndez married	El Méndez a una gitana
a gypsy girl.	en matrimonio se unió,
When night came,	y cuando llegó la noche
you should have seen them	habría que verlos a los dos.
both.	
He is eighty years old,	El tiene ochenta años
and we don't know if he went	no sabemos si atacó,
on the attack,	
but something failed to work	pero algo le fallaría
because she left him.	cuando ella lo abandonó
It was that the artillery	Y es que la artillería
never fired the entire night.	en tó la noche no disparó.
(Dormilones, 1979)	

When Méndez and the gypsy	Cuando el Méndez y la gitana
met and got together	se conocieron y se "juntaron"
in the store of "Balilla"	en la tienda del "Balilla"
they celebrated with special	con mucha gracia lo celebraron
pleasure.	
She said, "Juanito,	ella le decía "Juanito"
have these two drinks	tómate ya dos copas de menta
of mint and you'll see how	y tu verás en la cama
hot you'll get in bed.	la calentura que a ti te entra.
An old aphorism says,	Dice un antiguo refrán
that he who is horny	que morirá con la "pinga" tiesa
and sleeps with gypsies	todo el que no sea calé
will die with his penis erect.	y con gitanas se acuesta.
So if that it true,	Como eso sea verdad
then, the day Méndez dies,	el día que el menda se muera
they will have to open	tendrán que hacerle la caja
a hole in his coffin.	con un boquete en la tapaera.
(Los Travoltas, 1979)	

Four years later, in 1982, an older widower known by his family's nickname of Gallinito (little rooster) decided to remarry and in his own front yard had to face the taunting sounds of the *cencerrada*, the ringing of cowbells, and infuriating songs, including the following *cuplé* by the schoolteacher, Angel Guillén, sung by his *comparsa*, Los Primaveras:

The bachelor who was

sorry that he'd married a
spinster,
for she had, said her sweetie,
a washwoman's pussy,

nonetheless changed his mind
once he got raving sassy.
"My darling, oh how I love you!
Join me all the way.
Look at my hard-on:
it's as stiff as a stake.
Let them, Rosa, let them ring
the cowbells and tambourines.
The prettiest call still is
the one sounding retreat.
I'll sound out retreat for you
with a blow from my bugle."

(Comparsa Primavera, 1982)

El soltero que se arrepintió de
casarse
con la "solterona"

porque dijo el gachón que tenía
el "chumino" como una
fregona.
Sin embargo cambió de opinión
al entrarle pirula rabiosa.
Mi amada, ¡cuánto te quiero!
cásate por todas tus castas,
que tengo la "mamanduca"
tan tiesa como una estaca.
Deja, Rosa, que te toquen
cencerros y panderetas,
pero el toque más bonito
es el toque de "retreta".
Te lo pienso de dar yo
de un sopletazo con mi
trompeta.

Jesús Mañez and his *murga, Los Hijos de la Ramona*, provided another version for the occasion:

Gallinito finally married
that old woman,
and he liked it so much
that it gave him diarrhea.
They rang the bells outside his
house
for three whole nights,
and poor Gallinito
didn't get much sleep.
And the old woman would say:
" Paquito, please, go to the
police."
" Wait a little, honey,
because I just got it up now."
(Los Hijos de la Ramona, 1982)

Por fin con aquella vieja,
Gallinito se casó
y le entró hasta diarreas
del gustazo que le dio.
Le tocaron los cencerros

por tres noches de seguía
y el pobre del gallinito
el sueño no lo cogía.
Y la vieja le decía:
--Paquito, anda y ve al Cuartel.

--Espera un poco cariño
porque ahora la tengo en pie.

The wife in this instance, however, was not a marginal figure in the pueblo (as was the gypsy woman ridiculed two years earlier).

The couple refused to accept the taunts without protest, as one composer, Jesús Mañez, recalls:

"An old man here [Gallanito] married an old woman and so for several nights people rang cowbells. Like in the old days when a widower married, people rang cowbells for three consecutive nights. If the groom didn't invite them in, they would keep it up every night till they were invited in. So I came up with this *cuplé* about what happened."

["What did happen? Did they have you in for a drink?"] "Are you kidding? There was no invitation. Instead he turned us all in to the *Guardia Civil.*"

The Burnished Years

While expressions of esteem and admiration are sounded for towns and barrios, few phrases voicing love for the opposite sex find their way into carnival repertoires. On rare occasions, however, a *pasodoble* offers a tribute to enduring love.

I understand that some old traditions	Aunque comprendo se puedan perder
may die out with the passage of time	las tradiciones al pasar el tiempo
because life teaches us to see things differently	porque la vida nos enseña a ver
in different moments.	cosas distintas según el momento
However, I will never understand	yo sin embargo nunca entenderé
why some traditions were lost in this town.	algunas de ellas que aquí perdieron
In June, on Saint John's day,	recuerdo en junio el día de San Juan
we used to celebrate in a big way	se celebraba con gran lucimiento
a renowned fiesta	una fiesta renombrada
well rooted in the life of the village.	raigambre en el pueblo
Such traditions are dying out,	se pierden ya costumbres como aquella
customs which were like harbingers of spring,	que eran el presagio de la primavera

like when in San José	por San José con toda ilusión
we used to walk along the road	cogernos de la mano
holding hands	por la carretera
and sit by the river	y sentarnos juntos a la orilla del río
in the fresh shadow of a green eucalyptus.	a la sombra fresca de un verde eucalipto.
Drunk with love,	Emborracharnos de amor
just the two of us.	solitos los dos
Aren't these memories	mira si serán bellos
of those times beautiful?	los recuerdos de aquel tiempo
I still have on my lips,	que aún tengo yo en mis labios
Casaviejena of my soul,	casaviejeña del alma
the divine taste of those first kisses	el sabor tan divino de aquellos besos primeros
stolen from you in the shadow of the furze.	que te robé en la retama.
(Comparsa Payaso y Poeta, 1988)	

For devotees, however, carnival is an occasion for ridicule and mockery rather than affection. A carnival tribute is offered in its own inestimable style.

With love and affection they celebrated	Con cariño y afecto lo celebraron
their golden wedding anniversary this summer.	unas bodas de oro este verano.
The whole village was invited there.	allí fue todo el pueblo como invitado.
They auctioned off the groom's tie,	La corbata del novio la subastaron
everyone was well-oiled and they even danced.	se jartó todo el mundo y hasta bailaron.
The groom said	El novio decía
that he was nervous	que estaba nervioso
because the celebration reminded him	porque aquella boda le recordaba
of the years of his youth.	los años mozos.
And giving her a nudge	Y le dijo a ella
he said to her,	dándole un codazo.
"Prepare yourself,	Aprepárate que te "vía"
I'm going to stick it in up to your pacemaker."	meter hasta el marcapaso.
Segaores (1978)	

Carnival Ridicule

At times carnival song cuts close to the bone, laying the subject open to shame and ridicule and even placing the singer in some jeopardy.

> "I like carnival because I enjoy fooling around. When they poke fun at me, I joke back at them. . .In the future I doubt if I'll go out. Maybe I'll wear a costume, but I won't sing in a *chirigota* or *comparsa*. . . Because they'll beat me up. . .Because I infuriate people when I tell the truth. . .Because I say things that people would rather keep under wraps. They don't want gossip. . .gossip. Say a brother and sister are fooling around. Well, they don't want anybody to know. Boy! That's the sort of thing I like about carnival." (Juan Cazas)

The world has become	A estas alturas señores,
too modern nowadays.	el mundo se ha puesto
Even brothers,	demasiao moderno,
as soon as one of them	que hasta los mismos hermanos
turns round,	al volver la cara
cuckold each other.	se ponen los cuernos.
A boy in this town	Un muchacho de este pueblo,
was doing it with	a su propia cuñada
his own sister-in-law.	se la ventilaba
They didn't give it any	y no le dieron importancia
importance	
because it was just	porque entre familia
a family affair.	todo se quedaba.
Someone else from around here	Otro también de aquí cerca
sold his wife	vendió a la mujer
for three thousand pesetas;	por tres mil pesetas,
but he didn't see a cent	y después de no ver un duro
and had to console himself	tuvo que apañarse
with a nice pair of horns.	con la cornamenta.
Just two cases without any	Dos casos sin importancia
importance,	
or at least	y si es que la tuvo,
they didn't give it any.	ellos no la dieron.
But now these men need	Pero una gorra con mangas
a cap with sleeves	ellos necesitan
to hide their horns.	pá esconder los cuernos.
("Los Hijos de Ramona," 1982)	

Mateo, the estate guard, too was aware of the dangers of giving offense to specific individuals and of openly identifying anyone:

> "Not all matters can be sung about with humor. As one writes, one adds salt and pepper to flavor them. Sometimes you state exactly what happened. That isn't humorous. Regardless, people soon say, 'That song is about so-and-so Joe and Mary and Cathy Whomever.'"

Mateo referred to a scene in a local bar when a father's anger erupted toward a local swain. In a brief scuffle the father took a swipe at the young man. Mateo found the material ripe for carnival ridicule, but he inadvertently blundered by identifying the older man by his nickname. The young man left town temporarily without suffering any further consequences. The irate father, however, brought charges against Mateo, who was fined by the court. "So I wrote that he punched out his daughter's boyfriend," said Mateo. "I had to pay a fine and that was that."

But Mateo's stance found scant support in the pueblo. Townspeople, even fellow *coplistas*, sided with the family and against the songwriter. Pepe Colmena, the local doyen of carnival, observed: "I completely side with the father. One shouldn't involve those who sinned out of innocence." Mateo's friend Pepe, the mechanic, was also among the vocal opposition: "Sure, he's my friend, but I scolded him that it was wrong. That's why I don't enjoy carnival. Whatever happened to a family gets aired in public."

For his part, Mateo remained unrepentant, and the hefty fine imposed by the judge made him thirsty for revenge:

> "If the town were not familiar with carnival, with local events, one could easily take offense. But in a town like this one, so much into the fun of carnival, where people know what carnival is, nobody should take offense. Because I wasn't giving offense to anyone."

Mateo defiantly planned to pick up the theme again for carnival the following year, making the lyrics still stronger. But at the same time he promised to be more subtle as well:

> "I won't mention his name to avoid further charges. Because, if he catches me in a slip, he'll turn me in again, and I'll be in a bigger jam. I'll do it so that he'll say: 'That one was meant for me.' Yet he won't be able to turn me in because I won't use any names. No one will be able to bring up any charges."

This incident involving the local courts concerning libel, contrasts with censorship in past times under the dictatorship. Carnival composers no longer fear official reprisals and declare themselves free of any obligation to clear their work before singing in public.

> "You should not show the songs to anyone. Because now nothing is banned from the songs. If there's censorship, there's no freedom, no democracy. This would not be a democratic nation. With censorship we could not go out in carnival. If we sang a song about a guy who robbed a turkey and if he said it was a lie, then what would happen? Who'd be right? I'd get the blame. And that being the case, there shouldn't be censorship. There used to be censorship. Before singing the *coplas*, one took them to the barracks. If the *Guardias* said, "Change it!" . . .It would end up the same [meaning they would avoid changing anything but would be more careful where they sang it]."[4] (Jesús Mañez)

Jesús Mañez championed free speech on the local level as well, regardless of any personal animosity it might cause:

> "I'm planning to get up a quartet. I'll sing about everything that has happened in the town. Some will just have to take it. There are some who enjoy being sung about, and others who don't like it. You poke the most fun at those who don't like it. Understand? That's how I feel about carnival. If a silly remark causes someone to tell you 'Don't sing that!' and if you give in, then carnival loses all its fun. In carnival we must sing about what happened. Everything is fair game, names or no names, because that too should be up to the songwriter."

A *pasodoble* the previous year by another composer had stated it well:

The minstrels are not trying	Los Juglares no pretenden
to put anybody down.	a otros avasallar:
We try to perform well	procuramos hacerlo bien
and please our pueblo.	y a nuestro pueblo agradar.
We don't like fighting,	No nos gustan las peleas
although there's rivalry,	aunque haya rivalidad
since this is the spice	pues en esto está la salsa
in every good carnival.	de todo buen carnaval.
Our criticisms are wholesome,	Nuestras críticas son sanas
they're only meant for fun,	sólo buscan divertir

and if we succeed	y si además lo logramos
it will make us very happy.	eso nos hará feliz.
No one's dignity	Nadie se sienta ofendido
should be offended;	en su propia dignidad
we, the minstrels, respect the	los juglares respetamos
intimacy of everyone.	de todos la intimidad
But in every performance,	pero toda actuación
be it public or professional,	pública o profesional
we shall criticize some people	aunque algunos les pese
even if it bothers them.	sí les vamos a criticar.
But don't get angry,	Nada pues de enfados
everyone enjoy.	todos a gozar
It's only once a year	una vez al año
in the carnival.	con el carnaval.
(Los Juglares) 1980	

The desire to ridicule can seem to strain social ties to the limit, particularly when composers strike out at their fellow *murgistas*. One particularly offensive song is cited in Luis de la Rosa's history of carnival in Trebujena. The subject of the song was Francisco Galán Pérez, nicknamed "Paco de la Momita," a likeable and self-effacing vineyard worker, who also handwove brooms of palm leaves as his father had taught him. An earnest and responsible man, Paco cared for his wife, his aged and handicapped mother, and his aunt, and he hoped soon to have a son of his own. A devotee of the carnival, he participated each year as a singer, often composed songs and, when pressed to do so, occasionally served as choral director. In 1964, however, Paco's aspirations for fatherhood became the target for composer Miguel de la Lebrinjana's testy humor:[5]

The guy of the brooms	El tío de las escobas
is crazy to have a son,	está loco por un niño
but his tool	pero gasta un zoquetito
is more wrinkled than a honey doughnut.	arrugao como un pestiño.
Everyone in Trebujena knows this –	Eso lo sabe tó Trebujena
that he has a streak of pansy in him;	que de <<sarasa>> tiene una vena;
his poor wife is sick and tired of him,	a su señora, a la pobre, la trae frita

because she says he can't get	porque dice que no llega al sitio,
there – with what? with his	¿con qué? con su cosita.
little thing.	

Paco fielded the offense without blinking, and in time enjoyed a unique revenge. He had a son who became one of the most attractive kids in the pueblo. He quickly grew tall, was noted for his red hair, and even more so for his intelligence. In school he soon outdistanced his peers, was awarded scholarships, and, when I last saw him, was taking graduate studies in biology.

Even Jesús Máñez, however, drew the line at matters held sacred between a husband and his wife (influenced perhaps by his recent marriage to his *novia* from Alcalá de los Gazules):

> "It all depends on what's happened, right? If you stick your nose into a married couple's affairs, whose business is it? That's not for carnival. Things aren't funny concerning a man and his wife. Carnival deals with things one can joke about."

Notes

1. See Jerome R. Mintz, *The Anarchists of Casas Viejas*, pp. 69–71, 91–4.
2. Among the best known for the male are *bichillo* (small animal), *cola* (tail), *banano* (banana), *berejena* (eggplant), *nabo* (beet root), *pito* (whistle), *tranca* (stick that holds door shut), and *chorizo* (sausage). Commonly used to refer to the vulva are *almeja* (clam), *conejo* (rabbit), *coño* (cunt), *papo* (dewlap), *pandorita* (tambourine), *higo* (fig), *queso* (cheese), *fogón* (stove), and *anafa* (furnace). For a full range of sexual euphemisms, see Adolfo González Martínez, "*Eufemismos de la esfera sexual en las coplas de carnaval de Cádiz,*" *Boletín de la Academia Puertorriqueña de la lengua española*, vol. xiv. The following subject areas provide most of the euphemisms cited by González: animals, vegetables, musical instruments, processed foods (e.g. sausage), weapons, tools, utensils, clothes, holes, toys, among others. The author categorizes and analyzes euphemisms for penis and vagina in

the *coplas* of the Cádiz carnival between 1948 and 1976. The choice for this period, he argues, is because there was a strong censorship on everything pertaining to sexual matters, and this constraint forced writers to provide substitutes for forbidden terms. Political continuity made this period homogeneous culturally and linguistically. Critics would argue that the use of euphemisms precedes this period, as well as follows it, and that politics and censorship are less central to the use of euphemisms than culture, tradition, and style.

3. A mock serenade; a shivaree.
4. In the early 1960s in Trebujena, when the carnival was being restored, Luis de la Rosa observed: "Censorship only prevented groups from singing certain songs in front of the town hall or in the immediate surrounding areas; when they were further away from the official areas, they sang all their compositions, including the censored ones." *Breve Historia del Carnaval de Trebujena*, p. 37. Methods to circumvent censorship existed at every level of society. One ingenious subterfuge concerned reprinting anarchist and socialist writings in government journals. A network of young radicals, whose family connections had won them posts in the bureaucracy, correctly reasoned that material in government publications would automatically be passed by the censor. See the *Revista de Trabajo*, a publication of the Ministerio de Trabajo in Madrid, during the 1960s and 1970s.
5. Luis de la Rosa, *Breve Historia del Carnaval de Trebujena*, pp. 116–17.

Chapter 8

Women and Carnival

Rumor and Gossip

Gossip is generally thought to be the field of battle for women, but at carnival time it is the men who ride to the joust. The most popular rumor is unwanted pregnancy, whether it is the result of a supposed slip by young lovers, a tale of seduction (for example, by storeowner of innocent clerk), or accounts of emigrants from the town whose departure invites theories concerning their motives.

Of course from time to time the rumor turns out to provide an accurate account. An unplanned pregnancy is a common enough event, and everyone waits his and her turn as observer, participant, and commentator. As one middle-aged mother admitted after criticizing a young neighbor for carrying a baby before she was wed: "This is an emotional moment for me because you know the same thing happened to me."

Such tales when told by men draw the most opposition from women.

> "People say women are gossips, right? Yet men compose the songs, so they too gossip. They tell things as they want them to be – not the way things are, but the way it seems to them. Sometimes things aren't like that at all. When the criticism gets too specific, say, when a girl slipped up, then I don't like those songs as much as those about work, about happenings in the town, which are not so critical." (Carmen)

Young unmarried girls voice opposition not only to the songs but to carnival's overall concern with matters that should remain personal and private: "If a girl gets pregnant, it should be her business and nobody else's. If her neighbors learn about it, must the whole town know too?" Told that "The men say it isn't such a big deal," the girls, Natalia and María, reply: "That's because it's not about them."

The source for many carnival songs begins as bits of gossip that seem to float through the pueblo each day, year in and year out. Sounds of argument that filled the empty air at night or at midafternoon are soon amplified in every kitchen, shop, and tavern. The woman who took too many aspirins for a headache in the morning, by afternoon is said to have attempted suicide. The girl who left or entered the town hurriedly running is, within a few hours, the subject of a tale of rape or rapture. Some tales are quickly contradicted; other reports harden into generally accepted information. Ultimately some accounts are set to music and sung at carnival time, often with accompanying embarrassment and humiliation.

> "In all small towns it's like this. In a big city there is a newspaper that gives the daily news. Here the news is distributed by word of mouth. Every act is noted and exaggerated. A grain of sand is built up into a castle. People speak to annoy. They talk of things that don't exist, things they imagine." (Pepe Pareja)

Every rumor, from kitchen quarrels between in-laws, to neighbors dumping nightwater, to reports of illicit flirtation, generates a crosscurrent of opinions. To those who cherish privacy, gossipy townspeople become like barnyard fowl ruffling their feathers and pecking at a weakened opponent. Old Pinto says in disgust: "Jerónimo, don't you realize that this is a vicious pueblo?"

Townspeople with concern for their privacy or of a serious bent of mind, often find the vigilant eyes of the pueblo too much to bear. Juan says: "If I were born again, I would want to be isolated from everyone – to live completely isolated, because everything is a lie. Everything that people say to you is a lie. People say one thing and mean another."

Pepe Pareja, the old anarchist who believed in community, also wanted to be away from the pettiness of neighbors and family: "Sometimes I think I would like to live alone on a mountaintop. Instead of living in harmony, they pick away at each other. They exaggerate and create lies, and there's nothing you can answer to."

Those who have moved from the pueblo to the city find anonymity a welcome change. Emilia, the seamstress, is happy to be in the capital and away from watchful neighbors:

"People in the pueblo laugh at you when you go down the street. When I walk down the street, everyone stops me and starts to pick away at me. They try to get everything out of me. What my husband's doing, how he's doing. For that reason I don't want to return. There's a great deal of criticism in the village. Here [in the city] I don't know my neighbor. No, we don't like the pueblo [Emilia and her daughter] and we don't want to go back. Here I don't know anyone and no one knows me, and that's the way we like it."

La Crítica (Gossip)

Gossip in town among women is usually of a different cast than the harder news that drives carnival. Among women gossip often dwells on mundane household matters: whether the children are supervised and whether the men in one family are brutish, or if they are good providers. Some women are chided for their failure to improve their appearance and others just for looking poorly. Can the woman of the house be criticized for spending beyond her budget for fancy food, dress, or the beauty parlor? Do some want to appear too elegant, wear slacks instead of a skirt, or dress their children a bit too extravagantly? Have those in mourning worn black for a sufficient period of time? Have some lost their sense of proportion? "Look at Juana's mother buying all those clothes, and she doesn't have enough money for food."

Age is not a barrier: older women with families and younger unmarried girls echo each other's concerns:

"There is little contact between girls in the village. There's more between the boys. There's little friendship because of the criticism. There may be fifteen things I like about someone and one thing I don't like – and I keep my mouth shut. But no – they criticize: "Look, she's wearing the same sweater every day. Doesn't she have any other?" Or, "Look, she's changing her sweater all the time. How do they come to have so many?" There's no real friendship." (Ana)

"My aunt wants to walk for exercise, but she says she can't go by herself. People would notice her and talk and criticize. "Where's the old widow going by herself?" People are critical. There's a saying: It's not enough to be good; one must appear to be good as well." [*No hay que serlo, sino parecerlo.*] (María)

Under the threat of such notoriety, most mothers usually draw a strict line for their daughters to walk to avoid giving any excuse for idle talk.

"My daughter [age 15] doesn't go out in the mornings because if she did, people would talk. She's tall and pretty, and so people resent her a little. They have a lot of nerve. If she goes out in the mornings, the first thing they'll say is: "All day long on the streets, doing this. . . doing that. . .." In short, people gossip, so she'd better stay home. At night I let her go to the discotheque and to other places she likes. She's out for one or two hours. She goes out at about ten and is back by 11.30. . . If she's out late, they'll say: "Sure, she's out with a fellow. Sure, she's dancing too long, or maybe he's a married man or something." They'll talk about my daughter and about anybody else too. But I don't want them to talk about my daughter. If it were about me, I couldn't care less! I really don't care." (Dolores)

Fear of Childbirth

A major anxiety of women, to judge by its presence as a persistent and pervasive theme in conversation, is fear of childbirth. Women are in mortal terror over the pain of giving birth and are concerned over related matters such as birth control. This fear is as great among married women as among single girls.

"I really don't want more children but I'll have another because it's the thing to do, not to raise one child alone. But I fear giving birth more than rearing the child." (Juana)

"My biggest fear is giving birth. The first time I didn't know any better, so I really wasn't so frightened. But after that I've had terrible fear. Although the births have been easy and uncomplicated, thinking of the forceps and the range of possibilities, brings on a terrible fear. I just finished babyhood with my two-year-old, and I don't want to start again, but this is the lesser problem. I'm not fussy with my kids, and they don't really interfere. The first few months they sleep a lot and they're easy. But the fear of birth is overwhelming." (Dolores)

These concerns are discussed among women, but they rarely surface when men are present. They are never mentioned during madcap carnival where women are the subjects rather than the purveyors of carnival songs. The following *cuplé* is an uncommon example of providing a point of view sympathetic to females:

Two women assisted	A una burra en su parto
a burra to give birth	dos mujeres lo asistian
and with great gravity	y con mucha seriedad
one said to the other,	una a la otra decía.
"Poor little thing,	Pobrecita, qué dolor
so much pain she is bearing	está aquí pasando sola
here alone,	
without even remembering	sin que recuerde siquiera
when she was mounted,	cuando se montó en la ola.
and the macho simply enjoys---	Y el macho sólo disfruta
the son of a bi. . .."	el hijo de la gran pu. . ..
(Los Juglares, 1980)	

Work

The changing roles of women are most obvious in the city where opportunities for education and employment are greatest and women can find work in sales, business, and in the schools.

> "In recent years we have experienced an enormous change in women's perceptions of themselves and their roles. Women started to question the old idea that they should not work outside the home and so on."
> (Manuel Moreno and María López)

In Benalup women are locked in a narrower range of employment possibilities than is available in the city. Without industry in the area, and with so many men already unemployed, there have been few attempts to employ the largely wasted work force of young women. A few women have been able to utilize their sewing skills to fashion dresses for the well-to-do. More commonly, to help her family a young girl may seek work as a maid, a cook, or a babysitter. It has been commonplace before marriage for a young girl to spend a year or two in the city employed as a maid or babysitter. In an effort to provide employment for a large number of young women, the young well-to-do priest who served Benalup from 1968 to 1973 started a clothing factory. He managed to garner orders from the military and from civilian concerns, but the pay was low, orders dwindled, and the factory was turned over to the workers and eventually closed. In recent years the nearby settlement of Malcocinado has developed a successful flower-growing enterprise on land once reserved for pine trees. A large staff of young women drawn from Malcocinado and Benalup plant and cultivate the flowers and then box them for sale to restaurants and hotels in various cities.

Employment has sometimes come to the women of Benalup through marriage. Some enterprising couples have opened small shops in their front room, with the wives usually serving as clerks while their husbands took on the task of locating and transporting the merchandise to be put up for sale. The importance of marital teams can be seen in a variety of neighborhood stores and market stands selling groceries, vegetables, fish, chickens, bread and cakes, dry goods, and children's clothing. These small enterprises have enabled men and women to overcome the limited choices of household service for women or fieldwork for men and have anchored some couples to the town.

Up until the time of the rural exodus following the war, when men left to work overseas and sent their wages home to their families, women did not work in the fields. Without sufficient numbers of men, however, teams of women fieldworkers were brought from other regions still more impoverished than Cádiz to weed and cultivate the crop. Many local families have also picked cotton. With the husband away, the wife and children went to the fields to earn a bit of extra money.[1]

Traditional Roles

In the town of Benalup, relatively few women participate as fully as men in the festivities of carnival. They will help their men prepare for the holiday, but few women ever enlist as singers in a *comparsa* or *chirigota*. It is difficult to find a satisfactory answer to the question: "Why aren't there more women who compose carnival songs?"

Carmen: "That I can't tell you. Pili [her daughter], you explain it."

Pili: "Traditionally men sing and compose the songs. The women are always at home and the men are in the street. That's why women don't sing. What do you men say about this? Let's hear it from the men."

Pepe the mechanic: "Once a woman got together a group of young girls [named Triumfo Andaluz, 1979], and it's true that they sang at the movie house and elsewhere. But they weren't successful because their songs weren't as good as the men's. They weren't as good because they were less spicy, and so they weren't as funny. Because the men put more into it and compose spicier songs, people like them better. Some like it. I don't particularly like it. When this woman went out with those young girls, her songs weren't the least spicy, and so the people liked them less. But I'll say one thing – the songs were very nice. In fact, I enjoyed them more than the men's songs. I don't like it when carnival gets too vulgar. To put some punch into things to make them spicy, that's all right, but. . .not that spicy!"

The further irony of Pepe's observations lies in the fact that, unknown to him, the composer of Triunfo Andaluz was a man, Pepe Colmena. It is correct that the songs were less spicy. Colmena added or eliminated whatever he thought was appropriate for a woman.

Possible Themes

If women were to compose songs for carnival, they might choose themes similar to the men's but their perspectives would likely be completely different, as the following accounts suggest:

"Before I started going with my present *novio*, I had another *novio*. I spoke to a boy for twenty-one months. That's why I went to work in Cádiz. He began to work in Cádiz and couldn't return to see me often, and then he said there were the expenses of the trip. I was working here and he asked me to move there to work. But when I was there, he stopped coming to see me. I heard from others that he was taking walks with another. I never went out. I had two afternoons off, Thursday and Sunday, but I always stayed in waiting for him. I spent many Sundays like that – waiting. I told him that he should tell me if he wanted to break up, but he said, no, he didn't want to. He was my brother-in-law's brother and he didn't want to be known as a scoundrel. But he didn't come to see me. I lost my *ilusión* (dreams, hopes). I became ill. Everything was the same for me. I cried all the time. I lost the desire to eat. My sister took me to the doctor, and he gave me injections to give me the desire to eat. He said I was upset over something because there was nothing wrong with me, but I didn't tell him what it was. I lost my feelings for him very slowly. I had cared for him very much. I see him occasionally on the street, but he is like a stranger to me. My *novio* never asked me about my former *novio*. He asked me before we became *novios* if I was still walking with the other, and I said no, that we broke up. He never asked me anything again, out of respect for me. He knows that I don't want to talk about it." (María)

"Women here are not liberated. We can't go out alone. We have to go out with our husbands. Almost all husbands are jealous and ignorant. We can't wear pants or a shirt. I can't put on a pair of slacks. My husband ripped them up. I cried from being so angry. They think they work more than us, but we clean the children and take care of the house. If he walked in and I were sitting, I would get up and give him the chair. But if he were sitting on the chair and I entered, he wouldn't get up. They think they are the only ones that work. What you do is nothing." (Anita)

"At first I laughed about my young son's affair – he made a girl pregnant and ran away. The girl's employer went to his job and he had to go to court and pay a fine. Then the girl arrived here in the pueblo. My son said he would take down my *choza* and build a house and marry her when all was prepared. The girl said she'd go to work after the birth of the child to help him. It turns out now that they're fighting bitterly. He never takes her to the movies. He promised to take her to the fair in Vejer and didn't. The other night I heard his mother telling the girl, 'Look, my son doesn't care for you and you don't care for him. Otherwise you wouldn't have had to fine him.' I heard something like a smack and I looked in and said, 'Hombre, have you hit the girl?' She was crying. 'No,' my son said, 'She doesn't want to eat and we're urging her.' Who could eat? My older son bawled me out for looking in. The girl and my son hardly speak to each other. She lives and sleeps with his mother. The boy is in another place. They are not living together. This is not acceptable." (Juan)

Poetess

If women did compose, perhaps many would begin like Isabel R. We referred to Isabel briefly in a footnote in chapter two. She recalled the murder of the socialist mayor of Medina Sidonia and placed it in a religious context. Although the men in Isabel's family were radical-minded, like a fair number of women in the town she maintained a simple religious faith:

"I believe in God and in the Virgin, in the *Dolorosa*, and in the Virgin of this town. The *Dolorosa*, who is carried through the streets in Holy

Week, is the one we love the most. I do believe in these things. I think
that someone created the world. Jesús is a very good man who lived
many years ago."

"We had a priest here who was very funny. He thought only of
soccer. Once, on the day of the *romería* [pilgrimage], he entrusted the
statue of the Virgin to Palomita, a local woman, and skipped town to
go to Medina to watch a soccer game there."

"And I asked the priest once: 'Why does the virgin of Vejer have so
much jewelry? Why is she so rich and the one in Casas Viejas so poor?'
And he said, 'Do you think that a mother whose son has just been
killed needs so much jewelry? If your son were killed, would you sit
in front of the mirror and put on all your finery, and make up your
face and wear jewels, or would you just run out of the house wearing
whatever you have on?'"

Isabel, a handsome dark-haired young woman, was much sought
after as a *novia*, but she had been forced by circumstances to work
as a serving girl outside the town, and she did not marry until she
was thirty-three. Her husband, Pepe, was a slender, handsome man
of few words. He had a shy demeanor, but his physical agility
and sharp eyes gave him a quiet intensity. Seated on his powerful
motorcycle, he bore a trace of a daredevil pilot. Pepe was an *albañil*
(mason) who worked during the week on the coast. Everyone knew
him to be a skilled mason. During their yearlong *noviazgo*, every
weekend he had roared back on his motorcycle to Benalup to see
his *novia*. Isabel, an ample woman seemed to envelop her slim
sweetheart when he appeared. Pepe, too, doted on his *novia* and
was jealous of Isabel's every moment away from him. She relished
his attention and his jealousy, and each meeting was as fresh as
though they had just met in the *alameda*. Marriage was delayed
until Pepe could finish building and furnishing a house for them.
With the cost for bricks and cement at an end, he next saved to
purchase the furniture. Isabel already had the household linens
in hand. These matters were considered more essential to a
marriage than a license and a priestly blessing. Pepe's only
apparent vice was that he loved wine all too well. As Isabel
explained:

"My husband is very strange. He's a very good man. He's a hard
worker, clean, and good to me, but a bit weird at times. I have to
come here to my mother's. He won't. But I just won't stay home alone.
He's a very noble man. Everyone likes him. He built the market

precinct in Casas Viejas all on his own. He's been in a construction company for one and a-half years now. He's working in Marbella now. He built our house. It's a beautiful house with a great fireplace."

Isabel had a striking talent: although she could not read or write, she had composed hundreds of incidental narrative poems, principally concerning matrimony and romance, which she had committed to memory and could recite in a steady cascading rhythm. Her thoughts and insights are of the sort rarely if ever recorded in carnival song. It is from her poems, and not the songs of the composers in the raucous carnival, that we learn something of love and marriage from a woman's perspective.

Early one morning,
he left for Marbella,
carrying only a bag.
He didn't even say goodbye.
I looked out the window
and saw him walk away,
with very slow steps
and very sad eyes.
And I called: "My Friend."
But he wasn't listening.
The wind blew my
goodbye away.
I said so many things
without right or reason.
Each thing that he said
broke my heart.
His heart is so hard
it is as hard as cement.
No woman can break it,
not even the wind.
At night, when I go to bed
I may seem asleep
but I'm wide awake
and thinking about your love.
My head is spinning;
to the one who is far away:
my eyes cannot see you.
I'll carry you inside myself
until the day I die.

(1) Una mañana temprano
pá Marbella se marchó
con un bolso en la mano
y no me dijo ni adiós.
Yo me asomé a la ventana
y miré cómo se alejaba
con los pasos muy lentos
y muy triste la mirada.
Yo le dije: "Amigo."
Pero él no me escuchaba.
Aquel adiós que le di,
el viento se lo llevaba.
Yo le dije tantas cosas
sin motivo y sin razón,
cada cosa que decía
se me partía el corazón.
Tiene el corazón tan duro,
tan duro como el cemento.
No hay mujer que te lo rompa,
ni siquiera como el viento.
De noche cuando me acuesto
parece que estoy dormida
pero estoy muy despierta
y pensando en tu cariño.
La cabeza me da vueltas
el que está lejos de mí
mis ojos no pueden verte.
Te llevo dentro de mí
hasta el día de mi muerte.

Despite mutual love and affection, it is difficult to compete with the taste of wine from the Barberá bodega.

(Poem about wine).
When we were engaged
everything was promises and joys.
Now we are married
and I truly regret it.
I didn't know much,
and he said so many things,
and I believed him,
but everything he told me
was lies.
"Isabel, I don't like wine.
I'm going to make you very happy."
But now he gets drunk
to make me suffer.
I've been married for three months,
and my savings are gone;
and I curse the hour
we met.
I came home the other day
and he seemed greatly changed,
because he grabbed the bottle,
and he put it away.
And I said to myself:
"My God, how happy I am!
He finally hates wine.
I'm going to light up two candles
to thank you for your help."
I heard God's voice saying:

"Don't burn any candles to me,
because I didn't hear you.
It's just that he doesn't want
any more white wine;
he likes it bottled."
Oh God! What a wretched husband!
In the early morning

(2) (La del vino)
Cuando éramos novios
todo eran promesas y alegrías

ahora estamos casados
y yo estoy muy arrepentía.
Yo venía de no saber
y me decía tantas cosas
y yo me las creía,
pero eran palabritas falsas
todas las que me decía.
Isabel, a mí no me gusta el vino;
te voy a hacer muy feliz.

Pero ahora se emborracha
para hacerme sufrir.
Tres meses llevo casada

y los ahorros perdíos
y yo maldigo la hora
que lo hubiera conocío.
El otro día llegué
y lo encontré muy cambiado
porque cogió la botella
y él mismo la había guardado.
Y yo dije para mí:
Dios mío qué contenta
que el vino lo ha aborrecío.
Te voy a poner dos velas

por haberlo conseguío.
Escuché la voz del señor [que me decía]
a mí no me pongas velas
que yo no la he escuchado,
ya no quiere vino blanco,
que le gusta embotellado.
Dios mío que marido tengo
yo más desgraciado.

La madrugada llegó

he was lying on the ground.	y en el suelo se acostaba.
He stared at me	Me miró con unos ojos
with eyes that frightened me.	que miedo a mí me daba.
He told me so many things	Me dijo tantas cosas
without any reason	sin motivo y sin razón
that everything he said	que cada cosa que decía
broke my heart.	se me partía el corazón.
He told me: "I can't wait	Me dijo: que ganitas tengo
for you to die	de que te mueras
so I'll have some peace;	para yo quedar tranquilo
all the money that I earn	que todo el dinero que gane
I'll spend on wine."	me lo voy a gastar en vino.
And I answered: "You bastard!	Contesto yo: Mala sangre
Of all you earn,	que del dinero que tú ganas
you give me precious little.	tú me das tan poca cosa.
I cook for you	Yo te pongo de comer,
and do laundry for you.	yo te lavo a tí la ropa.
You abandon me.	Me tienes abandona(d)a.
You know that I pass the day	Tú sabes que paso el día
with one piece of bread.	con un pedazo de pan.

How can one cope with lost independence and control of the purse?

(I said to myself) [?]	(3) Dijeron entre mis gafas [unintelligible line]
I cannot buy from you;	que yo no puedo comprarte
I can buy from you,	que yo te compro las cosas
but then I cannot pay.	y después no puedo pagarte.
I don't own any money,	No soy dueña del dinero
he carries it all in his wallet,	él lo lleva en la cartera
and when he gives me a bill	y cuando me da un billete
everybody hears about it.	se entera hasta la portera.
I'm sick of him.	Hay que jartita me tiene
I can't take it any more.	ya estoy hasta la coronilla,
So when he comes in today,	y así cuando venga esta tarde
I'm going to give him a piece of my mind.	yo le leo la cartilla.
When he came in the afternoon	Cuando llegó por la tarde
and I saw the state he was in,	y vi yo cómo venía
I didn't say anything –	yo no le dije nada
it wouldn't have been good for me.	porque a mi no me convenía.
If I had told him anything,	Si le digo cuatro cosas

like how sick and tired I am,	que estoy hasta la coronilla
he surely would have grabbed a stick	seguro que coge un palo
to break my ribs.	que me parte las costillas.

The little garden behind the house where the wash is hung suddenly becomes the cause of grief.

"Just because I stepped	(4) Por una lechuguita
on a little lettuce plant,	que yo le pisé
our love suffered.	estuvo sufriendo
This little garden	ya nuestro querer.
is killing you;	Este huertecillo
whenever I need to hang	que te está matando
clothes up,	cuando tiendo ropa
I step on it.	yo lo estoy pisando.
If I hang clothes up on one end,	Si tiendo p'arriba
the dog barks at me;	el perro me ladra,
if I go to the other end,	si tiendo p'abajo
I step on your plants.	te piso las plantas.
Tell me, Pepillo,	Dímelo Pepillo
what can I do	lo que voy a hacer
with wet clothes	las ropas mojadas
if I don't hang them up?	no puedo tender.
Don't sow in the yard,	No siembres en el huerto
because everything is lost;	que ya está tó perdío
because even the ants	que hasta las hormigas
have eaten it all up."	ya se lo han comío.
(He answers)	(Contesta él)
"I will sow in the yard;	Sí que siembro el huerto
nothing is lost.	que no está perdío
Even the parsley	que hasta el perejil
is sprouting.	lo tengo nacío.
But the day when I die	Pero el día que yo me muera
don't start to cry;	no te pongas a llorar
even six feet under	que aunque esté bajo la tierra
I'll never forgive you."	no te voy a perdonar.
"And these songs I'm singing	Y estas coplas que yo canto
I always remember them,	yo las llevo en la memoria
and the day I die	y el día que yo me muera
I'll carry them to heaven with me."	me las llevo pá la gloria.

"All this really happened between a husband and a wife," Isabel adds.

"Now, I've been married for three and a-half years. These days I have a lot on my mind. We have a couple of pigs that I'm fattening to butcher them. I have to do laundry and take care of the house and all. It's not like when I was single – I didn't have anything to think about then. I was sweeping or working and then I would think up a poem. But it's harder now.

"Some couples get along really bad. Some men are horrible to their women. Some women are really good but their men are real dogs. Like a cousin of mine. Her husband – the guy who was here earlier today – beats her up. The other day he hit her in the head with a bottle. She just can't do a thing about it – especially with the six or seven children that she has. I like marriage, but I can't stand men who aren't thoughtful and nice to their women.

"My husband kisses me a lot. He's really affectionate. The first thing he does when he comes home is to kiss me. Sometimes I'm working on something around the house, and he sneaks behind me and gives me a little kiss." (Isabel)

Note

1. In 1979 a *cuplé* tells of a maid who took advantage of her vacationing employers and invited her friends to a big party.

When the owners returned
and learned what happened,
they told the maid
to go pick cotton.
(Los Dormilones, 1979)

Cuando llegaron los dueños
y se enteraron de "tó"
mandaron a la criada
que se fuera a . . .coger algodón

Chapter 9

Carnival in the Capital

City and Barrio

Cádiz, the capital of the provincial government, is an ancient maritime center founded a thousand years before the Christian era. The city fills a narrow peninsula poking northeast into the Gulf of Cádiz. It is a relatively small city with a contemporary population of roughly 157,000.[1] Further expansion of Cádiz is curtailed by the sea, which defines the peninsula's polygonal shape and limits its accessibility. A causeway built on the narrow isthmus running south to San Fernando, its only land tie to the mainland, is edged with a thin strip of undeveloped beach on one side (Playa de Cortadura) and salt flats on the other. Where the causeway begins, a bridge crosses northwest across the Bay of Cádiz to shorten the route to El Puerto de Santa Maria and Jerez. Seville lies 137 kilometers northeast. As a result of its geographical separation, Cádiz gives the illusion of a classical city-state, a municipality with commercial and political ties to the outside, but believing in its heart to be a self-contained administrative, economic, and social entity.

The city is composed of various barrios whose distinctions belie the city's outer semblance of unity and uniformity. The heart of the old city lies behind stone walls that protect it from the sea. Southward, beyond the old city gates, lie the city's beaches (Playa de la Victoria), its most modern buildings, and its newest and fastest growing barrios. On the northeastern side of the city facing the Bay of Cádiz lie the docks and shipbuilding facilities. Barrios in the old city such as La Viña, El Mentidero, Santa María, and Puerta-Tierra, each have a spirit of independence akin to that of small townships. La Viña, at the furthest edge of the city and the sea, is most closely associated with carnival. With a population of roughly 6,000, it is the equivalent of small towns such as Benalup or Trebujena. The barrio offers a crowded palate of Atlantic and (not too distant, 100 kilometers south) Mediterranean tastes, odors, and colors. The counters and tables of its cramped, bustling, street-side restaurants are always occupied with customers sipping wine or beer and picking at varieties of fried octopus, squid, sardines, and hake, or tasting hot sausage, salami, thin steak, meatballs, and chicken. Outside in the few spots ample enough for narrow sidewalks, pedestrians, pressed against the buildings, vie for space with baby carriages and parked cars.

Cobblestoned streets	Unas calles de adoquines
and the uproar of children.	un bullicio de criaturas.
Fewer schools than movie theaters	Menos colegios que cines:
and there are no parks	no existen jardines
in this neighborhood.	en su estructura.
The constant worry	La preocupación constante
about the sea	por la mar y por los vientos:
and the East and West winds,	el Poniente o el Levante
important gods	dioses importantes
who bring us our sustenance.	para el sustento.
Working with a net,	Con una red,
a hook or rigging,	un garabato o un aparejo;
and with great faith,	y su gran fé
the fisherman grows old.	el caletero se hace viejo.
In general, that is	En general
the popular barrio La Vina:	eso es el popular barrio de la Viña:
people who live, work, and keep going	
without property or privacy,	gente que vive, trabaja y sigue
and their joy and happiness	sin propiedades ni intimidad:
is a strange mystery indeed.	y el extraño misterio
(Paco Rosado, Los Cegatos, 1983)	de su alegría y su felicidad.

At carnival time the crowds are greater and the public air thickens with the smoke and odor of neighborhood fish fries. On some nights strips of fried fresh flounder and halibut are provided free to visitors by a *peña* (neighborhood association). A variety of crustaceans and crullers prepared on the spot are hawked for a fee by street vendors. Appropriately, the carnival singers offer a descriptive tour of sights and smells of the barrio.

I was strolling around	Paseaba apuraíllo
without a penny in my pocket	sin un duro en el bolsillo
one afternoon like any other one,	una tarde como otra
when a gentleman with a hat and a tie,	y se acerca un caballero
came to me	de corbata y de sombrero
in the Calle la Pelota.	en la calle la Pelota.
He asked me for directions to "la Viña"	Por la viña preguntaba
and as I was picking his pocket,	mientras yo lo aligeraba
I told him, smiling:	y le dije sonriendo:
"Just follow your nose,	mire usted que no hay cosa más sencilla
your nose'll tell you	si sigue a su naricilla
where 'la Viña' is."	ella se lo irá diciendo.
The [scent of] roses fresh each day	Las rosas frescas del día
will lovingly accompany one directly to	le irán llevando con mil amores derecho por compañía
Ay! what a Joy! the "Plaza of Flowers."	¡ay! qué alegría, Plaza las Flores.
The *churros* [fried dough] will guide him	Los churros le irán guiando
along Liberty Street,	calle abajito de la Libertad,
turn right	tuerza a la derecha
looking for the square "la Cruz Verde"	buscando la plaza La Cruz Verde
where one loses one's senses	donde el sentío se pierde
because you can smell carnival.	que ya huele a Carnaval.
Through the alleys	Por los callejones se irán
you will smell the jetties.	oliendo las escolleras
Take any way you will –	tire usted pá donde quiera
the smell of crabs	que el aroma de cangrejos
will tell you that you are in "la Viña, "	le irá diciendo que está en La Viña
the little house of the sea.	la casita del mar.
(Paco Rosado, Los Llaveros Solitarios, 1984.)	

The Fundación Gaditana del Carnaval

During the 1980s the *concurso*, the competition between the singing groups, became fixed as the defining element of the carnival in the capital. The enthusiasm aroused by the *concurso* through its preliminary rounds at the theater is akin to the excitement generated by a major soccer tournament. Of course there have always been informal competitions between groups as they saluted each other in the street or as they vied to hold court on a streetcorner. A formal face-off in a theater with winners and losers to be determined is another matter. In the smaller cities and towns of the province, a local *concurso* is held in some places and ignored in others. Some towns have organized a *concurso* but once and thereafter sworn off after having seen the rancor it created. In the capital of Cádiz, however, the *concurso* has grown in importance each year.

Since 1984 the carnival has been orchestrated by the *Fundación Gaditana del Carnaval*, a government creation keyed to official and commercial interests.[2] It has control of the town's theaters, the allotment of space on the street, and the presentation of parades, costume balls, and street feasts. Beginning months in advance, its staff handles the problems of organization and presentation. They plot the projected daily schedule of events; code an elaborate calendar detailing the times and locations of all official carnival events at each plaza, street, and building; choose the *pregoneros* (town criers); and arrange for the selection of the carnival goddess and the lesser deities comprising her court.

The *concurso* challenges the singers and their supporters, and rewards them, initially, with the raw elixir of participating in an intense and prestigious contest. For the singing groups a high standing in the competition is considered to be a major artistic accomplishment. With the lures of pride, fame, and possible financial gain, the *concurso* draws an ever increasing number of participants from the barrios of the capital, and from other cities and rural towns. In 1989, the total number of groups competing both from within the city and from outside reached 444. After the preliminary presentations, the juries of the *Fundación* culled the field down to fourteen finalists.

The competing groups rarely show a profit for their efforts, and the long hours spent memorizing and rehearsing are considered necessary contributions. In addition to costumes and instruments, the *coros* have to rent wagons and tractors to carry them through the streets. Most groups are fortunate if they can wrest back their basic expenses.

"...the great majority of groups don't make much money. Most groups spend money coming out in carnival. Last year I brought out a *chirigota* of fourteen people that spent 400,000 *pesetas* just on costumes. A *coro*, for example, is made up of forty-five people and can easily spend four and a-half million *pesetas* just to dress up its members. They make this money on raffles, for example, which start functioning already in December." (Eugenio Mariscal, vice-president of the Author's Society)

To aid and encourage the singing groups, public funds are allocated to help pay for costumes and for the publication of song pamphlets (*folletos*).

"Starting a few years ago, every *coro* that signs up for the contest receives a certain amount of money. As a result the prizes in the contest became honorific rather than monetary anymore. Each *coro* receives about 700,000 *pesetas* to help them with the expenses for coming out in carnival." (Eugenio Mariscal)

The *concurso* winners have the chance to turn a profit. There are invitations to perform in cafés and *peñas* [clubs] for a fee and often the opportunity to make a video or tape.

"Some of the most professional finalists may make recordings or even sign a contract to perform in Madrid, for example. There is a recording company in Chiclana, started fifteen years ago, that records songs by carnival groups. Both the carnival groups and this recording company make money from the sales." (Eugenio Mariscal)

The *concurso* presents dangers to traditional concerns. Many aficionados contend that emphasis on competition shifts the focus of the festival from the social criticism to achievement, monetary reward, and group rivalry. The enticement of winning the *concurso* dulls the poet's critical antenna and compromises his passion for free expression.

Teatro Falla

The site of the final *concurso* is the Teatro Falla, the largest and most beautiful theater in Cádiz. During the late 1980s, while the Falla was undergoing an expensive renovation, the *concurso* was held in Teatro Andalucía, which now hosts only the preliminary trials. The period of reconstruction gave everyone the opportunity to consider how best to minimize the damage done to the Falla during carnival time when the theater would reopen.

"The dispute comes from the fact that the theater belongs to the town hall. Since it is so heavily used for the carnival contest, it deteriorates quickly, and the town must spend millions of tax money on renovation and maintenance. The main reason for the deterioration of the theater is people bringing food and drink into the theater, practically having picnics there. So the theater suffers more in one week than during the rest of the year. In response to these problems, the town has come up with several proposals. One of them is to use the Falla only for the final days of the contest, while celebrating the rest of the competition in the Teatro Andalucía. This would cut on the heavy use, because sometimes there are up to 110 groups performing there, and it takes forever to listen to them all. Besides, I think that spectators should be more civilized and stop bringing whole meals, bottles of wine, cakes, and what have you in there. People protest the proposed restrictions because they are sentimentally attached to the Falla. Everyone wants to go there and use it the same way they always have." (Manuel Moreno and María López)

This excerpt from a *cuplé* cites a partial list of culinary offenses that aroused the ire of a councilwoman.

Josefina said	Ha dicho la Josefina
in a meeting of the council	dentro de un pleno
that if the Falla were given to us again,	que si de nuevo nos dieran el Falla
What crap!	¡me cachis en la mar![3]
They are going to set some norms	se van a dictar unas normas
so that no one thinks it is a beach party.	pá que la gente, joé, no piense que esto es la playa
What crap!	¡me cachis en la mar. . .!
And above all, she has said	Y sobre tó en el concurso
that in order to avoid abuses,	ha dicho que prohibirá
she will forbid	para evitar los abusos
eating an omelette	comer tortilla y papa aliñá.
and seasoned potatoes.	Fuera los bocadillos
Out with bologna sandwiches. . .	de mortadela..

and if someone wants to eat,	y el que quiera comer
let them go to the (stone)	vaya a las Canteras. . ..
quarries. . ..	
(Antonio Martín, Mar de Coplas,	
1990)	

Coros, Comparsas, Chirigotas

When the lights come up in the darkened theater, the audience is dazzled by the presence of the *coro*. The singers fill the stage in tiers and the lights reveal figures from a wide variety of possible scenes: an oriental palace, an ancient bark, or a rich oasis. An unexpected magnificence greets the eye in the variety of costume, make-up, masks, arms of war, or whatever else is needed to set the scene for their songs.

The more compact *comparsa* and *chirigota* can be equally imaginative in appearance, but their smaller numbers cannot provide the same stunning physical presence. The singers in the smaller groups stand together at stage center and rarely take advantage of the inviting emptiness of the space around them. Between songs the singers do no more than automatically pause to regroup for the next song.[4] The lack of movement indicates that only rarely have groups had the opportunity to rehearse in a large room let alone a theater. As a result few have given serious thought to the scope of a theatrical presentation and have paid scant attention to choreography. The singers, conscious of the jury as well as the public, often appear stiff and self-conscious, but we can anticipate that the singers will feel less inhibited when they hit the street.[5]

Attempts to condense the competition to a manageable schedule have been a continual source of contention. Groups waiting to appear are not only from the city; many have come from every corner of the province. Each group requires its time on the stage for at least one representative performance. Usually the most accomplished singers from their town, they are quick to sense any lack of courtesy or a hasty judgment. As the number of entries increases each year, it is difficult to be consistently fair and at the same time not drag out the competition interminably.[6]

Despite the long and late hours, the singers and the audience, and presumably the judges, try to maintain a steady level of enthusiasm for the singers. Much of the partisanship comes from those in the audience from their town or barrio and from those who may identify with one group or another. As a sign of appreciation, after a noteworthy song members of the audience (especially children, relatives and friends) approach the stage and throw flowers, paper streamers, and confetti to the singers. On occasion, the audience can also deliver a negative judgment and whistle a performance off the stage. It usually occurs when they sense a song is offensive to local perceptions, as occurred when a visiting group from Seville was suspected of parodying their city, or on another occasion when a group ridiculed some religious believers. The jury also has the authority, rarely employed, to signal sharp disapproval and to ask a group to stop performing.

> "Four years ago [1985] there was a *chirigota* called "Los Tontos del Capirote." Many of their songs made fun of the conservative bourgeoisie, the religious people from the upper middle classes who always come out in the processions. In no time at all they offended some sectors of the audience, naturally, and the radio station interrupted the broadcast." (Eugenio Mariscal)[7]

Basic Rules

The rules for groups participating in the *concurso* are laid down with precision and brevity in a small booklet (*Bases para el concurso oficial de agrupaciones*) prepared and published by the *Fundación*. It lists the number of singers and musicians pertaining to *coros*, *chirigotas*, *comparsas*, and *cuartetos*; the harmonies required; and the types of instruments permitted. According to the *Bases*, the *coros*, the largest of the singing groups, may include a minimum of fifteen to a maximum of thirty-five members. As a minimum they must sing in three-part harmony. They may include between four to ten instrumentalists playing the Spanish guitar, bandurria, and lute. Unlike the smaller groups who walk about the streets, the *coros* ride, usually on a tractor-drawn wagon or on a truck:

> These [*coros*] put on more serious airs. They prepare a pageant, with allusions to the theme that defines the group. The *coros* stand on top of the cart, and they sing as a compact group accompanied by string instruments. The *coro* tends to choose a *tanguillo* as their musical form, and their lyrics are, for the most part, more elaborate.[8]

The *comparsas*, smaller than the *coros*, can number from ten to fifteen. As a minimum they are required to sing in two-part harmony. The instruments employed can be the bass drum and cymbals, snare drums, up to three guitars, and *pitos* (kazoos). As we have seen, *chirigotas* are usually still fewer in number, from seven to twelve, and are less formal. The *chirigotas* are permitted to sing in a single voice. Accompanying instruments consist of the bass drum and cymbals, no more than two guitars, and *pitos*. Finally, the *cuartetos*, despite their name, can run between three to five (on one occasion a quartet was made up of three singers and a department store dummy). They are not obligated to sing part-harmonies, and they may use *pitos* and other instruments as their repertoire requires.

Written scores are not part of the musical scene, since usually neither composer nor singer can read or write music. The exception is the Cádiz composer Antonio Martín, who earns his living as an office employee in the shipyards but is acknowledged as a master of carnival music and lyrics. He learned to play the guitar when he was sixteen and already creating melodies for carnival. As he explained:

> "I have been writing for many years but I always conceived the melody by voice and guitar, and then I sang it for my group. After eighteen or nineteen times they would have it, or else I would put it on tape. The melody and rhythm are too complex for most *comparsas*. My group is the only one that can do it. I still can't give them the written music because they can't read it."

In recent years Antonio Martín has undertaken formal study of the piano, the guitar, and musical composition. He put his carnival *pasadobles* and *tanguillos* for a *coro* in writing for the first time in 1990.[9]

The Jury

In a dark corner of the balcony, cordoned off from the singers and the audience, the jury grades each group of performers for their costumes, music, the originality of their themes, their presentation, their placement on stage, and so on. Customarily, the jury, appointed anew each year by the *Fundación*, includes persons with a wide variety of experience in carnival activities: songwriters, directors of *murgas*, aficionados of every class, university students, and university professors. To those on the outside, the activities of juries and judges can be a matter of contention and derision: "I'm not a member of the jury because I don't want to have problems with anyone, and I don't like crayfish." (Implying that jurors spend a good bit of time stuffing themselves with delicacies.)[10] Since the juries keep their deliberations secret, to meet the interest of their readers the newspapers furnish shadow juries which offer their own assessment of the groups. Journalists and local pundits grade the performances for the press and offer their own predictions.

Between breaks in the performances, the doors leading to the lobby are frequently thrown open and patrons come and go, taking a wine or coffee break or making a trip to the bathroom. Gusts of tobacco smoke stream into the theater from the bar and drift upwards into the balcony where the judges sit in the darkness off to one side silently taking notes and marking scores.

The competing groups from outside the capital often view the proceedings with a suspicious eye, watching for signs of prejudice. With supporters from so many different barrios and towns, a jury decision is potentially always a flash point of controversy. Common complaint holds that nonresidents cannot hope to win even when they are clearly superior to all other contestants. Inevitably, they feel, a coveted first place will be denied them. Fears are most intense concerning prizes for the *coros*. They require the most rehearsal and are the most costly to produce. Usually they represent a city rather than a town because of the resources, skill, and personnel required. After so much effort and expense, it is painful to lose, particularly if in the eyes of the performers the judgment appears to be biased.

Order and Disorder

The preliminaries of the *concurso* are underway the week before the carnival actually begins. The last round of the finalists begins at 11 p.m. on Thursday night before the first weekend of carnival, and the city is awake the entire night as the competition winds down, with one audience cheering in the theater and another at home watching the countdown on television.

The performance in the theater is recorded by the television cameras on the final night of the competition, a marathon that starts just before midnight and ends at breakfast time seven and a-half hours later. For those watching on television at home, there is no noisy audience to distract one's attention. There are no commentators, analysts, or announcers to cover extended pauses or to slide one group exiting past another just entering. This is a theatrical rather than a cinematic presentation, and a single camera, set at a considerable distance from the action on stage and fixed in one location (at least at the performances I observed), does little to enhance the creative presentation. Changes in camera focal length are rare. After each number the groups stand around for some minutes catching their breath, tuning guitars, and waiting for their leader to signal the next song. Considering all the other regulations that the groups are required to obey, it is striking that there are no rules either encouraging imaginative staging or prescribing how long groups may pause between songs.

It is not until early Friday morning, around 7:30 a.m., that the winners are declared. In short order there are scheduled appearances of the prizewinning finalists (or representative singers from the groups) at various central points to celebrate their victory and entertain the citizenry. Soon afterward the other events of the festival get underway – the first receptions and public gatherings. At one o'clock in the afternoon on Friday, under the auspices of the *Fundación*, a large band of officials, writers, singers, and guests gather to honor the *pregoneros* and *ninfas*, the carnival's town criers and the young goddesses. After the mayor and other worthies speak, the guests partake of the *tapas* (titbits and appetizers) of cheese and pineapple, potato omelets, baked tunafish, potato salad, sliced ham, and other delicacies. In an echo of a distant Mediterranean prehistory, on signal a line of young girls in traditional dress carry out baskets of seafood while, with skillful flourishes, waiters draw wine from wooden casks with long slender dippers. A small band serenading the group is replaced by the singers of the *coro* that won first place. Later that evening the official *pregonero* inaugurates the carnival with a talk (or a song) in the Plaza Catedral. At 10 p.m., fireworks are set off in one of the plazas; at 11 p.m., an official ball is held.

On Saturday night the streets of the inner city fill with masked singers and other celebrants. Crowds swirl through the narrow street passageways. Performers engage an audience in a constricted street; celebrants are locked heel and toe until the singers conclude their serenade and surrender the spot to another group. Here and there, where space allows, a *romancero* sets up his banner of illustrations depicting some past event. Using a long wooden pointer, he describes the scenes on his banner and explains their implications to anyone willing to listen and drop a coin in his bowl. Singing groups hurry past on their way to perform at cafés and balls, and *peñas*.

Peñas, associations of neighbors and friends, play an important role in the celebration of carnival. The peñas came into existence in the early 1980s as private clubs created for sociability and savings. Apartments are small and crowded; for social life men, (and on occasion, their wives) gravitate to bar and café where the cost for food and drinks drain the family purse. The *peña* provides an alternative social setting for the membership and their families. Each *peña* manages its own bar where drinks are sold at reduced prices. The bar is usually open to the public, with the profits returned for the upkeep and activities of the *peña*. Most *peñas* afford a setting for meetings, games, and parties, including carnival festivities.

Some *peñas* are especially identified with carnival.[11] In carnival time in 1990, more than thirty *peñas* participated in carnival, organizing feasts and parades and offering prizes. Their efforts helped to create and sustain a range of singing groups, including *coros*, *comparsas*, *chirigotas*, and family *charangas* (informal bands of street singers). Not every *peña* sponsors a singing group, but frequently, like some restaurants, *peñas* pay favored ensembles to sing their repertoire inside the club. Unlike a public bar, a *peña* can close its doors to outsiders at any time it chooses, and so during carnival the audience at a *peña* has the opportunity to enjoy exclusive performances of the most popular groups.[12]

The *concurso* continues to spinoff during the week of the carnival with contests at various plazas, parks and streets for the most outstanding *estribillo* (refrain) and *piropo* (compliment) to Cádiz and La Viña (the popular barrio dedicated to the carnival). Other competitions decide the best of the different song genres: the *tanguillo*, *pasodoble*, *cuplé* and *popurrí* (medley). One contest in particular signals the great change that has taken place with the fall of the dictatorship and the entrance of democracy: in 1937 one rationale for closing the carnival was the fear of disguises; today there are contests for the best disguises among children, young people, and adults. At last there is belated recognition for the imaginative and sometimes sidesplitting humor involving the art of deception.

Midday on Sunday, after a night of release and excitement, there is a carousel of *coros* that winds around the Mercado Central (the central marketplace). The *coros*, with the members of each *coro* tightly packed in tiers on a tractor-drawn wagon, pause en route to sing samples of their repertoire. In counterpoint to the formality of the theater, on the street the singers are only a few feet, or at times a few inches, from their audience. Pedestrians, and those seated in chairs waiting for the singers to reach them, are close enough to bandy words, to purchase a song pamphlet, or to shout to a singer above the crowd. Bottles of wine are uncorked between songs to permit the singers to wet their throats and maintain their inspiration. On other occasions during the festival, by day and at night, the *coros* follow each other through the principal streets. Still the center of attention, but free of the bright, frozen lights of the theater, the singers are a "Night Watch" of shadow, color, and action.

Look out the window,	. . ..ven asómate
look how full the square is, so	mira como está esa plaza ya
full of people,	
and everybody is in costume.	todo el mundo con disfraz.
Forget about conquering.	Olvídate de conquistar
Join the rest.	rebújate con los demás.
The *coros* are passing by in	Ya los coros van en su carrusel
their carousel.	
They also want to conquer,	también quieren conquistar
singing their freedom.	cantando su libertad.
I've taken advantage of the	Aprovechó el disfraz
costume,	
and I go out into	y a la plaza "salió"
Freedom Square.	Plaza la Libertad.
I feel conquered by this carnival.	Me siento conquistao por este Carnaval
And a gaditano tango	y me ha quitao el sentío
has robbed my senses.	un tango gaditano.
My desire to do the carnival	Renacerán mis ganas
singing to my people	de hacer los Carnavales
will surge again.	cantando a mis paisanos
My favorite goal,	mi meta preferida
strolling through your squares,	recorriendo tus plazas,

strolling through your streets.	recorriendo tus calles.
And so on for a lifetime.	Y así toda la vida
And so on, for a lifetime.	Y así toda la vida.
(Paco Rosado, Los	
Conquistadores, 1988)	

Carnival Tamed

Despite its reputation for disorder and for turning the world topsy-turvy, carnival can tilt the world only so far. Carnival is not unleashed chaos that knows no bounds. Carnival has ties to the society in which it is celebrated. In the capital city, writers and singers must contend with formal rules and an official bureaucracy. With the ostensible help of the *Fundación*, few radical ideas or signs of protest can be found in the official urban carnival.

> "There are taboos in carnival. You don't criticize the church, the military, Easter, and the king, for example. Laws may have changed, but not institutions, nor the people in those institutions. The police and the army have guns and a lot of power. They are untouchable. Even if the law forbids it, they can be abusive and *franquista* if they want to, and there's mighty little one can do about it.[13] Most people are wary of the police, who have such a reputation for being brutal that when one of them is moderately nice to you, you feel ecstatic about it." (Manuel Moreno and María López)

Under the aegis of the *Fundación*, government censorship of previous times appears to have been replaced by a restrictive bureaucratic formalism.

> When the socio-political powers came to terms with their inability to end the carnival, they tended to control and regulate it. In so doing, the powers that be monitored carnival by restricting the festivities to certain specific locales.
> In this dangerous setting, the Cádiz carnival evolved. . . . One cannot corset the people during carnival; official intervention changes spontaneity into predetermined plots. In the case of the carnival groups, this danger increases: once there is a system of rules and a prize, everything turns around the two. . . .
> The *comparsista* incurs self-mutilation and self-censorship when he believes he is the protagonist of the festivals, and withdraws from the streets and the people, falling into the duality that can hurt the carnival most.[14]

On the surface, the new rules seem to have little to do with political opinion of one stripe or another; however, for those groups taking part in the *concurso*, the rules of the carnival have resulted in a kind of self-censorship. Instead of challenging political, social, religious, or sexual taboos, participating singers try to avoid offending both the juries and what has come to pass for popular taste.

Critics of the *Fundación* contend that the singers are too often tongue-tied by the lure of a prize. If a group has a radical or raunchy song or two in its repertoire, it is almost certain to omit them during the competition. Concerns with possible prestige and profit stifle the sharp criticism expected in carnival time. Singers popular with the *Fundación* are likely to treat even subjects as distressing as unemployment or a declining economy by indirection or by dousing them with romantic imagery.

By the sea	Que por la mar
ships no longer arrive,	ya no llegan los barcos,
by the sea	por la mar
love no longer comes,	ya no llega el amor,
Cádiz of the seas	que el Cádiz marinero
is unemployed,	está en el paro,
it sinks in the seas,	que naufraga por los mares. . .
the seas that gave them birth!	¡la mare que los parió. . .!

It often appears that in an effort to avoid giving offense, individuals cited in *coplas* for praise or criticism are usually famous but uncontroversial figures unlikely to raise passions. One *pasodoble*, for example, by an esteemed Cádiz carnival composer, concerns Manuel de Falla, the Spanish-born composer (1876–1946) who studied in Paris in the early part of the century, moved to Granada from 1921 to 1939, and then settled in Argentina. De Falla is identified with flamenco and Andalusian folk music, but he stirs no contemporary excitement, either symbolic or real. He is safe and agreeable, and the outrage displayed concerning his long distant departure from Spain seems synthetic, remote in time and space from contemporary concerns.

Who allowed you to	Quién dejó que a tu tierra
abandon your own land?	un día abandonaras,
Who disregarded the prelude	quién desolló el preludio
of love of your life. . .	de amor de tu vida. . ..

It is understandable that some partisans of the carnival as political theater are frustrated by lyrics skillfully wrought but cushioned from contemporary political and social issues. All too often this is what a tame official carnival has to offer. The lyrics fail to celebrate intense approval or disapproval. As two of the critics note of an adroit writer often honored by the *Fundación*:

"He has talent, but I think his talents are badly used because he tries to write in a manner that will not offend anybody, and he ends up saying what people want to hear. He doesn't criticize anybody; he seems afraid of bothering his listeners. He criticizes ETA [the Basque terrorist group], a pretty safe target, but other than that. . .. He is also very melodramatic and sentimental. If there's a child murder or a rape, he writes about it in very melodramatic tones. He can be criticized for being an opportunist. He started young, at seventeen or so, and I don't know his ideas or political background. He adapted to the majority with great ease. If the majority is stupid, he writes stupid, and unfortunately, that's often the case. His writing is very black and white – *piropos* [compliments] and songs of hate. People like *piropos* – they hide defects and present an unproblematic picture of things. I don't think that carnival should be so narcissistic and accommodating. It should tear off masks and be an escape valve. This fellow doesn't understand that. Carnival is a time for criticism. It's the time when you put yourself on the same level as those in power. We wouldn't dare say what we say in carnival at any other time of the year. Carnival cannot be colorless and bloodless. But he doesn't see it that way. He'd rather write about how everything's fine and in place." (Manuel Moreno and María López)

A voice complimentary to the *gaditano* songwriter just cited is that of the Seville journalist and writer Antonio Burgos, an aficionado of the Cádiz carnival. One of the very few outsiders to write for the Cádiz carnival, he too (understandably, as a sophist-icated visiting participant) chooses subjects to praise or to blame especially carefully. One tango of his, for example, written for the *coro* Batamonos Que Nos Vamos in 1990, exalts José María Pemán (1897–1981), the conservative Spanish poet and playwright who was a native son of Cádiz. A conservative Catholic and a royalist, Pemán had been a bitter foe of the Second Republic, which he had accused of creating an atmosphere of terror and violence. He had turned his pen and his poetry to further the cause of Franco. Pemán's literary works were conservative in ideology and style.

His light-hearted plays, usually set in the past, were full of picturesque detail and were written in a modernist style. For a time he was named president of the Royal Spanish Academy. A statue was erected in his honor. Pemán, however, had another sort of fame among those who recalled him as "that poet who after the fall of the Second Republic was responsible for purging school-teachers, intellectuals, and artists of the left." Following Pemán's death, someone decapitated his statue. It was a peculiarly carnivalesque action, but it did not sit well with Antonio Burgos, who admired Pemán's aesthetics.

Tango: To José María Pemán	
Of that event, the newspaper	De aquel hecho extraordinario
had tremendous photos,	trajo el diario
tremendous photos.	tremendas fotos, tremendas fotos.
And the little widow Naviera	Y la Viudita Naviera
was in shock, was in shock,	le dió un soponcio, le dio un soponcio.
when she saw them.	
The charcoal vender cried	Lloraba la piconera
through the Alameda,	por La Alameda
because in the park lies fallen	porque en el Parque tumbada está
the statue erected	la estatua que le erigiera
by our unique city	esta ciudad tan señera
to José María Pemán.	a José María Pemán.
Without mercy	Sin contemplación
they cut the head off,	le cortaron la cabeza
the same head which so nobly	tanto por Cádiz soñó.
dreamt of Cádiz so often.	Y la separó
And it severed it [the head]	del cuerpo que es cuerpo entero
from that body, the whole body	de gaditano puntero
of a leading gaditano.	cuánto salero de gran señor.
What zeal of great gentleman!	Como voz del pueblo
Like the voice of the people	dicen mis labios
my lips say	que un desagravio
that Pemán deserves to be	el gran Pemán ay, se merece
vindicated.	
If the authorities remain quiet	si callan las fuerzas vivas
La Viña says	dice la Viña
that the people still insist.	que el pueblo llano sigue en sus treces.
Pemán gave Cádiz	Pemán le entregó a su Cádiz

the best things he had, and now with my tango I raise to his poetry a monument full of life, so that no one can tear it apart.	tó lo mejor que tenía Y ahora yo en mi tango ya le levanto a su poesía un monumento lleno de vía para que nadie pueda arrancarlo.
Don't cry any more, charcoal vender. Seneca says so, because he's raising a choir for him, a monument with their throats, more *gaditano*, more *gaditano*.	No llores más, piconera. Séneca dice de esta manera porque ahora un coro ya le levanta el monumento con sus gargantas más gaditano, más gaditano.

On the more certain ground of local loyalty and male indignation, Burgos attacked Camilo José Cela, the novelist who received the Nobel prize for literature in 1989. No matter what his international literary attainments, Cela is best known in Spain as a journalist and television commentator who spits out vulgarities like cherry pits. He is unpopular in Cádiz ever since he accused the *gaditanos* of harboring too many homosexuals within their city walls. The tango, which never strikes fire, concludes:

I have enough of your millions and your novels. There are one thousand reasons to offer him my disrespect. Cádiz still remembers that story, that offense against our town. even if he won the prize one hundred times, I wouldn't forget that. Because keep in mind, old Camilo, that you insulted me, and you questioned my manhood, and there are a thousand witnesses to what I'm saying. Your Nobel doesn't do anything for us.	Me sobran sus libros y sus millones que hay mil razones para ofrecerle mi desprecio que Cádiz tiene memoria de aquella historia de aquella ofensa pá nuestro pueblo. Cien veces que lo ganará de aquello yo no me olvido, porque ten presente viejo Camilo que me insultaste que de mi hombría tú bien dudastes y hay mil testigos de lo que digo. Tu Nobel ya no nos vale

And since we are in carnival,   y como estamos en Carnavales
I tell you, genius, stick that   te digo genio métete el premio
Nobel prize
up where the cucumbers feel   que te hace falta por donde
the most bitter,   amargan
where the cucumbers feel the   más los pepinos, más los
most bitter.   pepinos.
(Antonio Burgos, Batamonos
Que Nos Vamos)

New Concerns

During the 1980s competing groups were seen first in the theater
and then on the official platforms erected in the street; but soon
afterward the contest winners disappeared inside bars and clubs
where they were contracted to appear for a fee. Carnival tradition-
alists vehemently objected to this growing custom of private
restaurants compromising the festival by denying to the general
population the festival's outstanding talents. From their point of
view this reserved the festival for the well-to-do and undermined
carnival as a festival of the people.

> "The high bourgeoisie, backbone of the political right, experiences
> the carnival in the expensive restaurants, like El Faro. . . .. In the last
> years, many of these restaurants hire *comparsas* to play there, especially
> those that have won prizes in the Falla contest. They pay them
> handsomely, and their act attracts customers to the restaurants, who
> in turn tend to tip the musicians. So everyone involved wins by this.
> Restaurant managers often arrange the performances, asking the
> *comparsas* to sing certain things first, others second, and so on. I think
> the real political right does not participate in carnival; they just do
> not get into it, [but] some *comparsas* actually cater to this type of public,
> and they shape their lyrics to accommodate their audience." (Manolo
> Moreno and María López)

Carnival critics consider it ironic that the singers often find
themselves entertaining those in higher social stations who have
contrary social and political views. There are many *gaditanos* who
fear that the contact of performer and cash sponsor cannot help
but soften the hard edges of some carnival lyrics.

Frequently *gaditanos* express concern that the capital's *concurso*
has become so inflated that it supercedes the carnival itself.

"Many *gaditanos* confuse the carnival with the contest. I don't have a problem with having a contest, but I don't want to make the contest *the* center of carnival. Some people think the carnival is the contest. We say it's not. Carnival hasn't even started yet, even though the contest at the Falla [theater] has been going on for a while. The contest is just a part of the carnival, but not the whole carnival. For us carnival is more spontaneous and improvised. . .more like anything goes. . .." (Manuel Moreno and María López)

As singing groups from around the province continue to pile into the capital to compete for the golden ring of the *concurso*, criticism swirls about the relationship of the *concurso* to the structure and function of the festival.

"The contest often demeans the carnival itself, because there are a lot of negative factors surrounding it, such as biased and unfair juries, nasty rivalries between groups, and other problems. It's like soccer. Soccer is about two teams kicking a ball. The big-business atmosphere – millionaire contracts, mafia, and corruption – are incidental, but they turn the sport into a quagmire. The sport itself is good – its circumstances may make it bad, though." (Manuel Moreno and María López)

Reaction to this tamed festival will be seen next in the resurgence of the urban street carnival.

Notes

1. In 1960 the national census recorded 117,871 inhabitants of the city of Cádiz. In 1970 the census listed 134,343 and in 1981, 157,766. The city census of 1989 recorded a slightly lower figure: 156,886.
2. Local government officials were instrumental in protecting the festival from obliteration by maintaining the fiction of allowing *fiestas típicas* during the 1940s, 50s, and 60s. Subsequently, the festival was administered by a series of government-appointed commissions. For twenty-five years, from 1950 to 1975, the

carnival in Cádiz was organized by *las Fiestas Típicas Gaditanas*. From 1975 to 1983 a *comisión de organización* was named each year to administer the carnival in the capital city.

3. *Me cachis en la mar* is a euphemism for *Me cago en la mar*: I poop in the sea. The expression is used as a Spanish curse to express disappointment.

4. Some *gaditanos* disagree with this appraisal and defend their *murgas*:

> "*Chirigotas* do [move], since mimicry and pantomime are part of their performance, and they are less serious and more theatrical. On the other hand, the *comparsas* are a serious affair. Even when they dress as something funny, as clowns, for example, they appear very serious, wearing rich costumes, made of luxurious cloth. The *cuartetos* also move around quite a bit; since they are less musical, their movements are a big portion of their act and their jokes." (Manuel Moreno)

5. Articles in the Cádiz press are peppered with comments on carnival comparable to movie and theater reviews in cities elsewhere. In 1989, Pedro Romero, a lyricist returning after an absence of some seasons from carnival activities, evaluated some of the current criticisms in a newspaper interview:

> . . .the *coro*, for one, is corseted and stilted. In it, costumes and ornament seem more important than the tango itself, king of the Cádiz carnival. . . .[he] doesn't agree that the *comparsas* are in crisis. What happens is that they are under attack from many angles at once, and they are suffering from attrition and misunderstanding. "There isn't such crisis, though. And proof of this is the fact that all the finalists are young authors, which is very stimulating for carnival." . . .[He thinks that] the *chirigotas* are living through a good moment right now, and thanks to new stimuli, the *chirigota* is recovering its great values. The *cuartetos*, on the other hand, are in a deep crisis of creativity and identity. We should help them out in maintaining their tradition, that seems to be gradually losing ground. (*Diario de Cádiz*, Jan. 28, 1989)

6. The *Fundación* has tried various schemes to try to speed the process of reaching the final few groups. Before 1980 the contest was handled in a single stage. Between 1980 and 1984 it became a two step process and in 1984 a third preliminary round was

held. In 1991, however, the third round was eliminated. See *Diario de Cádiz*, Feb. 23, 1992, Carnival Supplement, pp. 22–3.

Eugenio Mariscal Carlos and Rafael Parra Luna of the Author's Society added:

> Nowadays people criticize the *Fundación* [*del Carnaval*] because of the huge number of groups which take part in the contest. We presented a motion through the Author's Society a while ago proposing some changes in the procedure of the contest. We wanted to eliminate the preselection process, because it humiliates the people who are not selected after rehearsing for up to six months. We wanted a final with a few groups, like the four of five best ones in each category. In that way, we would have saved time and also we wouldn't humiliate those who are eliminated. But since we were in the minority, we were voted down. (*Diario de Cádiz*, Jan. 31, 1989)

Miguel Villanueva, president of the Author's Society, also attempted to streamline the early rounds.

> Eliminatory rounds make the contest unnecessarily long and boring, and they only contribute to humiliate the groups that do not pass it. The Author's Society proposed to return to the traditional formula: a semifinal and a final. We almost achieved this change, but in the last moment, someone threw their weight around. (*Diario de Cádiz*, Jan. 25, 1989)

7. In 1989 a trio from Seville called "Al compás de mi cohetello" was taunted with sounds from *pitos* played in the box seats. The intimidated singers began to sing softer and softer. During subsequent numbers the *pitos* sounded again, followed by murmurs from the audience, and finally shouts of "fuera, fuera!" ("out! out!") See *Diario de Cádiz*, Jan. 30, 1989.
8. R. Solís Llorente, *Coros y Chirigotas, Carnaval en Cádiz*, p. 18.
9. The music best suited for the *coro* is often in dispute. One champion of tradition insists that tango music should always be the same and the number and type of instruments employed should never vary. For other composers, both the beat and types of instruments may vary. A trumpet is sometimes introduced.

Antonio Martín is currently writing songs for pop singers and has produced a few records. He considers writing pop love songs to be much simpler than writing for the carnival with its varied types of songs and complex rhythms.

10. See José Rodríguez Chatín, *Diario de Cádiz*, Feb. 1, 1989, p. 8.
11. For example, El Charpa and Los Dedócratas in La Viña, Ramón Díaz Fletilla in El Mentidero, and La Perla de Cádiz in Santa María.
12. A federation of *peñas* coordinates the efforts of the groups involved. Not unexpectedly the *peñas* outside the old city complain of being ignored in favor of those from the more traditional barrios.
13. Manuel Moreno notes: "There was an amazing case with the military this year. General Armada, one of the leaders of the coup of February 23, 1981, was forgiven by the state and set free. This is outrageous! This man was one of the most prominent figures who tried to topple the democratic government a few years ago, and all of a sudden he's declared innocent. In spite of this, there haven't been many carnival lyrics about him. Only some newspapers in the country criticized this. Some even were in favor of the measure, saying that it shows that the government is confident in our democracy and in the citizens' political maturity, and for that reason is not afraid of antidemocratic elements."
14. A. Ramos Santana, *Historia del Carnaval de Cádiz*, pp. 5–6.

Chapter 10

The People's Carnival in the Capital

Protest against the *Fundación*

For the last two decades, *gaditanos* have had to reckon with the autocracy of committees managing the people's own traditions. To many it seems paradoxical to regulate rigidly a holiday so hostile to authority as carnival. Standards set by the *Fundación* for the size of the groups, the number and kind of instruments, the song genres permitted, and the harmonies, all tend to inhibit the freedom, candidness, and experimentation associated with carnival. While the *concurso* may serve as a temporary stimulant, ultimately the weight of its regulations and the pressure of its rewards undermine the essence of carnival criticism, frivolity, wit, and free expression.

Some organized groups, like the *Sociedad de Autores* (the Author's Society) formed in 1986 to represent the interests of a number of the city's lyricists and composers, maintain that they are given short shrift by *Fundación* officials. They are upset because their voices were ignored in the formation of rules. At the very least the *Sociedad* would like to select the jury that ranks the singing groups.

> "Our Sociedad bothers many people in the *Fundación* because we are often critical of their procedures. We want to preserve the purity of the carnival, and we criticize the *Fundación* for that same reason. We think that the carnival has become a little 'too corseted,' if you know what I mean. There are too many rules and regulations, and too little freedom for the *cuplé* writers. At present to enter the contest a group must have eight *pasodobles*, eight *cuplés*, the medley, and the introduction. And since they demand so much, sometimes the *coplas* are not well written – writers have to do so many *coplas* that they can't all be very good." (Eugenio Mariscal and Rafael Parra)

The irony of a carnival controlled by an academy of officials and businessmen is not lost on carnival aficionados whose numbers include many working-class intellectuals and students. They accuse the *Fundación* of wielding the scepter of a formal academy concerning poetic and musical genres and carnival activities. They maintain that carnival is not carnival if it is run by fiat and hobbled by rules, no matter who makes them. Their choice is to do away with the *Fundación* and all regulations.

"They don't want to enjoy, they just want to control. That's the essence of power. In the past the aristocracy wanted to control carnival through balls and dances. During the dictatorship, they wanted to exert control more forcibly: they changed dates, the name of carnival, and so on. Now, they still want to control things, but it is through more subtle means – through rules and regulations. Like then, some people nowadays would also like to get rid of carnival. People express too many things during those days.

"The people in that *Fundación* act like they are the carnival intellectuals. They claim to be the ones who know most about carnival and want everyone to pay attention to what they say, but they really just want to regulate and organize carnival as they please. It's a power trip. Power always wants to control carnival, no matter whether it is right- or left-wing. In the first democratic municipal government we had in 1979, the festival counselor was a communist and carnival had the same structures and the same sort of wrestling between control from above and the freedom of the people. I think that even if the anarchists were in power, the conflict would be the same.

"Carnival is one of those times, that all cultures have, when social rules dissolve. Now, to try to impose restrictions is completely ridiculous. It goes completely against everything that carnival stands for. What they want to do is to make the carnival into a spectacle for the tourists and for the people from here – but that's not the way it should be. . .The *Fundación Gaditano del Carnaval* acts like a state agency that tries to regulate the anarchy of carnival." (Manuel Moreno and María López)

The most effective response to carnival bureaucrats and academicians has been the formation of innovative groups and the creation of audacious carnival songs sung in the streets of the city.

Los Ilegales

As the *concurso* competition swelled in importance and influence, a countermovement began to take shape on the streets of the capital which had ramifications for both the festival and carnival song. Independent *comparsas* and *chirigotas* materialized whose members ignored restrictions established by the rules of the *Fundación*. Their numbers were swelled by informal groups called *charangas* composed of family, friends, neighbors, and fellow workers. In short order *gaditanos* began to recognize the existence of two distinct carnivals with discrete criteria of their own: one, the highly structured official carnival organized by the *Fundación* with its formal canon and competitions, and the other, the unbound carnival of the street – the people's carnival – comprising a variety of groups, including *ilegales*, so-called because they deliberately flout *Fundación* rules for participation in the *concurso* and express points of view of their own.

To the *ilegales* most questions decided by the *Fundación* are matters of individual taste and freedom. The composition of these groups varies, since they ignore with impunity official guidelines stipulating the precise number of singers, the type and number of songs, the instruments employed, and requirements for part singing. Some *chirigotas* list as many as eighteen members, disregarding the *Fundación*'s maximum of twelve. Matters are just as diverse concerning the required variety in their repertoires: some groups confine their repertoires to *cuplés* or to a few *pasodobles*. On one occasion a *chirigota ilegal* offered but two *pasodobles* and ten *cuplés*, and confessed they lacked the time to put together a potpourri, an offense that would keep them out of the formal competition.

As reported in a somewhat imperious account in the *Diario de Cádiz*, the range of costumes worn by the *charangas* illustrates their relatively amateur status, and at the same time their excitement and spirit:

> The numerous family *charangas* that paraded added color and humor to the event. Some of them sang to the crowd that flanked the streets. Despite the number of costumes, relatively few were truly interesting or original. However, the joy and enthusiasm of the *charanga* members more than made up for lack of originality in costumes.

Among the *charangas*, a group was dressed as parcheesi pieces, with dice as headpieces; another group dressed up as letter soup; another, as polka-dotted Spanish guitars, with a fan as *peineta*; there was also a group of "large and cool" snowmen; a family in altar-boy uniform; and some office calculators with a roll of paper on their heads. A group named "Bombos de Colón" showed the discoverer surrounded by pregnant Indian women ["*bombo*," or bass drum, is also colloquial for the round womb of a pregnant woman]. . . . Another group represented the new women *Guardia Civiles*. There were many other types and themes such as Dannon yogurt containers, cigarette packs, popcorn, sunflower seeds, witches, Indians, exotic tribes, water-carriers; all of them contributed to the festive atmosphere of the event.[1]

The *ilegales* champion the liberty of the carnival simply by being independent and pursuing their own course of action – refusing to conform to the rules and celebrating openly on the street. The *ilegales* thus far have resisted attempts to organize them into a contest (to be celebrated, to be sure, not in the theater but in the *mentideros* [places of gossiping and loafing]).

"A *chirigota ilegal* is a way to participate in carnival the way we have always understood it. Nowadays we, the *ilegales*, have total freedom to sing wherever we want and what we want. We say that if the *ilegales* disappeared there wouldn't be any carnival – just people walking around the streets, drinking. . . ." (Manolo Moreno and María López)

While the two traditions, the *legal* and the *ilegal*, frequently draw on the same fund of news, scandal, and politics, there are discernible differences in style and focus. There is a great range of poetic gifts on view, with both positive and negative results. Because they are able to play with themes without concern for the consequences of their place in the official competition, the best *ilegal* writers seem able to reach a high level of both fun and sophistication. Untamed and less fearful of giving offense to establishment powers, the *ilegales* attract working-class intellectuals and students to their ranks. While most groups competing officially are cautious to avoid barbed criticism, the *ilegales* sing out *forte* in the voice of the common citizen. Many songs are spirited, pointed, challenging, and at times piquant and disagreeable to the powers that be.

Fellowship

For those seeking a prize in the *concurso*, the quality of one's singing voice is a determining factor in being accepted in one group or another. Among the *ilegales*, however, the critical element is fellowship, and so groups of friends, fellow workers, neighbors, and family, regardless of talent, join together to sing and celebrate.

During the course of a day or evening, most *ilegales* gravitate to the local centers of carnival: the barrio La Viña where the traditions of the old carnival have their deepest roots, to La Plaza de las Flores, and to the steps of the Correos, the central post office. But they are not confined to specific streets and promenades nor to any set schedule. They sing wherever and whenever they choose, whether the audience is small or large, and they maintain their high level of enthusiasm and energy throughout the week.

> "You participate, and you are giving and giving, very altruistically. I think that helps a lot, because you are not working for anything in return. . .only for a smile, or for people's applause. . .and they appreciate it, they cheer, and that keeps you going. Alcohol helps a bit too, but without getting drunk. If you get drunk, goodbye to the festival; you can't do a thing. People don't drink too much. They just take little sips to keep the spirit up. Wine also helps people win over their shyness. It helps you make a spectacle of yourself. After all, you are being a clown in the eyes of many people – and without a mask, so everyone can see you. Wine helps one keep euphoric, even when people don't laugh or sing with you, or when they don't show any appreciation." (Manuel Moreno and María López)

Without the friction of competing for prizes and prize money, comradery attitudes can be maintained within the group and between groups. Comparisons between the two carnivals, the official and the unofficial, are easily noted:

> "Now that the only incentive in carnival is to get a prize, there is a lot of bad competitiveness and rivalry. . . .The newspapers yesterday criticized the *coro de la Viña* because they were at a certain spot too long [in a procession] and they did not let anyone else pass through or sing. They just want to monopolize the streets. In previous years, the *coros* ended up their rounds in the plaza, where they would sing to each other, cheer for each other, and so on. This year the papers reported as something exceptional that two *coros* sang to each other

in the street. But this used to be the norm in former times! The reporter's surprise just shows how far we have come from the conviviality and comradery of the original carnival.

"The *ilegales*, on the other hand, don't compete against each other; we sing songs to each other and with each other, and laugh a lot when we meet doing the rounds in the streets. The *legales*, however, don't do that, they are so envious of each other. . .." (Manuel Moreno and María López)

Café and Street

As we noted in the previous chapter, once the contests are decided for the best potpourri, the best libretto, and so on, the winners find it to their advantage to appear inside cafés for a fee. As is commonly observed, "The legal *chirigotas* don't go out on the streets, but to restaurants, bars, and contests." In contrast, the *ilegales* sing their songs at every corner and byway. The conflict over receiving fees from cafés, bars, and *peñas* is eliminated, as a statement in the *Diario de Cádiz* in 1989 affirms:

"We don't go into *peñas* or bars, or take part in any contest, because we don't want any money. We just want to amuse people while having a good time ourselves. We think that the family group is an important component of the Cádiz carnival; be it a good or a bad group, it doesn't matter, it's the best way to experience the festivals." These are words of Inmaculada Alonso Ponce and Milagrosa Díaz Martino, representatives of the whole *chirigota* [*No me pongas más peros*]. . ..[2] They started rehearsing their *coplas* after the epiphany [January 6]. Their locales have been a house in construction in Gallineras, San Fernando, and a garage in Cádiz. Before each performance, they distribute a few *pesetas* among the audience, and when they finish singing, they ask for applause from the claque."[3]

Participants claim that without the pressure and the rules of the *concurso*, the songs have improved.

"There are also singers and musicians who are disenchanted with the contests and the official scene, and they come out in *charangas ilegales*, and their songs are so much better now, much more sincere and authentic, since they come out merely to participate and are not under the stress of a contest, under the compulsion to win." (Manuel Moreno and María López)

Men and Women

The participation of men and women in carnival activities mirrors in great measure their place in the social life. In the city, as in the towns, the social life of men is largely outside of their apartments and is centered in the bar, café, *peña*, on the street, or in the *alameda*. Women's activities concern the home or subsidiary activities involving shopping, church, and children.

> ". . .among working-class people [in the city] without many cultural interests, for example, it is very typical for the man to come home from work, take a shower or something, eat and then go out to the bar, where he plays cards and talks to other male friends. . .while women are left at home to do the housework and stay with the kids, and so on. Things are changing a little, but they remain largely still the same." (Manuel Moreno and María López)

The limited role of women in the carnival is believed to result in some measure from the interest men have in protecting the fame and reputation of their women.

> "Because of the association of carnival and licentiousness, many men have discouraged their own women from participating in the carnival. Women should be handsome, loyal, motherly, and, last but not least, submissive. It's what many people say in Spain: 'all women are whores, except my wife and my mother.'" (Manuel Moreno and María López)

Women who accept their traditional role have found good cause to abide by the common prejudices.

> "As you know, women are often more chauvinistic than men, and the same happens here with carnival. They become proud of the roles that men have created for them. Older women have always had the notion that they were the wives and mothers of *comparsistas*. They tended to be proud of their husbands' participation in carnival, while they stayed at home, taking care of the children; they didn't go out, except on Sunday to see the parade. They have always believed in that role, and lived accordingly.
>
> For her part the mother all too readily accepts a carnival salute for the toil of washing everyone else's clothing, ironing, making beds, and preparing meals, usually without help from her children or husband. With her apron on, the woman may be celebrated as a

goddess, but at the same time she may be denied equality and an active role in the city carnival." (Manuel Moreno and María López)

Women in the *Ilegales*

In contrast to the official *concurso* entries, where women are rarely seen, among the *ilegales* there are many women who sing alongside the men. It is primarily the younger women who have broken into the ranks of singers, a circumstance which reflects their rejection of the old roles and their present desire to be part of carnival. Women who have entered the professional and business world as doctors, nurses, teachers, and office personnel are present and occasionally united in groups. Couples, married and unmarried, frequently participate. Of course, women and children take part in the family *charangas*.

The increased presence of women among the *ilegales* and family *charangas* adds new dimensions to the carnival. In recent years women have not only participated more in strolling bands of singers, but also have begun to write songs for the carnival. Adela del Moral, for example, has become a popular songwriter.

> "She brought out a mixed *coro* beginning five years ago – their name was "Italianas y Francesas." This year there is a group called "Imperio Inca," and Adela del Moral is writing for them. Some *chirigotas* are exclusively female and have links with the feminist movement. One of these came out once as widows; another time they ridiculed women who participated in beauty contests. They were members of the *Asociación Gaditana de la Mujer*. They went out in 1984 and 1985, but not last year or this one. They may be coming out still, but integrated in other mixed *chirigotas*. (Manuel Moreno and María López)

The women's groups had the advantage of rendering the scene with a fresh eye. A *chirigota* composed of women, and with lyrics written by women, mocked a notorious exam and complex questions put to women applying for janitorial work at the *Diputación* [a government building]. The exams inspired four women to compose "Qué peazo de oposición" (What a tough exam). It became the name of their *chirigota*. A newspaper account reported:

> They [the women] have been coming out in carnival for the last five years [since 1984]. . . ..for this year's carnival. . .they opted for dressing

up as cleaners at the *Diputación*. The best advantage of this *tipo* [costume] was that it consisted of a blue robe that only cost them 250 pesetas [$ 2.00]. They claim to be shy, which has prevented them from singing on the steps of the post office [*Correos*], the "*Falla*" [theater] of the *chirigotas*. . . .They state their objective is to have a good time. "We are not interested in providing a spectacle. We sing for five or for fifty people. We really don't care. The other day two women asked us to sing for them. We ended up singing almost our whole repertoire for them." . . .Although the group currently has eighteen members, they claim to accept anyone who would like to join, since few of them can show up regularly for rehearsals. Their repertoire consists exclusively of *cuplés*, because you really need to know a bit more [about singing and music] to do *pasodobles*.[4]

The *coplas* sung by most groups inadvertently assent in the portrait of family life set in the traditional mold. The *ilegales*, however, can challenge basic assumptions. A *chirigota* composed equally of men and women dedicated the following burlesque of conventional reality to one of their own singers. (The vulgar terms [*chochete* for vagina; *pichita* for penis] are considered affectionate when applied to children and other family members.)

My little pussy of my love,	Mi chochete de mi corazón,
you are glued to the stove day in, day out.	todo el día pegada al fogón.
There is nothing more sacred than my mother for me.	No hay nada mas sagrado que a una madre para mí;
I love my mother just as much as my anisette.	quiero a mi madre como a una copa de anis.
I remember her screaming as she washed the dishes:	Recuerdo sus gritos fregando los platos.
"You son of a bitch. If I catch you, I'm going to kill you.	Hijo de la gran puta, si te cojo te mato.
Who the fuck do you take after?"	¿A quién coño has salido?
she shouted at me with love.	me gritaba con amor,
"You are always such a slob. You look like a cauliflower."	siempre tan desaliñado este niño parece una coliflor.
And as I sing these lyrics, my heart skips a beat,	Y cuando entono estas letras mi corazón da un requiebro
because I pass out when I sing to my mother.	porque al cantarle a mi madre yo pierdo el conocimiento.

Notes

1. *Diario de Cádiz*, Feb. 6, 1989.
2. "This name '*No me pongas más peros*' is a pun. It means "don't
   hamper me any more" [*peros* are "buts": objections]; let me do
   whatever I want. In addition, we call apples *peros* in Cádiz, so
   in this sense, the group's name means "Don't put any more
   apples on my head." One of the group was dressed up as the
   legendary William Tell, with his bow and arrows, and another
   one came out with an apple on his head." (Manolo Moreno and
   María López)
3. *Diario de Cádiz*, Feb. 12, 1989: 10.
4. Ibid.

Chapter 11

Poet of the People's Carnival

Paco Rosado

To many *gaditanos*, Francisco (Paco) Rosado represents the highest attainment of the *ilegales*. Paco Rosado, who has been cited in these pages many times already, is a much admired local composer who speaks from the heart of the carnival:

With my guitar, my whistle, and my joy;	Con mi guitarra, mi pito y mi alegría;
the rattle drum, my voice, and my costume,	la caja, el bombo, mi voz y mi disfraz.
I am like the grasshopper, enjoying life.	Hoy soy cigarra que gozo de la vía.
I reject what makes me bitter, and I squander my sympathy, singing to my people, because this is carnival time.	Desecho lo que amarga, derrocho simpatía cantándole a mi gente, que estamos en Carnaval.
Everyday matters frighten us and cause us despair – a bomb, a kidnapping, a robbery, an epidemic, an assault on the Congress, or an invasion. But I disguise all this with that irony that is characteristic of our festivals when we turn our sorrows into a song.	Lo cotidiano asusta y desespera una bomba, un secuestro, un robo, una epidemia, un asalto al Congreso o cualquier invasión; pero yo lo disfrazo con esa ironía que es propia de la fiesta de tierra mía que hasta de sus pesares se hace una canción.
I don't want to sing about my laments, or to hurt your feelings, my dear paisano.	No quiero cantarte mis lamentos ni herir tus sentimientos, querido paisano.
I'd rather come to see you	Prefiero acudir a tu cita

with my best smile, and my heart on my sleeve.	con mi mejor sonrisa y el alma en la mano.
Here I am like a friend who will amuse you, will make you enjoy,	Y estoy contigo como un amigo que te divierta y te haga disfrutar
and will make you laugh.	y te haga reír
Because one shouldn't cry in carnival.	que en carnavales no hay que llorar.
(Paco Rosado, Los Cruzados Mágicos, 1982)	

For Paco Rosado, like many other Cádiz writers and singers, carnival is a way of life.

> ...I grew up in the belief that carnival was more than a superficial way to spend a few days. I thought that it was a philosophy rather than a science; an aesthetics of the abnormal, not of the mock-refined; an attitude, not an ability.[1] But above all things, I believed that carnival was freedom, with all the attributes the term has.

> ...I was told, and believed, that our festivals were a necessary escape from the everyday. It was the sublime possibility to criticize everything and anything, while keeping a sense of humor to laugh at oneself. Protected by the mask and the *copla*, I thought the *gaditano* had the chance of saying whatever he wanted concerning the surrounding world.[2]

A Composer's Reproof

Employed for many years as a shipyard worker in Cádiz, Paco Rosado is also a well-known personality on the local radio as well as in the press. It is principally through his songs, however, that he has become the champion of those who have struggled to maintain the freedom of the carnival. His best songs quickly attain wide currency and are memorized by aficionados.

Paco Rosado's point of view provides a strong philosophical base for defenders of traditional carnival. He has opposed the arbitrary rules of the *concurso*, commercialization of the festival, and any practices that have served to separate the people from the singers. In 1982 Rosado attacked the routine of paying the singers to perform in restaurants and clubs, thereby depriving the populace of their presence on the street. In his *chirigota*, *Los*

Cruzados Mágicos (The Magical Crusaders), Rosado sarcastically invited listeners to follow one such group inside to one of the city's fashionable restaurants:

To you, paisano, who are listening to our notes, with much love we are going to explain how we think of our *chirigota*	A usted, paisano, que escucha nuestras notas con mil amores le vamos a explicar como pensamos en nuestra chirigota
and where we are planning to take our *coplas,* in case you want to follow us during carnival. We'll visit the great restaurants,	y donde planeamos llevarle nuestras coplas por si quiere seguirnos mientras dura el Carnaval. Visitaremos los grandes restaurantes,
so don't be stupid and please go ahead. Reserve a table soon, if you want to hear us. After all, a plate of shrimp with half a bottle of wine is only ten thousand *pesetas.*	así que no sea tonto y vaya usted delante reserve mesa pronto si nos quiere escuchar: que una ración de gambas con media limeta no le cuesta más caro de diez mil pesetas
That's a bargain if you get to have a good time. We'll perform on different stages, a different theater every day. Buy your ticket soon. We think that art has a price.	y eso es una miseria si va a disfrutar. Iremos recorriendo escenarios teatros a diario, saque ya su entrada. Creemos que el arte hay que pagarlo
Don't forget that, and don't speak nonsense. We'll also say that	conviene no olvidarlo ni decir bobadas. Tambien diremos que intentaremos
we intend to go, if we have time, to some club with a stage in order to say that this is the most popular festival. (Paco Rosado. Los Cruzados Magicos, 1982)	si queda tiempo algún tablao[3] pisar pá después decir que esta es la fiesta más popular.

The following year, 1983, in his *chirigota Cegotas con Botas* (Blind Puss in Boots), he addressed the singers themselves, reminding them that carnival singing belongs not in private restaurants for the exclusive pleasure of its paying clients, but in the streets for the people to enjoy:

My dear *comparsista*,	Mi querido comparsista:
don't be surprised by my singing to you.	no te extrañe que te cante
I don't know much about conquests,	yo no entiendo de conquistas
and I'm not out for revenge,	no soy revanchista
nor to deceive you.	ni soy farsante.
Excuse my boldness,	Perdona mi atrevimiento
but I want to remind you	pero quiero recordarte
that you are wasting your talent	que se quema tu talento
appearing in a restaurant.	al servicio puesto de un restaurante.
I'll never forget	No olvidaré
the Plaza de las Flores (Flower Square)	nunca esa plaza de las Flores
where I sang to a people	donde canté
who provide endless honor.	a un pueblo que derrocha honores.
My heart	Mi corazón
melted in the street of la Palma.	se ha desgranao en la calle de la Palma
That's why it is my desire	Por eso quiero y es mi deseo
that you not spare yourself that emotion	que no te prives de esa emoción
and that you conquer the streets,	y conquistes la calle
with your throat filled with hope.	con tu garganta plena de ilusión.
(Paco Rosado, Cegotas con Botas, 1983)	

That same year in another *pasodoble* he argued against the excesses of the *concurso* itself. He urged that the capital *concurso* should be scaled back and that each town and city throughout the province should have its own *concurso* and leave the matter at that.[4]

The carnival has grown,	Crecieron los carnavales
now we are all happy.	ya somos todos felices;
From Cádiz to Trebujena,	de Trebujena hasta Cádiz
good branches grow from its	buenas ramas salen de sus .
roots.	raíces
We don't want to intrude,	No queremos ser intrusos
nor be presumptuous,	ni tampoco presumidos:
let each town have its own	cada pueblo y su concurso
contest;	
let each owl	que cada mochuelo
stay in its nest.	quede en su nido
. . . .	. . . .

The capital *concurso* continued to develop as the principal focus of carnival, and for some the abuses had become prosaic routines. Six years after his complaint against the *concurso* in song, Paco Rosado was still more blunt in prose.

> Year after year, the same comment crops up in every conversation on carnival: the contest is tedious and lacks quality. This feeling takes over carnival settings and participants as carnival days roll by and one discovers that lyrics, theatrical resources, humorous situations, types, and personal allusions repeat themselves. Furthermore, audiences become progressively tired of realizing that the great majority of the authors focus their critical abilities on inside carnival issues. Writers forget that carnival is the only chance a people have for denouncing what doesn't work and for pointing out those responsible for it. A carnival repertoire should contain general problems, not just particular complaints, bickering between *comparsas*, or accusations towards anyone who doesn't fervently admire our *coplas*.[5]

The Trials of Daily Life

One of the sources of Paco Rosado's popularity is his ability to seemingly transform the city into a small town. While Cádiz appears to be too large a city to treat private issues, Paco and his *chirigota* are able to relate the trials of the ordinary worker and to highlight details common to daily life. In one carnival *copla*, the poor are seen throwing their money away in lotteries and in slot machines when they can't even win a fried egg in their own kitchens:

This fellow doesn't do anything but gamble from sunup till sunset.	Este fulano desde que se levanta no hace otra cosa que no sea jugar;

This fellow doesn't do anything
but gamble
from sunup till sunset.

He plays dice, cards;

he is desperate, gambling his
money,
thinking only that he may win
some day.
He plays bingo and lottery;

he spends a fortune in the
Christmas lottery.
Wherever he goes he buys
numbers,
he fills in six *quinielas*

and he plays roulette.
And if he sees a *tombola*, then
forget it.[6]

He spends two months salary
playing with the gipsy with
the three cups.
It's tiring just to see him
throwing money into slot
machines.
Then at home, what a joke,

they raffle one fried egg among
them
and he never wins anything,
not even the smallest prizes.
(Paco Rosado, Los Cruzados
Mágicos, 1982)

Este fulano desde que se levanta
no hace otra cosa que no sea
jugar;
juega a los dados, también juega
a las cartas,
y anda desesperado jugándose
la pasta
pensando solamente que algún
día ganará.
Juega en el bingo y en cada
lotería;
ya sea de una pena o de una
cofradía
y si es por nochebuena se gasta
un dineral.
Donde quiera que vaya compra
papeletas
rellena seis quinielas y juega a
la ruleta
y si viene una tómbola es el no
va más.

Se tira el sueldo de dos meses
con el gitano ese de las tres
latillas.
Fatiga, fatiga da de verlo
tirando los dineros en las
maquinitas.
Luego en su casa, mira que
guasa,
un huevo frito se rifan entre tós
[todos]
y él nunca atrincó
ni siquiera la aproximación.

The mishaps awaiting those who must depend on social security for their health care are explored in the following potpourri of Los Cegatos con Botas in 1983.

. . .

This is about things that happen	Casos y cosas que suelen pasar
within the Social Security system.	dentro de la Seguridad Social;
Those of us who don't see any other solution	a los que no vemos más soluciones
have to go there for doctor's prescriptions.	y allí tenemos que ir por recetas.
Ballad	*Romance*
Early one morning I took my Social Security card	Muy tempranito cogí mi carné,
and I arrived at the Health Center	llegué al ambulatorio
at ten past eight.	a las ocho y diez;
Lucky me! I have a cousin working there	menos mal que mi primo trabaja allí mismo
and he could get me	y pudo sacarme
the number sixty three.	el sesenta y tres.
White border. . .black border	La orilla blanca. . . la orilla negra
Sitting in the room,	Sentado en la sala pude escuchar
I could hear the usual concert:	ese gran concierto que allí te dan:
"Ay, my bladder! Ay, my kidneys!	¡ay la vesícula, ay el riñón,
My bronchial tubes! Varicose veins!	los bronquios, las varices
Blood pressure!"	y la tensión!
And since my doctor is punctual	Y como mi médico es puntual
he was only four hours late.	sólo cuatro horas tardó en llegar.
But he is so smart	Pero es tan bueno
that the visit lasts only ten minutes	que pasa la consulta
(son of a Fleming) [Nobel Prize winner].	en diez minutos (hijo de Fleming)
He neither looks at you	el ni te mira ni te hace
nor asks you anything.	una pregunta.
What a genius!	¡Qué hombre tan listo
What a doctor!	qué peazo de doctor!

The poor patient has to pawn his boots to pay for the medicine and he is assigned a room in a hospital "with seven beds to a room and more visitors than in a nativity scene."

...	...
They rarely sweep there,	allí nunca se ve una escoba
and they don't even put	y en el caldo no hay ni avecrem[7].
bouillon in the broth	
They are always remodeling	Siempre está en obras, ¡vaya por
the building, my God!	Dios!
There's more rubble	Hay más escombros
than in an explosion.	que en la Explosión;
Many patients leave to go to	Muchos enfermos se van al cine
the movies.	
Oh, Jesus! What a mess!	¡ay! madre mía, qué descontrol.

Paco Rosado is sometimes joined in composing *cuplés* by his fellow *chirigoteros* who contribute their wit and humor. While Rosado writes all the *pasodobles* for his *chirigotas*, at times others compose *cuplés*, which require a somewhat different style. As the *gaditano* Manolo Moreno observed, "The *cuplé* is like the carnival costume: it mocks everything, but it is made with words instead of cloth and paper." With the *chirigota*, Los Cruzados Mágicos, the *cuplés* are signed by each composer.

> He writes a lot of the *cuplés* – the structure and most of the words – but even though he is a good poet, he apparently lacks the spark to create jokes and give the *cuplé* its biting wit. I didn't know that Paco lacked that. Apparently, a lot of the jokes in his songs are someone else's in the group. And the same with the music – both music and lyrics are written collectively by the whole *comparsa*, not just by him." (Manolo Moreno and María López)

One *cuplé* concerns the dilemma facing strollers on the sidewalks of land-poor Cádiz: how to avoid stepping into dog turds, not a favorite subject of the office of tourism but of vital concern to busy pedestrians.

With the new traffic lights	Con los nuevos semáforos
it's no problem to cross the	no hay problemas para cruzar:
streets.	
I just have to wait	sólo tengo que esperar
after hitting the button	que la sirena que tienen puesta
for the siren to sound.	empiece a sonar.
Now when I cross,	Ahora cuando cruzo
I feel safer;	voy más seguro;
not like before,	no como antes

when they crushed even my hair curlers.	que me aplastaban hasta los rulos.
I would like to ask whoever invents those contraptions,	Al que inventa estos aparatos yo le pido como cegato
to install sirens in the dogs' turds,	que si fuera posible una sirenita también pusiera
because I'm really fed up with	en las <<catalinas>> de los perros
stepping on dog shit.	que ya estoy harto de pisar mierda.

(Paco Rosado, Los Cegatos con Botas, 1983)

Los Cegatos con Botas takes to task a new breed of city inspectors in another *cuplé* for their excessive zeal in finding fault and for throwing their weight around.

What a sassy squad you see patrolling the city these days!	Qué patrulla más chula ronda por Cádiz hace tiempo ya;
How presumptuous they seem with their neckerchiefs and their brilliantined hair!	lo presumidos que van con su pañuelo y su brillantina por la ciudad.
They're really zealous about tramps,	Con los pordioseros son muy celosos
and they locked up Castelar because he's so ragged-looking.	y a Castelar me lo han encerrao por andrajoso.
They are real experts on picking out	Son expertos cogiendo huevos
eggs and foods that aren't fresh:	y productos que no estén buenos:
shellfish, sweets, marinated mussels;	las coquinas, los dulces, los mejillones en escabeche;
and in less than a year they have collected a full cargo of ill will.	y en menos de un año han cogío más de mil litros de mala leche.[8]

Criticism and Commentary

There is a range of criticism and commentary in the lyrics created by Paco Rosado and his fellow *chirigoteros*. The themes move from local incidents to larger social, class, and political concerns, as in the following *pasodobles*.

There are people in society	En la sociedad hay gentes
who look like insects,	que pudieran ser insectos
if you observe them coldly,	si se observan fríamente,
carefully, and with talent.	detenidamente y con talento.
The bosses are mosquitoes	Los patronos son mosquitos
who enjoy stinging us;	que las gozan con pincharnos
drones[9] and worms together	zánganos y gusanitos;
hope to govern us.	esperan juntitos
It has been proved	pá gobernarnos.
that the bankers are ants;	Se comprobó
no one will question	que los banqueros son hormigas;
that those in state Treasury	sin discusión
are lice;	que los de Hacienda son lallas
the clergy are crickets –	los curas son grillos
dark and monotonous.	de oscuridad y monotonía;
And the extreme right wing	y nuestros fachas
are cockroaches,	son cucarachas
who always live in some corner,	que habitan siempre cualquier rincón
afraid that one day	temerosos que un día
may leave them stiff from a	los dejen tiesos de un buen
stomping.	pisotón.
(Paco Rosado, Los Cegatos con Botas, 1983)	

The daily newspaper's ties to the status quo and its antipathy to progressive causes, are mocked in a *pasodoble*.

Among the good things	Entre tantas cosas buenas
we have in the capital,	que en la capital tenemos
the newspaper is the best.	el diario es lo que impera
It's always right	siempre está en primera
on the frontline.	línea de fuego.
Whether in priest's cassock	Con sotana o con chaqueta
or in sports jacket,	tiene expertos periodistas
its expert journalists	que defienden la peseta
defend money	contra majaretas
against nuts and progressives.	y progresistas.
They fight passionately	Con qué pasión
for old traditions!	lucha por viejas tradiciones,
When they lack reason,	cuanto calor
they make up for it with heat.	donde no alcanza las razones;
The newspaper has always defended	él defendió

the interests of certain *gaditanos*.	los intereses de algunos gaditanos.
And it remains in this position, vigilant and calm, to benefit the truths it upholds, always faithful to its motto: progress is mortal sin.	Sigue en su puesto celoso y quieto en beneficio de su verdad siempre fiel a su lema de que el progreso es pecado mortal.
(Paco Rosado, Los Cegatos con Botas, 1983)	

The history of Spain is rife with territorial invasion. New international foes are easily discovered among those who control the destiny of Spain and the rest of Europe – England (which governs Gibraltar, ceded to them following the Napoleonic wars) and the United States (with treaty rights for air bases and the naval station in nearby Rota). The U.S. agreement, which dated from 1953 and was tied in the popular mind to the past fascist government of Francisco Franco, was clearly in need of revision. The U.S. maintained three air bases on Spanish territory, including Torrejón near Madrid, that provided support, training and communications for U.S. and NATO operations. The U.S. naval facility at Rota provides both repairs and communication for ships and submarines in the Atlantic and western Mediterranean. In the 1980s the question of permitting U.S. bases in Spain became particularly heated. In the subsequent review (1987–1988) and renegotiation, the United States Department of Defense completely misread the mood of the Spanish people and the requirements of the Spanish government. The result was the loss of the air base at Torrejón.[10]

In an angry challenge Paco Rosado tied together past and present usurpers of Spain's territorial rights for the *gaditano* [citizen of Cádiz].

It's nothing strange, and perhaps it's repetitious to say that the *gaditano* is passionate; and one more year, remembers in its songs the pain that Cádiz [*la tacita*] gave	No es nada extraño y tal vez se repita que al gaditano lo guíe la pasión; y otro año en sus nuevas letrillas recuerde todo el daño que le hizo la tacita

to the terrible troops of Napoleon.

We were the glory and the pride of Spain,

and we have a place in history thanks to this feat.

But this is a feat that we must renew.

We should be ashamed to live on memories,

if no one here can follow the example

of those who knew how to fight for Cádiz.

We have new Napoleons

who are invading our land with neutrons.

Let's fight so that the *gaditanas* will curl their hair with the bombs they throw.[11]

Ay! How happy we will be when our *coplillas* celebrate the day

we expelled the invaders from Rota and Gibraltar.

(Paco Rosado, Los Cruzados Mágicos, 1982)

a las terribles tropas del mismo Napoleón.

Fuimos la gloria y el orgullo de España

y entramos en la historia por tan heroica hazaña

pero es una victoria que ya hay que renovar

vergüenza debe darnos vivir del recuerdo

si nadie aquí es capaz de seguir el ejemplo

de aquellos que por Cádiz supieron luchar.

Tenemos Napoleones nuevos

que invaden nuestro suelo hasta con neutrones.

Luchemos por que las gaditanas con las bombas se hagan más tirabuzones.

¡Ay! qué alegría si cualquier día nuestras copliyas pudieran recordar

cuando al invasor lo echamos de Rota y Gibraltar.

The waste and trappings surrounding the Pope and the Church were mocked in a Rosado *cuplé* which relied on the carnival's penchant for double-meanings. Rosado played with the phrase *totus tuus* (we are all yours), which was the slogan used to receive the Pope. Its first two syllables [which are pronounced *tós tus*] evoked the damning *tó[do]s tus muertos* (with all your dead – or, Go to hell). So without explicitly stating it, the last line in the composition, *totus tuus*, suggests a rebuke: *tó[dos]s tus muertos*. Of course the listener is implicated in the game by supplying the missing letters.[12]

The Pope's visit
raised a great polemic,
because of the expense,
and the coverage time

a visita del Papa
mucha polémica levantó,
por lo cara que costó
y por el tiempo

it was carried on TV.	que se llevaba en televisión.
Forty million spent on bodyguards!	Cuarenta millones
It seems that these bodyguards	en guardaespaldas
make good money	qué de dinero
as guardian angels.	cobran los ángeles de la guarda.
For nine days,	Se llevaron nueve diítas
the priests ate quite well.	papeando los capillitas,
That's why it doesn't surprise me	por eso no me extraña
that there were people at the airport	que hubiera gente en el aeropuerto
with a placard that said	con una pancarta que decía:
"We Say Farewell with `Totus tuus.'"	<<Te despedimos con Totus tuus>>
(Los Cegatos con Botas, 1983)	

Although Paco Rosado is sympathetic with the *Partido Socialista Obrero Español* (PSOE), like many other *coplistas*, he did not spare his criticism. During the first term of the Socialist government (1982–1986), Miguel Boyer, the *Ministro de Economía*, fell from grace. Boyer received a great deal of media attention for his vigorous measures demanding austerity and promoting enterprise. One of his first actions, and perhaps the most controversial, was the confiscation of Rumasa, the largest conglomerate in the country, which was headed by José María Ruiz-Mateos, considered to be the richest man in Spain. The conglomerate included department-store chains, hotels, banks, real estate, construction companies, vineyards, and hundreds of other concerns. Although confiscating Rumasa was a populist measure, it eventually brought down many government officials. Boyer, as well as many others in the Socialist government at the time, was subsequently accused of selling on the sly, parts of Rumasa's multimillion dollar empire to various corporations, investors, and competitors, and pocketing large sums of money.[13]

Boyer fell out of favor with the government and in 1983 resigned as minister. He soon became a socialite and jet-setter, a member of Spanish high society and the moneyed elite. His activities outside of government were constantly panned by the press. His marriage to Isabel Preisler, Philippine-born ex-Miss Spain and ex-wife of Julio Iglesias (and of another prominent socialite), helped to maintain his high profile. Boyer was regarded as the clearest example of the Socialist Party's forfeiture of its historical social ideology. His financial, social, and marital activities were the source of an infinite number of carnival songs that focused on hypocrisy and pretension.[14] Paco Rosado's reference to Boyer is offered in sarcastic advice to those interested in "easy" money.

. . .	. . .
If you want to steal don't be mysterious about it.	Si roba no lo haga con misterio
Stop fooling around and become a minister.	búsquese un ministerio, déjese de cuentos.
With flattery, you can become	Con coba es posible que ascienda
Minister of Economy, and that's quite a coup.	a Ministro de Hacienda y eso es un portento.
Steal in a grand style, without worrying	Robe a lo grande, sin preocuparse
if you take too much or rob without reason.	si roba mucho o roba sin razón.
If you steal in this way, you'll be treated like a lord.	Que robando así lo tratarán como a un gran señor.
(Paco Rosado, Los Cruzados Mágicos, 1982)	

Six years later, in his *chirigota*, "*Los Conquistadores*," Rosado's complaints against government corruption had been repeated so often that they seemed like birthday carols.

. . .	. . .
How can we live in peace, when the justice system washes its hands.	Como vivir tranquilo teniendo una justicia que se lava las manos.
Justice is horrified at a nude picture,	Cuando de un criminal pierde la pista
while at the same time they lose track of criminals	y en cambio de un desnudo se horroriza
and know nothing of human rights.	y no conoce los derechos humanos.
We all fight for democracy	Todos luchamos por la democracia
and it isn't funny	eso no es ninguna gracia
that the people have to thank	que el pueblo se la tenga que agradecer

a group of tyrants.	a unos tiranos.
(Paco Rosado, Los	
Conquistadores, 1988).	

Entering the *Concurso*

In 1984 Paco Rosado surprised everyone by entering his *chirigota* *"Los Llaveros Solitarios"* (The Solitary Turnkeys), in the *concurso*. Rosado's talents were so universally recognized that it was less of a surprise that the *chirigota* took first prize. The only mystery that remained was his motive for entering at all.

"That was to boycott the contest from inside and to silence the people who said that those who were against the contest were just no good at singing and writing. So when he entered the competition and won, he proved to everyone that he could speak ill of the contest and still win it. The jury might not have awarded Paco the prize, but the audiences pressed hard, because he had been so good." (Manuel Moreno and María López)

Paco Rosado's success in the *concurso* did not deter him from continuing his criticism at commercial corruption inherent in the *concurso*. In the 1986 carnival in this *cuplé* for his *chirigota*, "Los Cubatas," Paco Rosado took a swipe at the *chirigota*, "Los Carreros," for accepting a half-million *pesetas* to sing an advertisement for paint on television.

How shameless are the Carreros!	Hay que ver qué cara tienen los Carreros
They think they are TV artists.	que se creen artistas de televisión
It seems they made a lot of money;	por lo visto ganaron mucho dinero
what a shame, they gave them half a million.	qué vergüenza, les dieron medio millón
Since I am a *gaditano* I don't take very well	Yo como gaditano no veo bien
that those shameless people insult Cádiz	que esos caraduras insulten a to Cádiz
to announce some paint or another.	por anunciar no sé qué pintura
They made us seem such weaklings,	nos pusieron de flojos

no wonder people complain about them;	y con razón la gente se queja
it took them a whole month to paint one railing.	y es que estuvieron un mes pintando la misma reja.
(Paco Rosado, Los Cubatas, 1986)	

Having thrown down the gauntlet with his attack on commercialism, in 1988 in a *pasodoble* sung by the *chirigota*, "Los Conquistadores," he sarcastically advised those participating in the *concurso* of the *Fundación* how to finagle their way to victory.

If you want to be famous in carnival,	Si quieres ser famoso en Carnaval
to make it to the finals and be the first one,	estar en la final y ser primero
accept the advice of someone who is already becoming an "old timer"[15] in these matters.	admite los consejos que te da el que comienza a ser ya perro viejo.
Make sure that you let into your rehearsals	Procura que a tu ensayo pueda entrar
the most influential people.	la gente que más tienen influencias
Never miss a chance to show your patience,	y nunca pierdas la oportunidad
if someone criticizes your *coplas*.	de demostrar tu paciencia
Once the contest is over,	porque tus coplas van a criticar.
you can forget your decorum	Cuando acabe el concurso perderás tu decoro
if you sing in the streets.	si cantas en la calle.
That is only a resort	Eso es sólo un recurso
for the poor *coros*	para los pobres coros
and for the illegal groups.	y pá las ilegales.
If they don't have a nickel,	El que no tenga un duro
let them try to manage the best they can	que se busque la vida
with their tapeplayers.	con su radio-cassete
You should always attend with your *chirigota*,	tú vete siempre con tu chirigota
if the Federation organizes it,	si la Federación es que convoca
because that is what counts in the long run,	porque a la larga eso es lo que conviene
and if you don't want to be left aside,	y si no quieres que te den de lado

| give a flattering compliment to the jury, | dile un piropo al Jurado |
| even though sometimes it seems they have all been born in Albacete. | aunque parezca que hayan nacido tós en Albacete. |

Paco Rosado had now touched both sides of the carnival, as a critic of the *Fundación* and as a competitor in the *concurso*. He struggled with the criticism that his participation entailed.

"He's disappointed and hurt by the treatment he received in the Falla contest. He's always been so critical of official carnival institutions and of the Town Hall's influence on carnival, and a lot people have been trying to dethrone him and push him aside. And also, he may have gotten tired of battling problems year after year, you know." (Manuel Moreno and María López)

In *"Los Conquistadores"* Paco Rosado argued that he didn't care if he reached the finals of the *concurso*. He could walk away from such honors if he could be on satisfactory terms with his comrades and his community.

Pasodoble:

I want to do my cure of humility.	Deseo hacer mi cura de humildad
I have pondered this for a year,	durante un año he [recapacitado]
and I have realized that I don't care	y he visto que llegar a la final
if I make it to the finals or not.	es algo que me tiene sin cuidado.
If I come to participate here,	Si vengo ahora yo a participar
it is because I have a debt with you,	es porque tengo una deuda contigo
because I am eager to make up all the time I have wasted,	que estoy loquito por recuperar todo el tiempo que he perdido
and I want to thank your generosity.	y agradecer tu generosidad.
From this very instant,	Desde este mismo instante
what I need most	es gustar a mi gente
is to please my people.	lo que más necesito
What I need the most	y lo más importante
and what occupies my mind right now	que tengo yo en la mente

is to see you pleased.	es el verte agustito
I want to be in the square,	quiero estar en la plaza
with glasses of wine and fried fish,	con copitas de vino
selling booklets to my friends.	y pescao caletero
I'll have enough with this.	vendiendo un libretito a mis amigos
	con eso me conformo si consigo
If every February	acudir a tu cita cada febrero
I manage to come and see you,	son tu risa tu aplauso y tu
your laughter, applause, and your happiness	contento
are my only rule.	mi único reglamento
Why would I want all the rest?	para que necesito "to" lo demás
I don't need it.	ya no lo quiero.

The fact remains that during the remaining time this study was carried out, Paco Rosado did not continue to compete in the *concurso*. Perhaps he felt that he had proved the worth and the popularity of his lyrics. Perhaps he realized that he could take the argument no further. His world was about to change. Until 1989, when he was in his late thirties, he earned his living as a shipyard worker. That year he accepted a bonus pay for early retirement offered in the shipyard's effort to reduce personnel. Encouraged by friends and admirers he made plans to open a bar.

At that point Rosado saw the carnival feeding on itself, ensnarled in meaningless squabbles. He cited other offenses such as a flawed jury system and the decline of standards. Worst of all, he saw the *concurso* as a major culprit undermining the free spirit of the carnival. As he noted:

> All these schemes have gradually crumbled away for me, as I found out that carnival *coplas* are para-carnivalesque; that is, the carnival is censored and criticized by writers who don't participate in the festivals, by unfair juries, by commentators who render their opinions, and so on. In a way, each contest provides the subject matter for the *coplas* of the following year.
>
> It makes me sad to see great carnival writers entangle themselves in second-rate criticisms of fellow authors and groups. . . .Once we have won our freedom of expression, what do we use it for? How can some think that we can use our freedom of expression to coerce the expressions of others?
>
> If someone, well-qualified or not, dares to say he doesn't like a certain group, he's done for. If he's a media professional, he'll be

disqualified; if he's a fan of carnival, he'll be told he doesn't know the first thing about it (as if one had to study carnival); and when there are no reasons left, some will always appeal to the idea of the "sacrifice," of four months' work, as if time and difficulty were synonymous with quality. Should we give the first prize to whoever rehearses longer? Will that spare the contest?

His conclusion was unsparing:

I may be naïve, but perhaps by eliminating the contest we'll end up with a more authentic carnival.[16]

Notes

1. Here the author is playing with the similarity in sound between *actitud* and *aptitud*.
2. Paco Rosado, "Freedom vs. Expression," [Excerpts], *Diario de Cádiz*, Feb. 12, 1989, p. 8.
3. A restaurant with a stage for flamenco singing and dancing.
4. A few other towns and cities (such as El Puerto de Santa María) also hold local contests of their own, but they defer to the importance of activities in the capital.
5. Paco Rosado, "From Sung Journalism to Ennui," *Diario de Cádiz*, Jan. 29, 1989, p. 19.
6. *Quinielas* are forecasts of the results of soccer games. People fill them in with their forecasts, and if they have guessed right they win prizes in cash. A *tómbola* is a stand in the fairgrounds for raffles.
7. *Avecrem* is a popular brand of bouillon.
8. Literally, "more than three thousand liters of bad milk." *Mala leche* means resentment, ill-disposition against someone. The *cuplé* indicates that this squad has made many people resentful because of their zeal in carrying out their tasks.
9. In Spanish *zángano* is both the insect (drone) and a sponger, someone who lives off the work of other people.
10. The air base at Torrejón was particularly troublesome since it made Madrid a target in the event of future hostilities in the

hemisphere. It also increased the possibility of accidents at the nearby commerical air center at Barajas. The U.S. Department of Defense rejected the Spanish government's reasonable offer to relocate the American fighter wing in another less conspicuous part of Spain. As a result of the failure of the negotiations, in 1989 the Torrejón operation had to be transferred to a new location in Italy.

11. There was a popular *copla* from the time of the Napoleonic invasion that said that the *gaditanos* used the bombs the French threw at Cádiz to curl their hair.

12. A local *charanga* wrote a *cuplé* to then president Ronald Reagan incorporating similar language: "We sang to him, stating how happy we were he left. For the left here, Reagan incarnated the worst aspects of U.S. politics: conservative, right-wing, militaristic. . . .That's why in this *cuplé*, we say 'Go away, Reagan, *con todos tus muertos* [Go to hell, Reagan].'"

13. At the time of its takeover, Rumasa had liabilities of $2.9 billion dollars, and Miguel Boyer maintained he was acting to protect shareholders, bank depositors, and employees (including delinquent employee social security payments). There were fears as well for the nation's economy should bankruptcy be declared. In 1985 Ruiz-Mateos was charged with fraud and extradited from West Germany where he had fled.

Ruiz-Mateos countersued on the grounds that both the measure and the ways in which it was carried out were unconstitutional. Spanish judges, usually under the influence of the party in government, endlessly postponed the trial and eventually acquitted the government. The European tribunal for financial affairs thought otherwise and recommended that the Spanish government restore Ruiz-Mateo's properties, which has never been done. On the other hand, the government prosecuted Ruiz-Mateos and convicted him for tax evasion. He served short prison terms, interrupted by several escapes, using disguises, wigs, and doubles. He would typically escape, send postcards to government officials, prosecutors, judges, and newspapers from diverse spots in Spain, and finally turn himself in. Later he would escape again. In 1989 he won a seat as one of Spain's sixty representatives to the European Parliament. The election gave him parliamentary immunity and the warrants for his arrest were thrown out.

Ruiz-Mateos, a native of Jerez de la Frontera and a former sherry merchant, had well-known right-wing and *Opus Dei* sympathies. He had built most of his empire in the 1960s and 70s during Franco's era. (*Opus Dei* is a conservative Roman Catholic organization reputed to exercise political and religious powers.)

14. A thirty-two page illustrated article in *¡Hola!* in 1992 revealed that Boyer's luxurious mansion in the outskirts of Madrid featured an indoor pool and a heated kennel. It also had fourteen bathrooms and was therefore popularly christened Villa Meona (Piss Villa).

15. *Perro viejo*, literally "old dog": someone very experienced.

16. Paco Rosado, "Freedom vs. Expression," [Excerpts], *Diario de Cádiz*, Feb. 12, 1989, p. 8.

Chapter 12

Trebujena

Carnival in Trebujena

A final overview of carnival can be attempted in the town of Trebujena. Since the renewal of the festival in the 1960s, Trebujena has provided an imprint of the past and a guide to the future. Trebujena lies close to the capital, and similarities as well as variations of the rural and urban carnivals are clearly visible.

The town of Trebujena lies in the northwest corner of the province in the wine growing region.[1] According to oral accounts, carnival has been celebrated in Trebujena since at least the turn of the century.[2] The carnival singers of the town fell silent following Franco's prohibition in 1937, but when the carnival was renewed in the capital in the 1950s as *fiestas típicas*, Trebujena aficionados quickly found their voice. Luis de la Rosa recalls:

> In 1959, on the night before carnival, some former *murgistas* were at Cándido Borbón's bar. It had rained, as is frequent this time of the year. The grape juice was being passed around, when someone, possibly Manuel Gil, started reminiscing about the greatness of carnival in former times. José Chulán said: "I still have at home the bass drum and the snare drum from the last time we went out in carnival." Then Manolo Gil said, "If you get them right now, I'm going home for my violin to go out on the street." Chulan retorted, "Sure thing." The frying pan was hot. Soon afterwards, from the most distant corners in Trebujena one could hear the lyrics and the melodies from before the war sung by people like Antonio 'el Pantorrilla' [leg calf], el Galveta, Juaili, los Chulanes, el Venida, and others. On hearing the singing, the sergeant of the *Guardia Civil*, José Gil Guijarro, went to the bar to inquire what the din was all about. The answer was, "We were *murgistas* before the war and we are remembering the good old times. The sergeant then said, half-seriously, half-kidding, "Ok, go on, but make sure there's no trouble."[3]

After this expression of fond memories, several townspeople of Trebujena urged the mayor to obtain the permits necessary to renew the festival. The mayor and several town counselors carried their request to Cádiz to the governor of the province, while the townspeople anxiously waited in Trebujena's main square for their return. To their dismay the governor did not want to hear about the subject, and he followed up his verbal denial with a telegram reminding the town council of the prohibition against carnival. The townspeople and their representatives, however, would not accept the governor's judgment and circumvented his decision.

> They went out on the streets; they just could not restrain themselves any longer. It was all a matter of asking the mayor Ernesto Ceballo's permission, which was granted. It was this simple. The following year [1960], they came out as *Los Amantes de las Flores* (The Flower Lovers).[4]

The Carnival Costume

The carnival disguises that appeared on the streets of Trebujena lacked the elegance of the costumes worn at private parties in Cádiz. Given the postwar poverty of the rural towns, costumes were restitched from hand-me-downs and decorated by creative use of rags. Poverty was an incentive rather than a bar to invention. In the most difficult days of the dictatorship, for daily wear some *campesino* families had little more than a single change of clothes, and there were said to be some who when they washed their clothes were forced to wait in bed until these dried before they could dress again.

> The Trebujena costume – like that of surrounding towns – does not require any special materials, just a few rags that can be found in any house, wit, inventiveness, and cheek. The point of the costume is that, besides being surprising, it must stir the laughter of the observer and the wearer at the same time.
>
> The costume is one of the most important props of our festivals, and we must defend its vitality, in spite of the insistence of some sectors on using luxurious and refined costumes. That type of costume is more proper of the carnivals of Rio [de Janeiro] or [Santa Cruz de] Tenerife [on the Canary Islands], which have nothing to do with our own.[5]

As de la Rosa recalls, the most daring Trebujeneros renewed the custom of wearing disguises during the time of the latter days of the dictatorship when masks were still expressly forbidden. The Trebujena costume was a banner of opposition symbolizing the restored spirit of carnival. Masked celebrants were able to frustrate any overzealous police by virtue of the structure of many houses in the town, which allowed them to escape through a rear door that fortuitously opened on a different street than the front door entrance.

Los Pantorrillas

Two of the best-known composers of the Trebujena carnival have been the father and son known as *Los Pantorrillas* (leg calves): Antonio (Olivero Tejero) el Pantorrilla, the father, and Antonio Olivero Gómez, Pantorrilla *hijo* (son) – both workers in the vineyards of Trebujena.

During the Civil War the elder Pantorrilla had been drafted into Franco's army and had served for three years on several active fronts. In the 1930s before the war, he had composed for *murgas* and had sung on the streets. Luis de la Rosa characterized him as "a tight-lipped man" able to "express with subtlety the suffering of the people."[6] It was expected that Pantorrilla would be a leader of the revival of carnival in Trebujena in the 1960s and that his son would join him in composing for the *murgas*.

> Pantorrilla (leg calf), the father, was one of the shapers of the golden era of our carnivals. In 1959 he was in a small bar with a group of friends, and from there emerged the idea of going back into the streets to sing *coplillas* from before the war. He knew the carnival well, since he had participated in *murgas* in the 1930s along with those who were already veterans at that time. . ..[7]

The younger Pantorrilla, Antonio Olivero Gómez, recalled:

> "When carnival was reestablished in 1959, he started writing *coplas* and coming out in carnival. In 1959, that first year, I was twenty. It was two years before I went to military service. I was born in 1939, after my father got out of the army. *Los Amantes de las Flores* was the first *murga*. My father wrote the *coplas*, and I helped him a little. We

both wrote *coplas*. Some of the lyrics we sang were by him, some were by me. One thinks up the *coplas* in the country, at work. Then it's a matter of sitting at home and writing them."

The process of composition began with the melody rather than the words:

"We always do the music first. The music provides the melody, the rhythm, the cuts, the stops, the parts where the singers come in again. . .All this must be rehearsed before writing. Every year the music differs, so one has to start anew. The number of lines in the *coplas* changes depending on the music. Shortly after the carnival is over, we start to think up the music for the following year. Another fellow in the group usually makes up the music. In April or May, we start making up the music, bit by bit. When we have all the music, we record it on a tape, and then I write the lyrics. Before we had tape recorders, I had to learn it all by heart."

As Luis de la Rosa observed: "The 'saga' of the 'Pantorrillas' is a true institution in the Trebujena carnival."[8] From 1960 to 1974, corresponding to what is considered to be the golden age of carnival in Trebujena, the two Pantorrillas composed for nineteen singing groups, usually sang with them, and frequently served as director as well. From 1979 to 1991, Antonio the son composed for and appeared with seven additional groups. The elder Pantorrilla rarely sang in the street after 1973. He passed away in 1983 at the age of seventy-two, leaving his son to carry on the family tradition alone.

Trebujena and Cádiz

Since Trebujena lies close to Cádiz, its carnival was revitalized in the shadow of the capital city. In 1967 the equation changed when officials shifted the *fiestas típicas* to the springtime to attract greater numbers of tourists. Townships were prohibited from celebrating at the customary midwinter term. Subsequently they were discouraged from holding matching festivities in the spring. Officials feared that winter celebrations would undermine their arbitrary reordering of the ancient calendar, while a carnival-like spring festival would compete with the revelry ordered in the capital. For commercial considerations, rather than from political motivations, carnival once again was in danger of becoming moribund.

Trebujena ignored calls for restraint and conformity. While Benalup, like most of the other towns, bent to the will of the capital and for a time simply stopped celebrating carnival, Trebujena, less submissive and less fearful, hewed to the traditional pre-Lenten schedule. As a result, those disappointed by the disappearance of the midwinter carnival in Cádiz, flocked to the nearby wine-growing town to celebrate in the old-fashioned way. Unlike the capital, where singing groups were quickly captured for private parties, the carnival in Trebujena remained in the street.

> According to the testimonies of the elders in the town, before the war the carnivals were not celebrated with parties in closed locales, as in Cádiz, where everything seems to have started with bourgeois festivals. From this it follows that the authentic carnival in Trebujena is a manifestation of the people, the *campesinos*, who have no other way to express their feelings and ideas.[9]

Trebujena became recognized by celebrants and by the press as the site of the "authentic carnival."[10] Crowds began to appear in Trebujena at carnival time. Visitors included not only those from neighboring towns and from more distant points, but also frustrated *comparsistas* from the capital itself. Traffic piled up at the entrance to Trebujena, the taverns were so packed they had to close their doors, and the governor was required to order in extra guards to provide security.[11] The festival attracted a wide variety of people who liked to dress up for the occasion.

> "Something curious is the fact that all the homosexuals from Cádiz used to come to the carnival in Trebujena. Cádiz has a reputation for there being many homosexuals. Since costumes were forbidden in Cádiz, homosexuals used to come here, not only from the city but from all over the province. I remember as a child that this was something to see; there was nothing but gays in drag in the streets. Our mothers would tell us: 'You are not going out at night, because the town is full of queers.' There was a famous queen from Trebujena who used to live in Madrid, and he always came to town during carnivals, bringing with him ten or twelve friends from Madrid. They all dressed in drag, in very high heels, big asses, big breasts, heavy make-up, and with these big wigs. This was during the mid-sixties

to early seventies, year after year, until the strike discontinued the carnival." (Diego Caro Cancela)

The Close of an Era

The town's special notoriety continued for seven years from 1967 to 1974, when local conflicts caused the carnival celebration to be canceled.

> Beginning in 1975 the festivals were not celebrated for four years, a gap which made them lose some of their popularity. The causes for this break are not very clear: some say local authorities decided not to celebrate carnival for economic reasons; others say it was for political reasons. Apparently both versions are true.
>
> The vineyard workers strike of 1969 and its long-range consequences contributed to this climate of opposition. According to prevailing rumors, some had stated that one cannot feed the people with festivals. To top it off, part of the curtains of the queen's throne caught fire (it was not known whether it had been arson or an accident). Already in 1974 there was some controversy between the left and the town council regarding the goal of the festivals. All this led the mayor, José Alcalá González, to cancel the celebrations for fear that something might happen, and for lack of economic resources.[12]

Enthusiasm for carnival remained dampened until 1979. By that time the political scene had been transformed. A new national election would soon settle the composition of the government. Carnivals were now celebrated widely. This new freedom changed the constituency of the spectators attending the festival: when carnival resumed in Trebujena in 1979, the tide of homosexuals did not return.

> "In earlier years they were harassed and prosecuted by the police, so they took advantage of carnival to come out and show themselves in public. It wasn't only a matter of personal liberation, but also a chance to make themselves visible. Since this problem doesn't exist today, gays don't need to wait until carnival to show themselves. When carnival was celebrated again, in 1979, they didn't need to come to Trebujena to get in drag and parade the streets; they could do this anywhere they wanted to, in Cádiz or in their own towns." (Diego Caro Cancela)

The Vineyards of Trebujena

Most of the land of Trebujena is devoted to raising grapes. There are some cereal crops grown, but unlike Benalup there are very few *dehesas* (pastures for cattle). Most of the town's population of approximately 6,000 inhabitants are vineyard workers.[13] Agricultural work, however, is seasonal and limited to only a few months each year. In recent decades increased mechanization has permanently eliminated many agricultural chores, from cultivating the land to gathering the pruned vine shoots (*sarmentar*). Other tasks in the vineyards, however, still require skilled workers. Pruning the vines (*podar*), thinning (*castrar*), and grafting (*injertar*) can be done only by workers practiced in the agricultural arts. In Andalusia, to avoid the repetition of the destructive phylloxera epidemic of 1894 which wiped out European vines, varieties imported from California are planted which are stronger and more resistant to disease. For the taste of Jerez, local vines are later grafted on to them. Care of the vines requires knowledge, experience, and skill. Only the grape harvest (*vendimia*) can be done by relatively unskilled hands.

Workers in Trebujena complain that, as in all of Andalusia, most of the wealth of the community is in the hands of a very few. A member of the Communist local describes the common view of the workers, irrespective of party affiliation:

> "Four men own everything in the city and in the town. They have cars, chalets, vacations, and we have nothing. They own the land and do nothing with it. The land is empty and all they can do is ride across it for days." (Magalón)

Unlike most of Andalusia, however, much of the land surrounding Trebujena is divided into numerous small lots. As of the census of 1981, out of the township's 549 *fincas* (estates or agricultural properties), the overwhelming majority (472 fincas) comprise less than five hectares. The numbers break off sharply for slightly larger holdings (so that only thirty-nine families own between 5 and 10 hectares, and but twenty-five possess between 10 and 25 hectares). Just four estates are larger than 100 hectares, and of these only two run more than 250 hectares. (One estate, Alventud, is over 1,000 hectares, but this includes a considerable amount of marsh land.)[14]

The large number of small holdings does not mean that poverty and underemployment, endemic to the countryside, have been eliminated. During the 1960s and 1970s, emigration to other nations of Western Europe was required to survive. Antonio Olivera recalls:

"I was an emigrant worker for more than twenty years: I used to go to France to harvest beets for a few weeks every year. I went on my own and left my family here. Nowadays there's no more emigration."

A small plot cannot generate sufficient income to sustain a family. Low income and lack of work plagues Trebujena as it does every town in Andalusia and Spain in general. The small properties, however, provide a small measure of security. Workers cultivate and nurture their tiny plots on weekends. Some who own but cannot work their plots establish a sharecropping arrangement with others.

"People who work the vines usually own their own land, or they work the land of others for half the harvest. This is called *medianía*. Almost all the families own their own vines, though. Out of a thousand families in the town, at the most two or three hundred have neither land nor *medianías*. Nowadays very few *campesinos* are bad off here in Trebujena. Those who have neither land nor work live on unemployment pay. In this sense, the country here is very different from Casas Viejas, for example. All the land here is tilled." (Diego Caro Cancela)[15]

A wine cooperative was founded in 1957, with some help from the government, to purchase and market the harvest of small growers. The cooperative now has about seven hundred associates. There is a president, a treasurer, and a ruling committee of ten or twelve members. In good years the grapes produced on the small plots supplement the workers' income, but the good years are more than balanced by bad seasons and other problems related to market prices.

Antonio Olivera el Pantorrilla is an associate of the cooperative. The elder Pantorrilla had purchased half a hectare of land which after his death in 1983 passed to his son. In common with the other small growers, Pantorrilla the son continues to labor for wages in the vineyards and to tend his own vines in his free time.

"My father left the land to me. I have half a hectare where I grow vines. I sell the grapes to the wine cooperative in town. The cooperative doesn't want to buy it this year [1989], though, because they still haven't sold last year's produce. The market has been pretty weak lately."

Coplas of *Los Pantorrillas*

The most memorable *coplas* of the Pantorrillas, father and son, reflect the enduring poverty and repressed anger of the workers. In the year 1983 both Pantorrillas contributed to the songs of Los Príncipes del Cuento (The Princes of the Tale). Some lines we cite here:

. . .	. . .
It is so sad to see so many poor men	que da pena ver tantos pobres,
always embittered, weeping and crying,	siempre amargaos, entre llantos y clamores
when the fields of Andalusia are so rich.	siendo tan ricos los campos de Andalucía.
. . .	. . .
Even though they are not good, strikes are necessary	A pesar de no ser buena es necesaria la huelga
on some occasions.	en algunas ocasiones
If it weren't for them,	pues si no fuera por ellas
the agreements would just be piled up on some corner.	estarían los convenios amontonaos en los rincones.
They would have trampled on us often,	A la nuestra ya le habrian dao
thousands of times.	dos mil pisotones.
I'll never be able	Nunca podré,
to forget those moments	olvidar aquellos momentos
when the whole town was gathered in the square	cuando el pueblo se encontraba
under a melting sun	bajo aquel sol que derretía
confronting the armed forces.	frente a las fuerzas armadas.
. . .	. . .
I don't even want	Yo no quiero,
to think about it,	no quisiera pensarlo
that we may go back again	que otra vez volvamos
to those bitter times	a aquellos tiempos de sinsabores

when my siblings and I, naked,	cuando en cuerecitos lo mismos que mis hermanos
used to eat acorns by a fire of vine-wood.	comía bellotas junto a un fuego de chapores.

The elder Pantorrilla passed away later in the same year. The following year, 1984, there were no songs from *Los Pantorrillas*.

At times, Pantorrilla the son didn't come out during carnivals. Sometimes because of family problems – like when his father died; other times, because he didn't like the fact that the bars closed due to the huge carnival crowds; and on another occasion, because of the events in the contest of 1981. Eventually, he always went back to the street, because he knew he could not simply give up. It was, in a certain way, his life.[16]

Socialists and Communists

When Franco died in 1975 there was no party apparatus representing the left in Trebujena. The anarchist movement, which had enjoyed the support of the *campesinos* before the Civil War, failed to regain a significant following. Anarchist refusal to accept the existence of a central government or the need for an army or police, made the movement appear as an anachronism. The anarchists' inability to compromise, their refusal to participate in elections, their loose organization, and their failure to develop a political wing, made it impossible for them to win a foothold in the new democracy.

With the virtual demise of the anarchist movement, the workers of Trebujena had to choose between the Communist and Socialist parties. Many of the offspring of former anarchosyndicalists, the *campesinos* and rural workers, in a dramatic turnaround, now identified themselves as militant communists.[17] Forgotten were the ideological differences between communists and anarchists, and communist betrayal in the waning days of the Spanish Civil War, when faced with the certainty of the Republic's defeat, Stalinists treacherously shot down anarchist leaders to eliminate any threat to their future dominance. Instead, the communists were remembered for having continued the struggle against Franco. Outspoken and aggressive on matters of workers' rights and unemployment, communists were an immediate presence in 1975 and they held a commanding position of leadership of the left. The Communist Party, PCE – PCA (*Partido Comunista Español – Partido Comunista Andaluz*) was now the party of the majority of the vineyard workers of Trebujena.

> "The Communist Party had been functioning during Franco's time. In Trebujena, Francisco Cabrán, a *campesino* leader, had organized worker strikes during Franco's years. They had very few members until Franco's death in 1975. They started to organize the Communist Party in 1975, and it was therefore the first party to become organized. Since the Communist Party had been functioning all those years, it attracted the majority of the people in the town. In the first democratic elections of 1977, the Communist Party in Trebujena had one of the highest percentages in the country. One reason for this was that one of the candidates to Congress for Trebujena was Francisco Cabrán, the peasant leader. In 1977 practically everybody was communist in Trebujena. The communists came to power here [in the township] in 1979." (Diego Caro Cancela.)

The political struggle in the town between the communists and socialists engaged everyone's attention. The competition for adherents assumed an importance similar to the ideological rivalries before the war. Most members of the communist local were, however, like the anarchists they superceded, *inocentes*. They knew nothing of communist principles, plans for industry and agriculture, profits and wages, or the deeds of Lenin and Stalin. The courage of local leaders to protest proved to be more influential than party philosophy and international icons.

The enlarged *centro* of the local Communist Party became a popular nesting place for workers. The commodious room on the first floor contains a long bar, tables and chairs for cards and dominoes, and a television. A large fireplace gives the room a comfortable look, besides helping to reduce the winter moisture. An assembly room in the back serves for meetings (and for the performance of carnival songs). Upstairs, out of the way, are the business offices, mimeograph machines, and typewriters. A news bulletin (*Onda Roja*) is issued each month. Members pay monthly dues of 200 *pesetas*, but anyone is welcome to enter and there are people present with a range of views on the left.

Los Pantorrillas, father and son, while expressing the views of the workers in their *coplas*, remained on the periphery of politics. During the Civil War, Antonio the father had been drafted into the army and forced to fight for Franco. As his son Antonio explains:

> "My father was a *campesino*, like me. He fought the war on Franco's side. He avoided the military service for years, but when the war broke out, he finally had to go. He fought all over Spain for the three years of the Civil War; he was often relocated to wherever the front moved. He used to tell me about the war. He was a good man. He never spoke about politics; he didn't understand it. He was always out in the country, working the land. That was his thing – that and the carnival *coplas*, which he enjoyed the most.
>
> "He was a normal man, a pretty good man, always a hard worker. He was good to my mother, my sister and myself. He was well-liked in the town. I did not want to work the land. He tried to give me an education, and I went to the local public school until I had to stop and help my father to work the land. I was fourteen when I started to help my father in the fields."

Although he never committed himself to any political cause, the younger Pantorrilla was drawn to the party that attracted most of the vineyard workers.

> My father was a very independent man and didn't belong to any political party. I'm not interested in politics either, but I've liked the Communist Party a lot. It's a party of workers. But don't ask me anything about politics, because I don't know anything about it."

Partido Socialista Obrero Español (PSOE)

There were few socialists left in Trebujena at the time of Franco's death in 1975, and it took two to three years for the *Partido Socialista Obrero Español* (PSOE) to regain its strength in the town. Municipal power then seesawed back and forth between the socialists and communists. The Communist Party won the municipal elections in Trebujena in 1979 and again in 1983. Although the national elections were captured by the PSOE in 1982, municipal leadership in Trebujena eluded the socialists until 1987 when the Socialist Party won a narrow victory over the local Communist Party by just sixty-two votes.[18]

Township election results usually turn on commonplace matters rather than on ideological or broad political issues. The defeat of the communists in Trebujena in 1987 reflected differing attitudes toward a long-standing local tradition that cut across religion and politics. The conflict concerned the plaza de San Antonio in the paseo de Andalucía. It was the centerpiece of village life, and a communist project creating restrictions for pedestrians and traffic could not be tolerated.

> "This street has traditionally been part of the route of funeral processions on the way to the cemetery. It is also traversed by the Virgin de Palomares, the patroness of the town, when she is carried to her country chapel during town festivals. The Communist Party, then in power, decided to create closed space and cut the traffic. They did the same for burials and processions. Then everybody protested. Even CP members said traditions had to be respected. Some even said that when they died they wanted to be carried through this plaza, whether it was open to traffic or not. The image of the Virgin was carried through this plaza during the town festivals even though the street had been closed. All this shows deeply rooted sentiments. Besides, the communist project was very ugly. We [socialists] said that if we won, we would open this area to circulation again, and I think this position may have won us a few votes. On a more practical level, this street was the main traffic artery in the town. Once blocked, the traffic had to be detoured all over town. The Communist Party thought that no matter what they did, they would always govern this town; therefore, they made decisions that didn't respect local customs and traditions." (Diego Caro Cancela.)

When the socialists returned to power in Trebujena in 1987, they repaired the street and for good measure began the construction of a small edifice on the plaza containing a fountain. The work was delayed for many years and became the butt of jokes. It is usually referred to as *el santuario de San Antonio* and turns on the fact that Antonio, the mayor, had studied for the priesthood when he was a boy.

The Socialist Agenda

The principal agenda of the socialists concerned plans to reclaim the marshland of the nearby Guadalquivir River and to develop cooperatives to farm it. In this program they had the support of the town communists.

The land of the marshes by the Guadalquivir belongs to the Junta [township government]. On this particular topic, the communists agree with us. (Diego Caro Cancela.)

The design proposed for cooperatives bears a resemblance to the government-based programs of the defeated Spanish Republic.[19] The largest *cortijo* in the township, Alventud, which contains significant marshlands, is slated for expropriation. The soil will be expunged of salt and the land then divided into lots to be distributed among cooperatives. The cooperatives will have various bylaws and stipulations concerning rent and work. Tenants will be provided with long-term leases. Neither the individual farmers nor the cooperatives will have ownership of the land, which will be retained by the government.

A cooperative is made up of eight or nine families, and will receive ten hectares of land to be cultivated by these families. The cooperatives will later merge in order to sell the harvest, as the cotton cooperative does in Lebrija. These lots are distributed according to family income, number of children, and employment status. With a lot of land, a family can make 1,500,000, or even two million *pesetas* a year. The families who will cultivate the new lands by the Guadalquivir will pay a modest, almost symbolic, rent to the government. The property will not be theirs. It is leased to them, and the leases will be renewed indefinitely provided that certain conditions are respected: the families must work the land properly, they must remain part of the cooperative, and so on. If they do not fulfill these conditions, they lose the lease on the land, which is then given to other families. (Diego Caro Cancela.)[20]

The cooperatives are vastly dissimilar to the system of collectives once advanced by the anarchosyndicalists. The anarchists would have had the *campesinos* of the collective work the land in common, and then barter and trade goods with other collectives as needed. In contrast to the anarchist system of control by the collectives, both socialists and communists continue to rely on the state as the central agent of change and governance.

The anarchosyndicalists have quite a different idea, but they do not exist here any more. They were in favor of having collective property – like a Soviet kolkhos." (Diego Caro Cancela)

The local communists, who have a streak of political independence not unlike their counterparts in Italy, have learned to
temper their voices:

> "We're not for revolution as in the past. We respect the democracy,
> but we have to change from the few who own everything. We would
> work the land. We would divide the land into cooperatives and work
> it." (Magalón)

On national issues, the great majority of the workers of
Trebujena, socialists and communists, have been united and often
at odds with the rest of Spain. In 1986, for example, when Spain
voted to join the North Atlantic Treaty Organization (NATO), 75
percent of the votes in Trebujena were against the *referéndum*.

Carnival Changes in Trebujena

Shortly before the elections of 1979, the communists won a march
on the socialists by deciding to revitalize the carnival. At that point
the festival had had a hiatus of five years. Although the town
council of Trebujena agreed to permit the revival, they declined to
be involved in it. The townspeople, however, were ignited by the
agreement and five singing groups prepared repertoires to go out
on the street. This new beginning in a now democratic country
would introduce many innovations in the Trebujena carnival, as
Luis de la Rosa recounts:

a) Censorship was abandoned in favor of new norms of freedom of
   speech.
b) New rules were introduced to choose the "First Maid of Carnival,"
   although it was still popularly called "Queen."
c) String instruments were used for the first time, in imitation of the
   groups from Cádiz.
d) *Murgas* and *comparsas* were sponsored by the town hall for the first
   time.
e) The parade was emphasized.
f) The traditional *murga* died out, while *comparsas* and *chirigotas*
   gained strength.
g) Small groups appeared.
h) The festivals became longer due to the organization of a costume
   ball.[21]

Innovations were usually counterbalanced by tradition and engrained habits. Although censorship was declared eliminated, for example, for a time the groups continued to submit their songs to officials for review.

New styles, Luis de la Rosa observed, had transformed the singing groups and shifted attention from the *murga* to *chirigotas* and *comparsas*, with greater attention on musical accompaniment and choral part-harmonies.

In the old carnivals most groups were *murgas*; nowadays, there are more *comparsas* and *chirigotas*, which has resulted in a certain loss of identity.[22]

A costume ball, previously privately organized, became an accepted municipal activity. A contest for carnival queen became standard fare. The final parade, which heretofore had been composed of the *murgas* followed helter skelter by the children of the town, was now given special importance as an organized pageant, with prizes awarded for the most outstanding floats and costumes. Children always played a part in the *murgas*. A young boy often accompanied the group. He carried the group's songs on sheets of paper or printed in a booklet, and he emulated the leader in conducting the singing. The carnival concluded in a traditional vein with the burning of the straw image of Piti the witch, as always dressed in black and with a broom.

Despite the restored vigor of the festival, long-time participants maintained that the carnival would never again reach the intensity and the importance of the celebration of 1967 and the few years following when Trebujena stood in the place of the capital and kept carnival in tune with the traditional calendar.

"Corazón de Hielo" (Heart of Ice)

In 1988 Antonio Olivero Gómez el Pantorrilla, the son, composed the songs for the *comparsa "Corazón de Hielo"* (Heart of Ice) with Eskimos as the central symbolic figures. The judges of the capital *concurso* of 1988 rewarded the singers of *"Corazón de Hielo"* with a place in the semifinals ahead of hundreds of other groups. Listeners recognized that these were the songs of a *campesino* poet who expressed the problems and the pain of the people of the pueblo.

Sweat,	Sudores
we have to sweat a lot	tenemos que derramar sudores
to get a piece of bread to eat.	para comernos un trozo de pan
The sweat of the miners	los del minero
falls among the rocks.	entre las piedras están
The sweat of the boatmen	los del barquero
falls into the waves of the sea.	en las olas del mar
Tell me, good plowman,	y dime tú buen labrador
tell me, good plowman,	y dime tú buen labrodor
how many times your brow	cuántas veces tu frente
must have been drenched,	se habrá encharcao mojando
wetting the handle of your hoe	el cabo de tu azuela o de tu
or spade.	azadón
The sweat of the laborer who	el que labra la viña
cultivates the vines,	
of the worker in the mines, the	el de la mina y el camionero
truck driver,	
the fisherman who gathers	el que va por coquinas
shellfish,	
the sailor and the woodsman.	el marinero y el leñador
Sweat	sudores
comes from their entrails,	le salen de sus entrañas
sweat	sudores
drips on their land.	que por su tierra derrama
Sweat,	sudores
but how badly paid that sweat	pero que mal se lo pagan
is,	
because in this blessed nation	porque en esta santa nación
those who don't work	el que come y vive mejor
are the ones who eat and drink	es quien no trabaja
the best,	
and it just breaks our heart	y te rompes el corazón
when a guy in an armchair	cuando a un tío en un sillón
wants to live on our sweat.	queriendo vivir de tu sudor.
How bitter,	Qué amargo
how bitter it is to wake up,	qué amargo es despertar
how bitter,	qué amargo
and not to have enough for	y no tener para desayunar
breakfast,	
see your little girl	ver tu pequeña
hugging the pillow,	que abraza la almohada
and hear your young boy	y al mayorcillo
asking for milk and bread.	que pide leche y pan
You know this better than I,	lo sabe usted mejor que yo

You know this better than I,	lo sabe usted mejor que yo
forgive me, my president,	mi señor presidente y usted perdone
but the poor man cries in anger and pain	que el pobre
when he doesn't have anything to eat.	cuando no tiene llora de rabia y dolor,
We don't doubt that being born poor	no ponemos en duda
may be natural law.	que nacer pobre sea ley de vida
But why,	pero por qué esa ley
if we are all born naked,	si en cueros al mundo venimos todos
life,	la vida
for those who are being born poor,	para los que nacen pobres
life	la vida
has no value and no name,	no tiene valor ni nombre
life	la vida
is for your gentleman	es para ustedes señores
who can toast with champagne	que podéis brindar con champán
while thousands of other Spaniards	mientras están pidiéndole pan
are begging for bread.	miles de españoles
With this situation, you are going to succeed in making	y con esto vais a lograr
a free Spain	que una España con libertad
break up again in two halves.	se rompa otra vez en dos mitad.

With a few strokes Antonio could also satirize the tortured sentiments of someone who could kiss a dog on his behind and in the next breath put a man in jail.

Cuplé

Be careful, oh, oh,	Tenga cuidado señor, ojú, ojú,
when you drive, sir,	al circular
don't run a stop sign, oh, oh,	y no se salte un stop, ojú, ojú,
don't kid around.	por chulear
The other day a guy killed a little dog	que el otro día un cachondo mató a un perrito
when the little animal wanted to pee.	cuando el animalito quería mear
When the old spinster (who owned the dog) saw	cuando vio la solterona

her little doggie lying on the ground	a su perrito en el suelo
her hair stuck stiff	como el bigote de una foca
like a seal's moustache.	se le pusieron los pelos
She kissed the little dog beside the tail.	besando a su perrito junto a la cola
With her hair down and her sleeves rolled up,	con el cabello suelto y arremangá
she told a policeman:	le decía a guardia
"Throw him in jail.	métalo en chirona
It is the fault of a guy	que por culpa de un gachó
that once again I have to sleep alone."	tengo otra vez que dormir sola.

Antonio explained his personal style of writing:

> "The *coplas* vary depending on the type of *comparsa* one writes for.
> My coplas are more personal, more like expressions of my life. When
> I write them, I can feel them in my heart. There has to be feeling in
> what one writes. And the *coplas* have to make people feel that what
> one talks about has happened. Like when I make a *pasodoble* about a
> mother who lost a child, or about a catastrophe with many casualties,
> I have to feel it. And then the people who listen to it have to feel it
> too.
>
> I don't like joking around and making fun of things in the *coplas* so
> much. I also write about work. I'm not a very serious person, but the
> *pasodoble* is serious. The *cuplé* is more obscene. The *cuplé* is merely a
> small fragment that makes people laugh. Nowadays, it's harder to
> make people laugh, though."

City and Town

The *Cádiz concurso* is part of a carnival interchange between the
capital and the towns of the province. For the *concurso*, the most
adventurous groups from nearby San Fernando and Puerto Real,
as well as more distant Trebujena, Ubrique, Benalup, and elsewhere, bring their songs and voices to the capital hoping to place
well in the contest. They must impress listeners and judges with
their artistic skill, their sophistication, and the quality of their lyrics.
It is frequently charged, however, that it is virtually impossible to
snatch a prize in the jealously guarded local hierarchy. Antonio
Olivera is well aware of the odds:

"Almost every year the groups who make the finals in the Falla contest are from Cádiz. I think the judges are prejudiced against people from other towns outside Cádiz."

Groups from the capital have obvious advantages. Those in the capital usually set the standards that others must follow. The use of stringed instruments to accompany the singers and complex harmonies were experienced first in the city and then were carried into the rural areas. Opportunities for competition, training, and honing one's skills are greater in the city than in the towns. Rural festivals are usually marked by simpler traditions:

"We [in Trebujena] don't have guitars, and Cádiz does. We don't have a *concurso*. We had it one year and there were too many arguments. We don't sing in harmony as they do in the city. We sing in one voice. We don't dress in elegant costumes but make them from hand-me-downs. (Juan A. Cordero Moyano)

Two Audiences

Antonio was well aware that he now wrote for two masters: the townspeople of Trebujena and the city dwellers in the capital. It was difficult to satisfy both. City audiences expect carnival singers to speak to themes of national interest and to cite in their songs the famous or the infamous who have already won notoriety in the press and on television. Townsmen can chronicle the antics of neighbors and draw on the gossip of the market place and the café concerning seductions, pregnancies, and late marriages; however, since the individuals involved are unknown outside the town, their affairs are of little interest to the city dweller. He has to face the question, as one writer put it, "What happens here to report on?" Antonio Olivero recalls:

"I started writing a *piropo* (compliment) which turned into a joke. It's a *copla* about women who are big and have started walking around town a whole lot to lose weight, but after they are done walking, they go home and eat their fill. So walking around so much doesn't help them very much.

"These are *coplas* in the old style. People like this old style in *coplas*. People like *coplas* about things that happen in town; but there is little to say about the town. Not too many things happen here. Elderly people are usually the ones who want to hear the same old things in the *coplas*."

Both writer and audience, he adds, are more mobile than in past times.

> "When the carnival is over in Trebujena, the *comparsas* are invited to go to Arcos, or Jerez, Chiclana, El Puerto, Puerto Real, Sanlúcar. That's why we don't really start to do anything for the following year's carnival until April or May. Then I write about whatever happens during the year. I compose the songs as things happen. If a girl in town got pregnant, it used to be a subject for carnival jokes. Now this sort of thing doesn't shock anybody anymore. Some people still make fun of this type of thing, though. We have almost always talked about the same things: the workers, things that have happened in town. The songs are different from year to year, but the topics are very similar."
>
> "In recent years we have started imitating Cádiz, bringing up national news in the *coplas*. Before, people didn't go to Cádiz as much. We were always here. Nowadays people go to Cádiz. They leave [our] town. Nowadays the *comparsas* also go to El Puerto, Cádiz, and elsewhere. And we must talk in the *coplas* about things people know about. This year, for example, we have been rehearsing six months for something – in order to leave town, to go to other contests, and become known outside of Trebujena."

To appear to be as cosmopolitan and well-informed as their urban counterparts, carnival composers from the towns are under pressure to reject rural themes in favor of subjects with national notoriety and to enlist images and details that show them to be sophisticated and clever in their art. Confronted with the same problem years before, Manolo Lago of Benalup decided to remain with his own vision of circumstances in his town (see chapter 6, p. 116.) He saw the carnival as his opportunity to express himself on local matters. Antonio Olivero moved in the opposite direction: to open his *coplas* to events outside his pubelo and to reach a wider audience throughout the province.

Jaque Mate (Checkmate)

In the Cádiz *concurso* of 1989, Antonio Olivero's *comparsa* was singled out for attention in the newspaper *Diario de Cádiz*.[23]

The *comparsa Jaque Mate* [Checkmate] from Trebujena, represented with its *tipo* a chessboard and pieces. They came to the contest last year as *Corazón de Hielo*, and they made it to the semifinals. They hope to repeat such an achievement this year, or, as its director Manuel Ramírez stated, to go even further in the contest.

This is the third year that the *comparsa* comes to the Cádiz contest. They have been taking part in the carnivals of Trebujena for nine years and in the contest of El Puerto for six. The group needs money, and their main sources of income are their carnival performances in the bars and discos of Trebujena, where they pass the hat after each performance.[24]

To command the attention of a more sophisticated audience, Antonio utilized chess, a game he had never played, as a metaphor for public struggles for power:

The more I think about chess	Lo pienso más cada vez
the more I realize	viéndolo sobre el tablero
that there is something in common	que el juego del ajedrez
between the game of chess	con el mundo del obrero
and the world of the workers.	algo en común puede haber
Black and white chess pieces	blancas y negras a la vez
move at the same time.	se van moviendo
and study each other	y se estudian a su vez
so as not to fall.	por no caer
Sometimes it takes a month	tal vez un mes
to make a move	para mover
because a false step	porque un falso movimiento
would cause the pawns	hará que en cualquier momento
on both sides	vayan cayendo poquito a poco
to start to fall one by one at any moment,	los peones de un lado y de otro
while the bigger pieces remain standing.	mientras sus figuras están de pie
Tell me if it is not true	diga si no es
that this is a game of kings and queens	un juego de reina y de reyes
where the pawns always lose	donde es el peón quien pierde
regardless of their color.	porque su color no importa
But why is it that the pawns	pero ¿por qué han de ser los peones
always suffer	los que siempre sufran las
defeat?	derrotas?

The desire to please his larger audience, however, could not tame Antonio's views of the social struggle nor temper his criticism of the deployment of nuclear submarines at the American naval base in the nearby town of Rota.

Life is a checkmate	La vida es jaque mate
between the poor and the	entre pobre y burgués
bourgeois.	
Listen to me,	Escúchame
my beautiful land,	mi tierra hermosa
neither Yankees nor missiles	ni misiles ni yanquis
will make you any prettier.	te harán maravillosa
And let me tell you	y sepa usted
another thing;	otra cosa
what will happen to my Cádiz	ahora que va a ser de mi Cádiz
if Rota explodes.	si explota Rota.
I let free	Eché a volar la paloma
the dove I raised.	que yo criaba
It flew across your skies;	voló surcando tu cielo
it kissed the foam of the waters	besó la espuma del agua
of your raging sea.	de tu mar brava
I put a message in its beak,	Puse un mensaje en su pico
just two words:	simplemente dos palabras:
peace and hope.	paz y esperanza.

As always Antonio Olivera expressed the community's cynicism concerning government plans to alleviate unemployment:

It was said in my city	Lo dijo en mi ciudad
by the president of our Junta[25]	el señor presidente de nues
that there's nothing quite like	que como Cáiz no hay ná
Cádiz,	
and that this little corner of	y que este rinconcito era
Andalusia	
is the best place in Europe.	era lo mejor de Europa
But we all knew	pero todos sabíamos
that it was just talk,	que aquello era un pegote
because all the towns	porque todos los pueblos
under his jurisdiction	que entraban en su lote
have already one hundred	ya tiene cien paraos por cada
unemployed	pelo
for each hair in his moustache.	que tiene su bigote.

Parting

Despite the *comparsa's* acceptance in the capital, some old-timers of Trebujena expressed disappointment that the songs Antonio wrote for *Jaque Mate* were too general, that they were about matters of interest in the capital, and that they did not contain sufficient news of the pueblo. They missed references to townspeople and more familiar local themes. Their complaints discouraged the singers of *Jaque Mate*, who then nursed grievances of their own against the town. Antonio too sensed the loss of contact with some of the older townsmen who were unwilling to accept the need for new themes in carnival songs. A few were unwilling to move beyond the cobbled streets of the pueblo, he said:

> "People in Trebujena hardly even clap when we sing. They tell you it's all very pretty and that's it, but they don't mark the beat with their clapping. In Cádiz they clap in the theater. People here [in Trebujena] don't appreciate the singing very much."

Antonio now measures his talent by his place in the *concurso* of the capital city, by the plaudits he receives in other towns, and by the empathy of his fellow townsmen. He continues to express the concerns of the pueblo in his songs even as he searches for new subjects to interest a larger and more cosmopolitan audience. As happens every year when carnival time arrives, this vineyard worker assumes a traditional and grander identity. He is an inspired poet who speaks for himself and his pueblo. The streets of Trebujena provide the theater and the carnival costume his Muse and inspiration.

A moonlit night,	Noche de luna
singing and a disguise:	cante y un disfraz
such is the cradle	así es la cuna
of our carnival.	de nuestro carnaval

Notes

1. Trebujena is far older than Benalup. In 1494, to encourage settlement after the Reconquest, the Duke of Medina Sidonia gave Trebujena its municipal deed and its independence from Sanlúcar de Barrameda.

   Trebujena townsmen participated in the activities of the Federación Regional Española in the latter part of the nineteenth century. In January 1892, armed with hoes and clubs, workers from the towns around Jerez, including Trebujena, participated in the march on the city to decry social conditions and to protest the imprisonment of their *compañeros*. See Jerome R. Mintz, *The Anarchists of Casas Viejas*, pp. 22–5, especially notes 8–10. See also Temma Kaplan, *Anarchists of Andalusia, 1868–1903* (Princeton: Princeton University Press, 1977); Manuel M. Cañas Moya, et al, *Trebujena, Los Pueblos de la Provincia de Cádiz* (Cádiz: *Diputación de Cádiz*, n.d.), pp. 78–87.
2. Luis de la Rosa, *¡¡Esto es Carnaval!! Breve Historia del Carnaval de Trebujena* (Trebujena, Cádiz, 1992), pp. 16–17.
3. Ibid., pp. 27–8.
4. Ibid., p. 77. A second *murga*, *Los Reaparecidos* (The Reappeared), also came out that first year under the leadership of Pepe la Gordita.
5. Ibid., pp. 51–3.
6. Ibid., p. 77.
7. Ibid., p. 77.
8. Ibid., p. 77.
9. Ibid., p. 58.
10. Ibid., pp. 51–3.
11. Ibid., pp. 29–36. The author notes that there was widespread coverage in the press. The cover of the *ABC* of February 25, 1971, printed two pictures (the pageant of the carnival queen and the burning of the witch Pitti) under the headline, "The Trebujena Festivals."
12. Luis de la Rosa, *Breve Historia del Carnaval de Trebujena*, p. 45.
13. In December 1981, the population of Trebujena was 6,287 inhabitants. Population growth is relatively slow: in 1970 the population was listed as 5,857, an increase of only 430 over the course of a decade. See Manuel M. Cañas Moya, *Trebujena*, p. 101.

14. Ibid., p. 116.
15. Diego Caro Cancela served as a Socialist councilman of Trebujena. He is a professor of history at the University of Cádiz.
16. Luis de la Rosa, *Breve Historia del Carnaval de Trebujena*, p. 77.
17. As early as 1921, visits by anarchists such as Ángel Pestaña, the secretary of the CNT, to the Soviet Union, warned of the loss of freedom in the acquisition of absolute power by the Bolsheviks. During the Spanish Civil War, although they were ostensibly allies against Franco, the anarchists and communists had been deadly foes.
18. PSOE, 1897 votes; PCE, 1835 votes; and AP [Alianza Popular, the conservative party], 257. (In 1989 the Alianza Popular was absorbed by the Partido Popular representing the center-right.)
19. Only four estates have more than 101 hectares. (See Manuel M. Cañas Moya, *Trebujena*, p. 116.) The two biggest *cortijos* are Alventud and Cascadejo, and Alventud is slated to be expropriated by the government and the land distributed among the workers. This *cortijo* owns the land of the marshes by the river. The plan is to drain the land by the Guadalquivir.
20. For example, "Now the town government has some land that has never been worked before. It is an estate of fifty-three hectares called 'La Debosilla.' This has been given to the Junta [Andalusian government] in exchange for conditioning the marshes. We are going to distribute them among eight cooperatives, with six or seven families each. Each will have a five-hectares lot to build greenhouses, where they will grow flowers, fruit, or whatever is suitable. This project will be finished by next year." (Diego Caro Cancela)
21. Luis de la Rosa, *Breve Historia del Carnaval de Trebujena*, pp. 45, 56–7.
22. Ibid., pp. 54–5.
23. *Diario de Cádiz*, Jan. 22, 1989: 12.
24. Ibid.
25. This is federal government for Andalusia.

Chapter 13

Epilogue: The Structure of Carnival Song and Celebration

There is widespread agreement on the essential properties of carnival. The festival is identified with freedom by scholars and by participants of every class and locale. As Cádiz historian Alberto Ramos Santana describes at the outset of his historical account:

> For me the history of carnival is the history of a struggle for freedom, since carnival has always had to struggle for its own existence. Reviewing the dispositions that those in power imposed on the carnival, one reads a long history of bans and impediments which tried to erase, or at the very least to control, a popular manifestation which has traditionally developed only in the frame of political liberties.[1]

Taking its mission a step further, the Seville anthropologist Salvador Rodríguez Becerra sees carnival as a challenge to entrenched community rules and to personal mores:

> Carnival fulfills social and psychological functions that no other festival does. It breaks with the social order, pits social classes against each other, frees the instincts, and shatters repressions. All this is realized through costumes, the upturning of the social order, through food and drink, irony, satires of society and authority, and, in sum, giving free rein to fantasy and freedom.[2]

Contemporary carnival singers in the capital and elsewhere agree on the broad scope of these powers. They insist on the right to test authority with their criticisms and revelations:

> "During carnival one should do everything the law forbids in other times – the laws of manners, politics, ethics. . .Carnival should have no limits – as long as you don't trespass on other people's freedom.

When the groups sing on the streets, people have the freedom to listen or not, but I need the freedom to sing what I want. After all, words don't break bones.

"Carnival is a celebration of freedom. No matter how democratic a society is, there is always something forbidden and taboo. Sex is one of the main taboos in our society, and carnival is the time of busting inhibitions. Carnival should be a time of freedom bordering on licentiousness. Here in Spain, the church and the military are two big taboos. Carnival is about the loss of respect for them. That's the essence of carnival. That may be one of the most important qualities of human beings: that they always rebel and don't conform. This may be the only source of faith in humanity we have left." (Manuel Moreno and María López)

For some, freedom in carnival means a transitory period of liberty without restraints. For others carnival is a catalyst for social change. Portents of social protest have resonated in carnival source materials since earliest times. In his analysis of sixteenth-century carnival and popular culture depicted in Rabelais' *Gargantua and Pantagruel* (1534), Mikhail Bakhtin saw symbolic signs of destruction and regeneration in the carnival's reversal of the social order. "Bakhtin's carnival," explains Michael Holquist in the prologue, ". . .is not only not an impediment to revolutionary change, it is revolution itself."[3]

Although it is tempting to conceive of carnival in such a grand role, there is this caveat to its identification with revolution: carnival is shadow play. Its social dynamite lies in its wit and poetry and not in its deeds. Carnival is the wellspring of song, theater, and costume; however, despite its eloquence and vitality, it is only playacting and not open rebellion. That fact defines its limitation and provides its fascination.

In the past the true radical children of Andalusia, the anarchists and anarchosyndicalists, thought carnival to be a foolish distraction from the education and action necessary for social revolution. The Great Day for which they waited was not carnival but the general strike and the eradication of government – revolution with political and religious authority destroyed.[4] Rather than touch off rebellion, carnival has a place in the flow of ritual.[5]

Through the year composers and singers have anticipated their moment:

"I didn't say anything before because they'd say I'm crazy. I waited until carnival to express my criticism. That's what carnival is for, right? I don't write smutty songs or little light-hearted ditties. I deal with matters I want to criticize." (Manolo Lago)

"For fifty-one weeks of the year, we live under laws and repressive forces, so why not have one week of total freedom? Carnival critiques are our only possible response to the abuse we get from the bigwigs in this society. I can't touch them, but I can criticize them." (Manuel Moreno and María López)

Criticism of moral issues raised by the collective voices of the *agrupaciones*, rather than defiance of church and state, is the carnival's metier. Belief in social justice is the moral compass that steers *campesino* and worker. The songs express indignation and fury at acts of exploitation and deceit. They mock those individuals great and small who breach established codes of behavior. Carnival drollery, turned on those miscreants, can redress grievances and reassert local values and natural law. An underlying motive of the criticism and public ridicule is to put things right and to hasten a return to traditional, righteous ways. This is evident when *campesinos* protest against the failure of landowners to cultivate their estates, thereby denying work to the *campesinos*, or when a government official is found to be pandering his integrity for personal gain.

During the few days of misrule, the world appears to be standing on its head. After a week of hilarity, however, instead of realizing social and political change, carnival closes for Lent. After Easter, life then picks up again as before until the succeeding winter when the singers will return in new costumes to sound similar complaints with renewed humor, vulgarity, and wit.

Despite its unofficial place in the calendar, carnival is as antithetical to accepted religious doctrine as it is to Lent itself. Carnival is an impious holiday, without prayers and without reference to God, saints, heaven or hell. For carnival singers, judgment cannot wait to be meted out in eternity. Official representations of law, too, are regarded with skepticism. The truth is to be determined only by the people's own keen view and their ongoing suspicions.

Carnival in the capital contrasts sharply with the carnival we have seen in the towns. Some dissimilarities reflect social distinctions between the urban and rural worlds. The urban celebration is socially more complex and more subject to bureaucratic controls. While the town and capital carnivals are the creation of their working-class constituencies, the capital carnival is strongly influenced by upper- and middle-class tastes and by commercial concerns. Moreover, the official urban carnival is organized and directed by government appointed officials. Sharp reactions against official and commercial controls, however, have resulted in the creation of more varied *agrupaciones* and the renewal and regeneration of the street carnival.

The essential elements of the festival for the townsmen are defined by Pepe "Colmena," a carnival poet and the youthful operator of a bar in Benalup known as "the beehive" [*colmena*]:

"Carnival is a newspaper. It gives the news of what happened during the year. It criticizes, it comments. It concerns itself with politics. . . with someone who took a comical fall in the street. It's all of that. Carnival is made by poor people. Perhaps it attacks most the political bosses in power, who give only what they must, the councilmen, the leaders, anybody who did something wrong, and anybody who did right is sung about in a *pasodoble*. Carnival speaks about all that happened in the town and elsewhere in the province."

Carnival resembles a newspaper in its verve, spirit, tempo, and range of themes. In its timing, however, it is a yearbook, an annual summary of events and opinion. In the towns, local events and circumstances are usually of paramount interest, be they disputes between neighbors, revelations of clandestine sexual encounters, or criticisms of an irritating municipal ordinance. In contrast, carnival in the city can claim songs of a wider scope than those of the towns, although the underlying subjects may remain essentially the same. Content is defined by time: songs of the Franco period recall hunger, economic depression, and the exodus of rural workers to the cities of Spain and Western Europe. In the new era of democracy, unemployment and emigration continue as crucial themes; other subjects touch on national and international politics, the hunger for equality and justice, and demands for regional and local independence. During the dictatorship, problems were never tied to the head of government; today, specific officials are cited for corruption and ineptitude.

It is possible on occasion to reach across generational and geographical boundaries and touch every listener with the same song. Shared beliefs and common ties of town, land, and labor bind the composer and the audience. At carnival a half-century ago in 1933 and 1934, *coplas* relating the tragedy at Casas Viejas stirred collective fear and anger. Reference to the event in song today rouses similar emotions and ties to the past. A similar nexus occurred in 1981 with songs of Lieutenant Colonel Tejero storming the Cortés and holding it captive. In the same year, laments over those dead and infirm from the peddling of tainted cooking oil, evoked universal outrage.

Carnival composers reveal both comic and tragic sides of life, setting side by side the serious and the bizarre, and mirroring the realities of daily experience. Art as well as coarseness flourish. *Gaditanos* are remarkably conscious of the levels of significance in carnival. Even those who are less cognizant of its sober side sense the intrinsic importance of the festival. As Manuel Moreno Riobo and María López Liboreiro, who sing in an informal *charanga*, observed of many participants:

> "Carnival has been resurrected in many places in the last few years. I think that carnivals are now just an excuse to have fun, but at the same time, people are reviving them because, somehow, they touch us way deep inside."

The carnival costume helps the singers create a fresh vision of commonplace events. Assuming a new identity is meant to surprise and provoke laughter. The disguise is also a scrim that separates the performer from the audience and from society. It enables the singer to be larger than life, to take a comic turn, and to risk appearing foolish. Some choose the enduring illusion of a clown; others dress as pirates, tourists, or, perhaps with a touch of social satire, appear as priests or as soldiers. Anonymity provides a shield to sing brave words, to criticize, to sound an alarm, or to ridicule a politician or a neighbor. Some men and women take the opportunity to cast aside etiquette and inhibition, and switch to costumes of the opposite sex. A few young men and staid elders dress as brides or as painted hussies and even swagger with lewd song and dance. On occasion the spectacle offers, without comment or quarrel, a tableau of hidden sensuality.

The art of dissimulation is ingrained in Andalusian culture. It has been suggested that, during the final years of the dictatorship when the festival was reawakened, censorship and the constraints of fear encouraged rhetorical slights of hand, including the increased use of euphemisms for sexual terms.[6] It is also true that these poetic defenses were not a wholly new pattern. Guile is a fact of daily life. Mastery of euphemisms, double-entendres, and allusion have always been necessary rhetorical skills for Spanish writers in repressive periods throughout Spanish history.[7]

Ambiguity and innuendo are often needed for sensitive subjects outside the realm of politics. Although carnival is famous for its raucous humor and vulgar interests, the Cádiz festival is the most subtle of all carnival celebrations. Subjects covered in carnival song are often already well-known locally and have been gossiped about during summer ambles and winter encounters. A matter previously concealed can be an unpleasant surprise to the principal subjects. It may be taken as a joke or a sharp jab. But as the costume disguises the singers, so too may the poet conceal the identity of his characters. This can be seen in part as artistry and in part as a strategy of self-defense should a song arouse anger without laughter. If a composer fails to protect his subjects and himself, he must prepare for fines for slander or worse, depending on the subject matter.

The expression of artistic skill remains paramount. The purpose is to say what you mean in a way that can tickle your friends and frustrate your enemies. More often than not the sensibility and the skill of the songwriter are revealed by his ability to deliver a barb and evade a hot reply. Like most matters in Andalusia, artistry in the carnival is based on misdirection.

> "[In composing] One should maintain the spirit of Cádiz. I don't say Andalusia because Andalusia is too large. Carnival should have the spirit of Cádiz. For carnival belongs to Cádiz, and in Cádiz one must have wit – to put things with wit, with merriment, and with feeling in the *pasodoble*. Criticizing but making the people laugh – criticizing them subtly, in a way that no one can be offended. To say: 'You did this, you did that. But look: I do not say it was you. It wasn't you. It was someone whom I made up. But everybody knows it's you!' It's that simple." (Pepe Colmena)

Notes

1. A. Ramos Santana, *Historia del Carnaval de Cádiz*, p. 5.
2. S. Rodríguez Becerra, "Cultura Popular y Fiestas," *Los Andaluces*, p. 81. Also cited in Santana, *Historia del Carnaval de Cádiz*, p. 13.
3. Mikhail Bakhtin, *Rabelais and His World*, p. xviii.
4. Jerome R. Mintz, *The Anarchists of Casas Viejas*, pp. 2–5, 25–8.
5. Concerning the European carnival, in her study of social life in sixteenth-century France, Natalie Davis writes: ". . .rather than being a mere `safety value,' deflecting attention from social reality, festive life can on the one hand perpetuate certain values of the community (even guarantee its survival), and on the other hand criticize political order. Misrule can have its own rigor and can also decipher king and state." *Society and Culture in Early Modern France* (Stanford: Stanford University Press, 1975) p. 97.

   The view that carnival is a source of social integration and continuity may be based in part on world-wide observations of mechanisms of social change. In his *Rituals of Rebellion in South-East Africa* ([S.L.]: Free Press of Glencoe, 1963), Max Gluckman's description of the mechanisms of Zulu ceremonies bore striking similarities to the European carnival: ". . .rituals of rebellion proceed within an established and sacred traditional system in which there is dispute about particular distributions of power, and not about the structure of the system itself. This allows for instituted protest, and in complex ways renews the unity of the system." (p. 112) For other parallels see pp. 118, 127.

   During field research in Andalusia in the 1960's, 70's, and 80's, I independently came to the conclusion that "social controls in rural Andalusia were achieved not through government regulation and police surveillance but, rather, through social sanctions that were enforced by gossip and by various forms of criticism and public censure. At carnival questionable conduct was trumpeted to the public in song." *The Anarchists of Casas Viejas*, p. 83.
6. See Chapter 7, note 2.
7. See, for example, the dualities in Marrano existence as depicted in Fernando de Rojas' *La Celestina* and discussed in Yirmiyahu

Yovel's *Spinoza and other Heretics, the Marrano of Reason* (Princeton: Princeton University Press, 1989), chapters 4 and 5. Yovel writes: "In this game which the author plays with his readers and all the characters play with one another, it is hard to know whether language serves to communicate or to disguise; but in any case it serves both to amuse and to realize an artistic conception. Of course, this is the only way Rojas could protect himself and ensure the survival of his work." (p. 113)

Other Works by Jerome R. Mintz

Books

The Anarchists of Casas Viejas

Hasidic People, A Place in the New World

Legends of the Hasidim, An Introduction to Hasidic Culture & Oral Tradition in the New World

In Praise of the Baal Shem Tov [Shivhei ha-Besht], The Earliest Collection of Legends about the Founder of Hasidism (tr. & ed. with Dan Ben-Amos)

Documentary Films

Carnaval de Pueblo (Town Carnival)

Romeria: Day of the Virgin

The Shoemaker

Pepe's Family

Perico the Bowlmaker

The Shepherd's Family

Jerome R. Mintz is Professor Emeritus of Anthropology at Indiana University, Bloomington, Indiana.

Index